Sex Work, Labour, and Empowerment

This book presents an analysis of the concepts of female empowerment and resilience against violence in the informal entertainment and sex industries.

Generally, the key debates on sex work have centred on arguments proposed by the oppressive and empowerment paradigms. This book moves away from such debates to look widely at the micro issues such as the role of income in the lives of sex workers, the significance of peer organisations and networks of women, and how resilience is enacted and empowerment experienced. It also uses positive deviancy theory as a useful strategy to bring about notable changes in terms of empowerment and agency for women working in this sector and also for addressing the wider issues of migration, HIV/AIDS, and violence against women and girls. The focus is on moving beyond a victimisation framework without downplaying the extent of the violence that women in this industry experience. It conceptualises the theories of empowerment and power which have not been tested against women who work in this sector, combined with in-depth interviews with women working in the industry as well as academics, activists, and personnel in the NGO and donor sector. In doing so, it informs the reader of the numerous social, political, and economic factors that structure and sustain the global growth of the industry and analyses the diverse factors that lead many thousands of women and girls around the world to work in this sector.

The work presents an important contribution to the study of citizenship and rights from a non-Western angle and will be of interest to academics, researchers, and policymakers across human rights, sociology, economics, and development studies.

Sutirtha Sahariah is an independent development consultant and researcher focusing on issues of gender, migration, sanitation, human rights, and violence in South Asia. He has previously worked as a freelance journalist and covered stories on human trafficking, gender, and development for *The Guardian* (UK), the BBC, *NewsDeeply*, Dutch Public Radio & Television, and NPR. He has a Ph.D. in international development from University of Portsmouth, England.

Studies in Citizenship, Human Rights and the Law

The series Studies in Citizenship, Human Rights and the Law encourages a pluralistic vision of citizenship. The aim is to promote inclusiveness and rights at the local and global levels while approaching citizenship from a socio-legal perspective. The series may include comparative approaches along with books that focus on single jurisdictions, and brings together research monographs and edited collections which allow the expression of different schools of thought. Grounded in law and legal theory, where relevant, the series also welcomes contributions that take an interdisciplinary approach to rights and citizenship.

Series Editor:
Leïla Choukroune is Professor of International Law and Director of the University of Portsmouth Research and Innovation Theme in Democratic Citizenship. Her research focuses on the interactions between international trade and investment law, human rights, development studies, jurisprudence and social theory. It is also applied to emerging countries, India, China and East Africa in particular.

Titles in this series:

The Development of Child Protection Law and Policy
Children, Risk and Modernities
Kieran Walsh

Sex Work, Labour, and Empowerment
Lessons from the Informal Entertainment Sector in Nepal
Sutirtha Sahariah

For more information about this series, please visit: https://www.routledge.com/Studies-in-Citizenship-Human-Rights-and-the-Law/book-series/StudiesCHRL

Sex Work, Labour, and Empowerment

Lessons from the Informal Entertainment Sector in Nepal

Sutirtha Sahariah

Routledge
Taylor & Francis Group
LONDON AND NEW YORK

First published 2022
by Routledge
2 Park Square, Milton Park, Abingdon, Oxon OX14 4RN

and by Routledge
605 Third Avenue, New York, NY 10158

Routledge is an imprint of the Taylor & Francis Group, an informa business

British Library Cataloguing-in-Publication Data
A catalogue record for this book is available from the British Library

Library of Congress Cataloging-in-Publication Data
A catalog record has been requested for this book

ISBN: 978-0-367-74249-2 (hbk)
ISBN: 978-0-367-74254-6 (pbk)
ISBN: 978-1-003-15679-6 (ebk)

DOI: 10.4324/9781003156796

Typeset in Galliard
by Deanta Global Publishing Services, Chennai, India

In memory of my late mother, Sarmistha Sahariah.
Your values continue to be my guiding force in my life.

Contents

Illustrations

Tables

Figures

Foreword

Professor Leïla Choukroune[1]

When Simone de Beauvoir daringly asserted that "one is not born a woman, but rather becomes one", she opened the door to the possible.[2] In distinguishing sex and gender, she allowed women to choose an identity, a destiny, and a life of dignity. In interrogating the cultural elements which determine the fate of human beings, she also questioned their ability to exist as autonomous and equal individuals. In her seminal work, *The Second Sex*, Simone de Beauvoir also insisted on the necessity for women to be economically independent to achieve freedom.

While not many women would naturally choose sex work as a means to reach this objective, some may well deliberately engage in a monetary transaction which does not always come from, nor result in coercion. There is liberty in reclaiming one's body. There is also pride and honour if not sometimes a form of transcendence in being in control of one's sexuality. In medieval South India, *Devadasi* women were dedicated to God and considered as respected independent artists who chose their partners but married none. Over the centuries, the practice transformed into the sexual exploitation of young Dalit girls, who now serve as a mere tool for their untouchable families to survive.

The complexity of human nature and the multitude of situations in which women can engage in prostitution deserve an honest and nuanced discussion, one deprived of prudish preconceptions and other religious or cultural bias. In engaging at the grassroots level in Nepal with dozens of women who sell their bodies for a living, Dr Sutirtha Sahariah has produced a unique and remarkable piece of research. He has listened to these women's stories of violence, domination, and patriarchy but also understood their aspirations and their ability to reinvent themselves in a life which might not conform to the social norms in place and the general expectations of what it is to be a modern woman but has provided them with the means for emancipation.

1 Professor of international law and director of the Democratic Citizenship Theme, University of Portsmouth. Routledge series editor, *Studies in Citizenship, Human Rights and the Law*.

2 See Simone de Beauvoir, *The Second Sex*, and Judith Butler, "Sex and Gender in Simone de Beauvoir's Second Sex", *Simone de Beauvoir: Witness to a Century*, Yale French Studies, No. 72, Yale University Press, (1986), pp. 35–49.

It is not anecdotal that these women can proudly say: "Through my association I have learnt that literacy and early marriage are the main cause of women's problem. I have learnt not be supressed by men".[3]

or

> Earlier I was afraid of everything around me: the police, society, people. But now things are different. You see I can speak confidently. People might abuse me but that is momentary, but I know that I am standing on my feet. I am not begging. I don't care what society thinks of me. Society is made by us. Society does not provide me food or shelter.

All of the testimonies collected, year after year, based on the meticulous work of investigating and building trust and confidence must be heard for what they are. Leftist feminists might find sex work degrading and against the gender equality cause, but there is much more to these women's lives than selling their body to a man. This complication lifts a veil of hypocrisy and questions an economic reality as much as it interrogates large pieces of scholarship and other gender studies. Recognising these women as workers is also a way of acknowledging their existence as the rights holders of the very rights to life, health, and education of which patriarchy had deprived them.

Without ever judging their choices, in conveying their words, in observing and narrating their lives as agent and not necessarily victims, and in placing these issues in a rich theoretical framework, Dr Sutirtha Sahariah has managed to write a new type of study, one that will make a great difference.

3 See pp. 103–104 – women's testimonies and peers networks.

Acknowledgements

This book is the outcome of four years of research work in Nepal. So, firstly I would like to express my gratitude to all the brave participants of this research and the leaders of the four organisations listed in the book: Shanti Tiwari of SWASA Nepal, Shova Dangol of SWAN, Menuka Thapa of Raksha Nepal, and Bijaya Dhakal of JMMS. All of them were very cooperative and provided immense support in collecting information, even when the COVID-19 pandemic was severely disrupting normal life in Nepal. All four leaders said that they are passionate about their work and hoped that through this book the movement for the rights of sex workers and violence against women in Nepal and around the world would be furthered strengthened. I am also grateful to the Government of Nepal, Department of Women and Children, for its help during the early stages of this research.

I am eternally grateful to Dr Bindeshwar Pathak, the Stockholm Water Prize winner and founder of one of India's largest non-governmental organisations, Sulabh International Social Service Organisation, which has been working in the field of sanitation, water, waste management, human rights and social reform through education for five decades. In 2014, I met Pathak as a journalist while producing a radio story on India's sanitation challenges for NPR. Inspired by his work, I later joined Sulabh as a consultant. He showed immense faith and confidence in my abilities and supported my PhD programme at the University of Portsmouth, UK. I shall forever be grateful to him for his generosity.

My special thanks to my academic colleagues, Professor Tamsin Bradley (who was also my PhD supervisor at the University of Portsmouth), Dr George Byrne and Leïla Choukroune, professor of international law and director of the University of Research and Innovation Theme in Democratic Citizenship, University of Portsmouth – she proposed the idea for the book and connected me with Routledge.

The research would have been very difficult without the support of Anita Subba and Tritiksha Magar, who patiently helped with translations, and my friends in Nepal, Pramit and Bobin, who supported me during my field work in Nepal – I remain very thankful to them.

My family has been a pillar of strength throughout this work, and I feel privileged to express my appreciation for my wife Dr Karabi Pathak, my father Sarada Kumar Sahariah, and my two aunts Sujata Mukherjee and Bijoya Upadhaya, for all their love and support. And equally, I thank our close family friends, Dr Hannah Simcoe-Read, Dr Devendra Saroj, Alamder Hussein, Saran, and Nitin, for being a constant source of motivation for me.

Finally, I would like to thank Routledge and Taylor & Francis, especially Alison Kirk and Emily Summers, for their continuing support of my work.

Abbreviations

CEDAW	Convention on the Elimination of all Forms of Discrimination Against Women
CLS	Community legal service
CoID	Commission of Inquiry on the Disappearances
COYOTE	Call Off Your Old Tired Ethics
CPN-Maoist	Maoist Communist Party of Nepal
CSW	Commercial sex workers
DFID	Department for International Development
DOE	Degrees of empowerment
ECP	English Collective of Prostitutes
FCSW	Female commercial sex workers
GBV	Gender-based violence
GWP	General Welfare Pratisthan
HCMC	Ho Chi Minh City
HDR	Human Development Report
HIV	Human immunodeficiency viruses
HIV/AIDS	Human immunodeficiency viruses/acquired immunodeficiency syndrome
ICTJ	International Centre for Transitional Justice
IDPs	Internally displaced peoples
ILO	International Labour Organisation
INGO	International non-governmental organisation
INR	Indian rupee
IRP	Interim Relief Programme
JMMS	Jagriti Mahila Maha Sangh
NDHS	Nepal Demographic and Health Survey
NGO	Non-governmental organisation
NPA	Royal Nepal Army
NR	Nepalese rupee
NSWP	Network of Sex Workers Projects
OHCHR	Office of the United Nations High Commissioner for Human Rights
PLA	People's Liberation Army

PTSD	Post-traumatic stress disorder
SPA	Seven-Party Alliance
SWAN	Society for Women Awareness in Nepal
TADA	Terrorist and disruptive activities
Tdh	Terre des Hommes
THB	Trafficking in human beings
TIP	Trafficking in persons
TJ	Transitional justice
TJRA	Transitional Justice Reference Archive
TMER	Transconceptual Model of Empowerment and Resilience
TRC	Truth and Reconciliation Commission
UN	United Nations
UNICEF	United Nations Children's Fund
UNMIN	United Nations Mission in Nepal
UNODC	United Nations Office on Drugs and Crime
USAID	United States Agency for International Development
USD	United States dollar
VAMP	Veshya Anyay Mukti Parishad
VAW	Violence against women
VAWG	Violence against women and girls
WATCH	Women Acting Together for Change
WEE	Women's economic empowerment
WHO	World Health Organisation
WNU	Women's Network for Unity

1 Introduction

1.1 Origins of the study

Researcher engagement with issues of violence against women and economic empowerment of women in South Asia

In the summer of 2012, I was recruited by the BBC World Service as a researcher and producer for a newly commissioned documentary on human trafficking. The documentary investigated how girls from eastern states of India were being trafficked and sold for marriage in states such as Haryana and Punjab, the more prosperous northern regions that have a skewed sex ratio resulting from female foeticide and infanticide. The documentary is titled: *India's lost girls.* Just as the documentary was being aired worldwide on the BBC, another incident took place that made global headlines: a 23-year-old female student was brutally gang-raped in a moving bus in south Delhi (see Burke, 2013). The incident outraged India's civil society, and thousands took to the streets in protest against the growing number of rape cases and other forms of violence against women (VAW). The protests were historically significant because they forced the Indian government to make wide-ranging amendments to the county's criminal law in order to deal more severely with sexual assault cases. Following this, there was a sudden surge in the reporting and analysis of incidents of rape and VAW in India, especially by the international media. Many such reports were written by foreign journalists, and the stories revealed an incoherent narrative and inaccurate portrayal of rape in India (Bradley, Sahariah, & Siddiqui, 2016). Many international journalists who flew to India to mine stories of VAW demonstrated a lack of understanding of the complexity and diversity of India's culture and value system.

The BBC documentary and the Delhi rape case inadvertently steered me towards reporting extensively on issues concerning gender-based violence (GBV) across the South Asian region. Over the following five years, I researched and wrote about issues of human trafficking, violence against women and girls (VAWG), and women's economic empowerment (WEE). These stories were featured in media outlets including *The Guardian* (UK), the BBC, Dutch Public Broadcasting, *The Huffington Post*, *Women and Girls Hub: News Deeply*, and the World Economic Forum.

DOI: 10.4324/9781003156796-1

During this time, I came into contact with a number of global organisations that worked on women's issues. One such organisation was Freeset, which worked to create alternative livelihoods for women sex workers in Sonagachi, Kolkata – India's largest red-light district. The project was started by Kerry Hill who had moved to Kolkata from New Zealand in 1999 with his wife Annie and their four children. Kerry said he had been inspired by Mother Teresa and wanted to help the poor. He had rented an apartment in the Sonagachi area only to realise later that he was living in the midst of a thriving red-light area with over 10,000 sex workers as his immediate neighbours. When Kerry started interacting with the women in the area, he found himself profoundly affected by the tales of suffering and exploitation of women working in the sex industry: "Their stories moved me so much that I would cry for days feeling helpless". Kerry realised that many women stuck to the profession despite the abuse because they were unskilled and had no alternative livelihood options, and so he began to document their lives. With the aim of offering some of the women a different means to make a living, Kerry set up a production unit for jute bags for the export market with the help of 20 women from the area who no longer wanted to do sex work. It was a huge challenge to teach unskilled women to sew quality bags, admitted Kerry, but with consistent training and quality control the problems were overcome. Over time, the business grew in size, eventually employing over 200 women producing over 1,000 high-quality bags a day.

I visited Sonagachi a number of times and interacted with sex workers to learn about their lives and aspirations. I later met members of the Durbar Mahila Samanwaya Committee (DMSC) – a large national network representing over 50,000 sex workers. The organisation has been campaigning on issues such as the inclusion of sex work in the Ministry of Labour, the protection of the labour and the human rights of sex workers, and the recognition of the self-regulatory boards of sex workers in the interest of stepping up the fight against trafficking and improving the quality of life of sex workers (Kotiswaran, 2011). My interactions made me realise that the sex and adult entertainment industry is an integral aspect of any economy, and in India it is a major part of the vast informal labour sector. It is predominantly occupied by women workers but remains unprotected by legislation relating to wages or labour despite its substantial contribution to the economy (Rajan, 2011).

My early field visits were eye-opening and provided me with insights into the wider livelihood and social issues facing the women working as sex workers. However, during my frequent visits to Kolkata, I began to recognise the differences in perspectives on sex work and how approaches to engaging with sex workers were driven by ideological positions. Freeset, for example, was essentially run by Western missionaries who were evangelical Christians. It vehemently opposed sex work or any efforts to legalise it. The organisation argued that sex work was the root cause of human trafficking and classified it as a form of modern slavery. Freeset did create a sound business model and, through its global network, developed overseas markets for the products the former sex workers made, but in the process of doing so they also sold the stories of the women they were employing. Freeset paid a reasonable salary to its employees (former sex workers) with healthcare benefits, but the business was ultimately profit driven. Women were strictly discouraged from going back to sex work, and the promoters of Freeset argued that they created a mechanism that allowed women to choose to live a life of dignity and freedom. On the other hand, the DMSC maintained that human trafficking and sex work are two distinct issues and disapproved of any attempt to conflate them. It called for the decriminalisation of sex work and argued that sex workers cannot be judged through the lenses of religion or morality as there are myriad legitimate reasons why women choose this profession. They further argued that sex workers – like everyone else – have their own agency and are capable of making their own life decisions. In this book, there are constant echoes of these polarised positions, and they are particularly visible in Chapter 8, which talks about the human rights of sex workers.

In 1995, the DMSC established one of the largest multipurpose cooperatives known as Usha with the aim of providing financial security to sex workers. One of the immediate benefits of the Usha programme is that large numbers of sex workers are able to regularly save significant portions of their income. They are also able to secure loans at low interest rates without any onerous conditions. In the past, women in their position had to depend on unscrupulous money lenders who often exploited them and even subjected them to violence. The data provided by Usha (as cited in NSWP, 2014, p. 12) states that thousands of sex workers have taken out loans of varying sizes for diverse purposes, ranging from purchasing land or other real estate assets to financing the education of their children or for health care. Usha's model has been replicated by other organisations discussed in this book. For example, Raksha Nepal, an organisation that works for the rights of women working in Kathmandu's informal sector, sent teams to Kolkata to learn from Usha's experience. Raksha Nepal then set up its own savings and credit scheme in Thamel, Kathmandu, which has realised a number of benefits for women and girls. The project is discussed in more detail in later chapters.

In 2016, Britain's Department for International Development (DFID) commissioned a comparative research project across three countries (Pakistan, Nepal, and Myanmar) on women, work, and violence to investigate how approaches to WEE can tackle violence at the same time. The project was part of a wider portfolio of research on VAWG in South Asia. The key objective was to understand the complex two-way relationship between VAWG and WEE. The project was commissioned against the backdrop of a shift whereby significant resources in the developing world had been directed towards enhancing the financial independence of women in the belief that women who earn their own income would have control over how they spend it and would be given more leverage in decision-making at the household level. This, in turn, would empower women to take control of other aspects of their lives, including building resilience against violence. Unfortunately, however, this has not always been the case. Part of the reason is that income earned by women can also lead to potential negative outcomes for them: the transgression of traditional gender norms (through employment and/or earning, for example) may actually lead to increased oppression at home and even a violent "backlash" that seeks to redress the shifting power balance (see e.g. Goetz & Sen Gupta, 1996). As such, the objective of the DFID research was to avoid this and instead to establish ways in which approaches to WEE can contribute to tackling violence.

The aims of the DFID South Asia project were

1. To understand how normative violence in specific societies shaped women's economic engagement patterns and to ascertain how best to address this issue.
2. To uncover the complex ways in which earning or generating an income shapes/alters (both positively and negatively) the forms of violence that women experience and how it affects their levels of vulnerability.
3. To unpack and describe how approaches to enhancing women's economic activity can support the prevention of and responses to VAW.

The overall impact objective was to generate new research that offers a clear policy and programme direction on how WEE can be used as a vehicle to mitigate VAW.

The University of Portsmouth, UK, was the academic lead on this project and, as part of my doctoral research, I carried out the scoping study in Nepal and Myanmar. The purpose of the scoping work was to map in detail the demographics of the field sites through identifying key gatekeepers and the potential risks of the research (such as participants who might be distressed by it) and to gain insight into the enabling environment in terms of the community organisations that might be able to support the research (in facilitating interviews, for example). This phase also focused on gathering more detail on key organisations and programmes that exist and identifying gaps in provision. From discussions with the DFID, United Nations (UN) agencies, and the government, it emerged that no law exists in Nepal relating to acts of sexual harassment at work against female employees working in places such as dance bars, cabin restaurants (where customers are served by waitresses in tiny individual rooms), or massage parlours, which are referred to in this book as the "informal entertainment industry" (Thapa, 2018).

Whilst there is a lot of focus globally on the rights of sex workers who are engaged in street-based prostitution or who operate from brothels or in red-light districts, very little research exists about women working in closed establishments such as spa centres or live entertainment restaurants, which in Nepal (as in many parts of the world) are where sex work is often done surreptitiously. Within the realm of the wider hospitality and tourism industry, it is well known that sex work is not restricted to brothels or street-based prostitution but includes exotic dancing and other exchanges of sex for money, which sometimes occur in massage parlours and through escort services. Fortunato (1973 as cited in Bryant & Palmer, 1975) describes massage parlours as places "where anything goes and states that they offer wide a repertoire of sexual services for an appropriate fee". As such, studying forms of sex work in the informal entertainment industry (such as exotic dancing in restaurants or prostitution in massage parlours) is important because it not only makes up a large and lucrative part of the sex industry, but its scope is also increasing, particularly in Nepal where this study was conducted (Estébanez, Fitch, & Nájera, 1993).

From the voices of the women and girls documented in this study, it becomes clear that the levels of violence, exploitation, and abuse that women and girls face within the closed spaces of informal entertainment establishments can be equally as traumatic as that experienced by women who operate from brothels or on the street. Sex workers who work on their own and operate on the streets are potentially at greater risk of violence and harassment, even from state actors such as the police, but what goes on behind closed doors remains unknown, and women rarely talk about it for fear of backlash and stigma. The organisations documented in this book, e.g. Raksha Nepal and Biswas Nepal (see Chapter 6), categorically state that their activism is focused on the rights of women working in the "informal entertainment sector" and they treat "sex workers" as a different category. Other organisations, such as the Society for Women Awareness Nepal (SWAN), Jagriti Mahila Maha Sang (JMMS), and Social Work Allies for Sustainable Approaches (SWASA), work with sex workers but do so in the context of implementing human immunodeficiency virus (HIV)-related health programmes, promoting the human rights of sex workers, and raising awareness of issues related to VAWG. This is because sex work is illegal in Nepal, and no organisation wants to be seen openly supporting sex workers' rights for fear of public reprisal. Many organisations also rely on funding from donors that, in principle, do not support commercial sex work, and recipients of such funds are expected to ensure that their staff members refrain from engaging in any form of sex work (discussed in detail in Chapter 6). However, there is a consensus (as is evidenced during the course of this book) that both groups (i.e. sex workers and those women working in informal entertainment) are engaged in bodily labour and commercial sex work. There are no fixed criteria regarding who works where, says Menuka Thapa of Raksha Nepal, who campaigns for the rights of women working in the informal entertainment sector. Young women are far more likely to be employed in informal entertainment establishments, such as dance bars and spa centres, than older women who mostly work as independent sex workers: "Not all women who work in these establishments are involved directly in sex work, but then the level of violence is really high, and women are sometimes coerced into selling sex", says Thapa. During the COVID-19 pandemic (see Chapter 8), the informal entertainment centres were badly affected, leading to the closure of many businesses. Thousands of women lost their livelihoods, with many choosing sex work (including the online sex industry) as a means to make a living.

In this book, I use the term "informal entertainment industry" to denote all aspects of sex work. All women working in this sector – in closed establishments such as massage parlours or working as a street-based sex worker – are exposed to similar levels of vulnerability and challenges. Their aspirations are largely the same, and there is a commonality of factors behind their reasons for being in the industry. The book demonstrates that income from engaging in the informal entertainment sector is fundamental for survival, and this income, coupled with support from peer networks, enables them to build their resilience to daily adversities.

1.2 The question of autonomy and self-determination

The strategic need to study the relationship between violence and empowerment in the informal entertainment and sex industry

Definitions of women's economic empowerment generally include elements of economic activity (such as sufficient economic and personal resources to be economically productive), power, and agency (the ability to make and act on decisions and control resources) (see Kabeer, 2001). Although it represents only one aspect of overall empowerment, in addition to economic gain, WEE has the potential to balance gender inequities and gender norms. Whilst programmatic frameworks generally recognise that in order to achieve economic empowerment, women need skills, capacities, and resources, only a few programmes acknowledge the importance of transforming the normative environment, which includes reshaping gender norms and ensuring women's right to earn a fair wage and live free from violence. Whilst a number of studies have explored the extent to which money in the hands of women can lead to empowerment, this has rarely been addressed in respect of the women who engage in the informal entertainment industry using their body as a primary "resource" to earn an income and doing so without labour rights and while constantly exposed to risk (Baltiwala, 2013; Busza, 2004; Murthy & Seshu, 2013; O'Connell Davidson, 2006; Overs, 2013). A key reason for this is that sex work is illegal in many countries, meaning women who work in this sector do so in secrecy and have limited access to legal recourse should they face exploitation, violence, or rape while working. Moreover, social stigma and gender inequality also make them a "hard-to-reach" group (Onyeneho, 2009 as cited in Moret, 2014).

The situation of sex workers globally is further complicated by the ongoing global debates regarding their right to work and self-determination. This resonates among radical feminist groups in South Asia that strongly oppose any form of sex work and view it as a typical expression of patriarchy and unequal gender relations. This is in line with twentieth-century Euro-American perspectives on sex work, which affirmed that exploitation, subjugation, and violence are intrinsic to and ineradicable from sex work (Dworkin, 1993; Jeffreys, 1997; MacKinnon, 1993). More recent articulations have conceived of sex work as a form of "modern slavery" and have suggested that all sex workers are victims of exploitation, rape, and/or human trafficking, and have claimed that the idea of consensual transactional sex is a misplaced notion (Halley et al., 2006, Sullivan, 2007). Such groups strongly demand abolition of sex work on the ground that sex workers lack agency and are coerced into prostitution, meaning all aspects of the sex industry, which I argue elements of the work conducted by many women in Nepal's informal entertainment sector, must be "condemned uncompromisingly" (Sagade & Forster, 2018, p. 36). Liberal feminist and sex worker rights activists, on the other hand, argue that consensual sex work should be treated as work. From this perspective, it is a form of labour whereby a woman detaches herself from her sexuality and offers her services purely on a commercial basis, and it should be treated as such. Proponents of this view tend to focus on the human rights of sex workers, and their legal interventions have been geared towards the self-determination of sex workers, including decent working conditions and freedom of movement (Sutherland, 2004). In her book *The Industrial Vagina*, Jeffreys (2009) states that the pro-sex movement has gained momentum in recent decades in part because of the vast amount of "AIDS money" that has been allocated to controlling the epidemic. The funding has been crucial in creating a strong sex worker movement globally, which has been leading the call for the decriminalisation of sex work around the world. Further, studies have demonstrated that flexible working hours and the potential for higher monetary gains in contrast to other alternatives within the socio-economic environment are also reasons why women choose to work in the informal entertainment sector (Sandy, 2009). The findings presented in this volume support these observations.

Advocates of this position strongly oppose the notion of conflating human trafficking with sex work and argue that counter-trafficking policies that conflate trafficking with sex work are counterproductive and have not yielded the desired results (Bradley & Szablewska, 2014, p. 271). Sex worker activists have further argued that it undermines their efforts to deal with issues of violence and protect the rights of women working in the sector and empower them. They claim that excessive focus on human trafficking means that the problems of the women working in the sex and informal entertainment industry get sidelined and systematically ignored by both governments and donors (Hahn & Holzscheiter, 2013). The demands of this group reflect and resonate with the aims of international agencies that seek to guarantee "free choice of profession and employment, (Article 11 (c) CEDAW)"; "just and favourable conditions of work and [...] protection against unemployment (Universal Declaration of Human Rights, 1948)"; "the right to work which includes the right of everyone to the opportunity to gain his living by work which he freely chooses or accepts (International Covenant on Economic, Social and Cultural Rights 1966)" (Sagade & Forster, 2018).

Prominent advocates of sex work in South Asia, Laxmi Murthy and Saraswathi Seshu (2013), argue that though many sex workers may have a sad story to tell, several tenets of patriarchy are also challenged within sex work, not least because women's decision-making power is significantly increased at home, giving them a sense of control and independence that would otherwise be denied (discussed further in Chapter 4). Seshu and Murthy go on to stress that there is a greater need to understand sex work from the perspective of sex workers themselves in order to gain deeper insights into whether or not earning an income can be an empowering experience. They also point out that even liberal feminists who advocate for the liberation of women from restrictive sexual mores have generally not addressed commercial sexual transactions. However, women who are engaged in sex work present a different picture: they increasingly question the binary characterisation of sex workers as victims versus sex workers as sexually liberated agents and allege that such notions undermine understandings of the agency, choice, and consent of those working in the sector. The activists define the business of sex as a transaction of multiple sexual partnerships within a commercial framework and contend that it can exist devoid of emotion, such as love or guilt (Seshu & Murthy, 2013, p. 23; Hahn & Holzscheiter, 2013).

Hakim (2015, p. 339), commenting on how the sex industry is becoming increasingly pervasive and stronger by going digital, disagrees with the views expressed by pressure groups that look at the industry as something that normalises violence against women. He argues that such arguments are "outdated" in the context of Western countries. He criticises studies that come to a conclusion by merely focusing on street-based sex workers as a typical group as they are easier to study (Weitzer, 2005; Brooks-Gordon, 2006 as cited by Hakim, 2015). The author points out that street-based sex workers are estimated to account for no more than 10% of the industry as most of the trade has moved indoors and, as such, has become invisible to researchers and the general public.

The world of the informal entertainment industry is complex, and a range of interests and power dynamics operationalise it. Skeldon (2000), whose research looks at market development and trafficking as a business, points out that the "woman as victim" interpretation, as favoured by many anti-prostitution activists, might not always be true. The author argues:

> the industry is divided into many sub-sectors, each catering to different markets, each with their own geography, price structure and organization. Those who have studied the various sectors are virtually unanimous in their assessment that most women entered the sex industry voluntarily.
>
> (Skeldon, 2000, p. 18)

The same study reports that in Thailand only 13.5% and 7.5% of the women in brothels and massage parlours, respectively, were introduced by agents or middlemen, thus questioning the assumption that trafficking and the sex industry are tightly linked. Most of the women entered the sector through a person they had known previously and tended to come from provinces that are economically less developed with few options for alternative work.

This draws a rather different account of the circumstances in which sex workers are most likely to be abused and by whom (Szablewska & Bradley, 2014, p. 249). Often, those working in the industry highlight that it is the social and legal structures created to address the matter that lead to secrecy. In fact, non-reporting causing the impunity of the offenders and the perpetuation of violence, as well as abuse by the police, authorities, and organisations involved in the "clean ups" and the "raid and rescue" operations are more of a concern than violence from clients. Violence perpetrated by the police is a recurring theme that also emerged in this study. In her study in Vietnam, Binh (2006 cited by Szablewska & Bradley, 2014, p. 249) concluded that sexual exploitation mostly takes place not in venues "established for prostitution" but rather in "nightclubs, bars, beer halls, and other entertainment venues". Also, in most of Southeast Asia and South Asia, victims of trafficking are often labelled as criminals and there is insufficient state support for them. Sex workers tend to be treated as "dirty" women who lack morality and, because of this, attract abuse and are neglected by people in authority. As has been reported in other countries, the stigmatisation of the profession, along with blaming sex workers for their choice of occupation (often by disregarding the underlying structural and socio-economic factors), leads to their further marginalisation and discrimination. This is used by state officials to justify police brutality which, in turn, promotes further violence and abuse of these women. Szablewska and Bradley (2014), therefore, argue that it is not only the causes of prostitution and the diversity of motivations to enter the industry but also the diversity of the sex work services that require further comprehension before decisions can be made on sex work and how it should be regulated.

Studies that have documented the voices of women working in this sector have shown that, owing to a variety of reasons, many women engage in informal entertainment or sex work out of choice. Ditmore's (2014) study examining despair in the lives of women engaged in the informal sex industry in Cambodia found that despite limited choices of alternate employment and their marginalisation and exclusion, women working in this sector do their best to uphold culturally valued social obligations such as paying-off debts and supporting their families. This point was strongly reinforced by the participants in this study who asserted that they were willing to tolerate humiliation and stigma for the sake of a better future for their children. Weitzer (2011) criticises international agencies, non-governmental organisations (NGOs), and those that toe the abolitionist line, particularly for inflating the extent of trafficking by linking it with prostitution and the sex industry rather than analysing it within the wider issues of migration and livelihood. She challenges the assumption that prostitution aids the trafficking of women and girls and suggests that the theory cannot be substantiated due to three fundamental problems:

1. the clandestine nature of trafficking (which makes it difficult to obtain data),
2. the lack of a solid baseline from which changes over time can be measured,
3. possible market saturation, especially for sexual commerce.

She further asserts that numbers are exaggerated and reproduced in the media with the intention of causing alarm, shocking the world, and convincing governments to commit greater resources to fighting sex work, to funding rescue operations, and to enhancing penalties against traffickers and clients.

Literature that examines the growth of the sex industry in the context of globalisation points out that in many fast-growing economies, the proliferation of sex work and the emergence of the informal entertainment industry has happened alongside economic growth, which has created a new class of people with disposable incomes who increasingly look for leisure and erotic entertainment (Hakim, 2015; Wilson, 2004). However, economic growth has also been inequitable; it has resulted in the large-scale internal migration of young women and girls to larger cities to find employment in the new symbols of growth such as dance bars, pubs, malls, and massage parlours.

The sex industry took root and flourished under the aegis of globalisation long before the internet era. For example, Lim's study (1998) examining the economic and social basis of prostitution in South Asia (which was incorporated into an International Labour Organisation [ILO] report) illustrated the sheer size and role of the sex and informal entertainment industry in East Asian economies. The study documented that in Indonesia, Malaysia, the Philippines, and Thailand, the sex sector accounted for between 2% and 14% of gross domestic product (GDP). Beyond the women directly engaged in this sector, tens of millions relied on the industry for their livelihood, thereby raising an array of different issues relating to basic human rights, morality, employment, gender discrimination, and criminality. According to Lim, the growth of this sector provided local government authorities with substantial revenue in the form of bribes and corruption in areas where prostitution thrived illegally, and from licensing fees and taxes where it was legal, as well as from the hotels, bars, restaurants, and game rooms that flourished alongside the sex work and informal entertainment. It is precisely for these reasons that it has been extremely challenging for governments to separate morality and the economic regulation of the sex industry. This trend is visible in Nepal where sex work remains illegal, but the government recognises the informal entertainment industry. Questions arise regarding why this is the case, and particularly whether it is due to the government's inability to create decent jobs in the economy or the government turning a blind eye to the issues within the sector because powerful and politically connected stakeholders run the industry.

In the South Asian context, women in this sector say that far more serious issues than the binary debates about whether sex work is oppressive or empowering need to be addressed, such as recognition of their basic human rights and particularly their right to earn a livelihood without experiencing violence. Studies from neighbouring India – where the legal and social attitude to sex work is similar to Nepal – have found that spaces where sex work is practised are highly abusive. There is systematic police violence, petty criminal gang harassment, abusive money lenders who charge compound interest, and business owners who ruthlessly use the system for monetary gain (see e.g. Seshu & Murthy, 2013, p. 16). It is therefore essential to understand how women working in this sector respond to such abuse. What are the factors (if any) that help them to be resilient?

This book examines the life histories of the participants to explore the following questions:

1. What are the social, cultural, and political factors that lead women to work in Nepal's sex and informal entertainment sector?
2. What difference does income make in the lives of women working in the informal entertainment sector?
3. What does empowerment mean for the women working in this sector?

4. How do women in this sector build their resilience in order to cope with trauma and daily violence?
5. How significant is the role of positive deviance?
6. What is the overall role of peer networks in addressing the violence that women face?
7. How important are local women's organisations in supporting and driving change for women in this sector?

By addressing the above empirical questions, this book explores the relationship between earning an independent income, empowerment, resilience, and the significance of peer organisations and networks for women who work in the sex and informal entertainment industry in Kathmandu, Nepal. I investigate the various sociocultural and political factors that compel women to migrate and to join the sex and informal entertainment industry, placing themselves in a highly vulnerable situation. I found that many factors, particularly political armed conflict disproportionally affect women, especially in societies where they are already subjugated and oppressed due to gender norms and patriarchal structures.

The study tested different models of empowerment in the context of the participants' lives and found that income from the informal entertainment industry is critical for the participants as it gives them decision-making power and allows them to take control of their income and make strategic choices pertaining to their future aspirations – these factors put them on the path towards empowerment. Resilience emerges when their inner attributes intersect with external resources provided through peer networks. In such networks, the participants found support and camaraderie, which gave them the confidence to assert their rights and even to confront violence. The book attempts to reframe the sex and informal entertainment industry by moving beyond a victimisation framework, but it does so without downplaying the extent of violence that women in this industry experience. It further attempts to build a counter-narrative that challenges the notion that sex workers are devoid of agency and outside the bounds of acceptable moral behaviour. In particular, I reflect on how the women struggle with their own ambiguity regarding their profession but find ways to remain positive about their future.

1.3 Thamel, Kathmandu

Overview of the sex and informal entertainment industry

Thousands of women work in massage parlours and dance bars, which often act as a conduit for sex work in Thamel, a vibrant business centre chosen as the primary field site for this book. It is hugely popular with tourists and locals alike in Nepal's capital, Kathmandu. Although no official figures are available on the number of women working in what is largely regarded as "informal entertainment" in Nepal, a 2009 study by the Swiss Agency Terre des Hommes (TdH) estimated that 11,000–13,000 girls and women were engaged in the industry in the Kathmandu Valley alone. The actual figure is believed to be much higher across Nepal. A 2013 Nepal Human Rights Commission (NHRC) study found that four in five workers reported that they had joined the industry through friends, and the study indicated that 73% of these women reported being verbally abused by customers, while 60% had experienced physical abuse.

Another report by TdH (Aguettant, Basnyat, & Fredrick, 2010) points out that not all women working in this sector work as sex workers, but they do work under conditions in which they are subjected to sexual harassment and abuse in order to please the customers so that they can buy food and drink. However, those who sell sex directly often do so under compulsion and coercion from the employer or the customer. A 2002 study by NGO Shakti Samua shows that "73% of the respondents stated that they 'performed additional' duties due to force from the employer or the customer" (as cited in Aguettant, Basnyat, & Fredrick, 2010, p. 24). Activists interviewed for this research say that the situation has not changed and that the number of female commercial sex workers (FCSW) in the country has actually increased since the outbreak of the COVID-19 pandemic. However, due to unreliable data sources and discrepancies regarding the definition of commercial sex workers (CSW), the actual number of FCSWs in Nepal is difficult to ascertain. Those interviewed for this study suggest that it is likely that the true number of women working in this sector is severely underestimated.

Responding to the surge of women working in this sector and reports of severe exploitation and trafficking, the Supreme Court of Nepal issued procedural guidelines in 2008 (Forum for Protection of Public Interest, 2009) giving protection against the economic and sexual exploitation of women and girls in the entertainment sector in a bid to curb sexual harassment. Recently, during its observations of the sixth periodic report of Nepal, the Committee on the Elimination of Discrimination against Women (CEDAW) expressed serious concern over the non-implementation of guidelines and noted that women in the informal entertainment sector continue to face extreme violence and abuse from clients and law enforcement bodies. CEDAW has directed the Government of Nepal to formulate a comprehensive legislative and regulatory policy framework that ensures monitoring and legal protection from exploitation for women who engage in sex work and to ensure that they are not prosecuted for engaging in such activities (Thapa, 2018).

In Nepal, sex workers and all women engaged in the informal entertainment sector are extremely marginalised, looked down upon, and severed from mainstream society. Economic opportunities for women are highly constrained, and sex workers are routinely prosecuted under the guise of public order offenses (Harman, Kaufman, Menger, & Shrestha, 2016). They are viewed as a group that do not conform, or who under conform, to the normative expectations of society (Heckert & Heckert, 2002, p. 456). Furthermore, dominant discourses in Nepal have linked the sex industry and prostitution to human trafficking and the HIV epidemic, leading to added stigma. Thus, women working in the industry are perceived as a category that is infected and therefore needs to be controlled (Basnyat, 2014).

Liechty (2005) situates the emergence of the informal entertainment industry in Kathmandu by drawing a relation between sex and food in Nepal's social context and describes the cabin restaurants in the Thamel area of Kathmandu that "service the carnal appetites – culinary and sexual – of a middle-class male clientele", documenting how Kathmandu emerged as a hub for prostitution and male entertainment in the early 1990s (Liechty, 2005, p. 17). Part of this transition was fuelled by the expansion of consumer practices brought about by growing global trade, which brought with it significant changes in the local economy and social texture. This was coupled with a steady growth in tourism and the carpet industry, which created thousands of new jobs (Liechty, 1998, 2003 as cited in Caviglia, 2017, p. 13).

In more recent years, the remittance economy that transfers funds to Nepal from the millions of Nepalese workers worldwide has created a new middle class, which has caused a significant shift in the sociocultural makeup of the country. Against this backdrop, Kathmandu became the consumption hub and the nation's centre of popular culture. Liechty argues that the evolution of new market forces transcended the barriers of caste and class that had firmly dictated social relations for centuries. The "restaurants of dance" were potent symbols of a new culture in Kathmandu and were places in which food and women were equally commodified in the private spaces that the restaurants offered. Liechty's study (2005) is significant as it analyses local and structural factors in relation to redefining gender relations and the emergence of an informal entertainment industry. It considers how gender relations change as transactions and sex move increasingly from the private, domestic sphere to the commercial sphere. In the market domain, however, especially in dance bars and cabin restaurants, the gender hierarchy was reinforced as women became the objects of male control and desire. Women were paid to perform intimate acts or entertain customers (who were mainly men) for their pleasure. Liechty also notes that within the sphere of the market, the traditional norms of food consumption and sexual behaviour dictated by socio-religious practices were often diluted. The women working in the cabin restaurants and dance bars came from diverse castes and backgrounds and were essentially serving a category of local men who could afford such services. The new zones of entertainment became hotspots where bodies lost their caste-based moral meanings and became anonymous parts of a "free market" of commercial exchange. And in this context, the women who were part of the informal entertainment industry used the market economy as the basis for building autonomy by selling sexual services (Liechty, 2005, p. 11).

Commenting on how sex work in Nepal can be seen as a social and analytical category, Caviglia (2017) examines how sex workers negotiate their identity in an urban space where they are detached from their immediate communities and social norms that undermine the lives of women in Nepal. The women working in this sector in Kathmandu offer different opportunities for anonymity and possibilities for a different kind of freedom (Kristvik, 2002, p. 114). Through ethnographic study, Caviglia deconstructs the "sex worker" category against the backdrop of global influences and how they come into conflict with local urban surroundings and points to the contradictions therein. Although sex workers are judged harshly by the media and social commentators, Caviglia also points to various contradictions in Nepalese societies that are constructed and upheld to keep women in a subordinated role and where male dependency largely affects women's subsistence. The author also critiques the labelling of sex workers as a category of women who are victims and also deviant, describing it as an "othering" strategy that occurs at the caste–gender nexus and often becomes the basis to reaffirm subjugation and further marginalisation of sex workers.

Some women simply see sex work as an option to make a living and justify the suitability of their profession in various ways in the face of widespread stigmatisation. Caviglia questions the notions of moral value usually linked with intimate relations, which in Nepal and in a wider South Asian context are usually defined by material exchanges (such as a dowry) that generate a "continuum of sexual-economic" exchange and engender asymmetrical relations (Tablet, 2004 as cited in Caviglia, 2017). For example, Kathmandu's original inhabitants, Newars, see marriage as a contractual "affair between wife-takers" marked by a large number of exchange rituals (Gutschow & Michales, 2012 as cited in Caviglia, 2017, p. 147). The point the author is making is that in a culture where women's identities, voices, and agency are often subject to limits imposed by patriarchy, sex workers are aware of the value of their sexuality and body and that expressing this value also involves a form of exchange. Whether or not sex is a commodity depends on the context. For example, it can be a gift in marriage, a symbol of emotion in a love marriage, or simply a commodity in the context of sex work. As Kristvik (2002, p. 261) argues, for Nepali women economic independence can pave the way out of the debilitating bondage of patriarchy and an abusive marriage, which this study supports. For many, entering sex work is one of the very few chances they might have to earn their own money and thus live an independent life in which they can exercise their agency.

1.4 Scoping work and qualitative research

There is a need to employ sensitising concepts to explore and better understand the backgrounds of individuals and how these have led to the current situation of the participants in my research. Qualitative methods are useful tools to study the knowledge and practices of participants. It is critical to understand how they normalise their work and to analyse interactions and ways of dealing with violence. As suggested by Flick (2014, p. 16), qualitative research takes into account the viewpoints and experiences of the participants and the different subjective perspectives and social backgrounds related to them. Qualitative research is frequently used in feminist studies in order to open up space for women's voices and needs in general.

For the purpose of this study, extensive scoping work was undertaken during the initial phase of the research. The objective of the scoping work was to scan the external environment in order to see first-hand the realities relating to WEE and VAWG in Nepal. Accordingly, a list of key stakeholder organisations was mapped. The mapped organisations were then divided into two broad categories in order to gain institutional perspectives and actor perspectives. The institutional perspectives refer to suppliers of services or those who are duty bearers for addressing issues such as children's and women's protection, poverty reduction, WEE, and VAWG. These include the Government of Nepal, UN agencies, donors, industry associations, and consulting organisations. The actor perspectives include those of individual women and girls, their associations (such as unions and financial or business cooperatives), and NGOs that work with them. The institutions that were interviewed in Nepal made several statements relating to policies, norms, and institutions or the legal, official, and social policy environment, of which many are related to institutional initiatives or needs.

Since the women in the entertainment industry are a "hard-to-reach" social group, the scoping work enabled me to select originations that were suitable for the study. The key challenge was to get access to the women working in the sector and to ensure that the research was conducted in a safe and secure environment. Whilst government agencies, international non-governmental organisations (INGOs), and NGOs provided valuable information about the type of VAWG and WEE projects that were already in place, it was, however, clear that no research initiatives were in place to explore how WEE can also potentially tackle violence in relation to women who work in Nepal's informal entertainment industry.

Accordingly, four well-known NGOs working in the informal entertainment sector, Raksha Nepal, Biswas Nepal, Jagriti Mahila Maha Sangh, and the SWAN, were contacted. During the scoping work, I visited all four organisations and had conversations with members of their staff. I also attended a meeting of union members. The exercise familiarised me with the general policy and legal enabling environment vis-à-vis women in the informal entertainment sector and the day-to-day challenges they face. For example, all four organisations emphasised that no laws are in place to deal with crimes related to VAWG in the informal entertainment sector, which they attributed to the industry being seen as synonymous with sex work, which is not recognised as "work" by the Nepal government.

According to Raksha Nepal, among the women with whom they work, approximately 57% are victims of conflict, and others have also experienced domestic violence, sexual violence, and caste discrimination. The four organisations also stressed that since sex work is illegal, police officers are known to extract money from the owners of massage parlours, dance bars, and other establishments in the informal entertainment industry. The points raised and documented during the scoping process were complemented by intense observation, and together these were instrumental in formulating the research questions as they gave some indication of what participants might reveal during the actual interview process. Accordingly, these issues were raised with individual participants as well as with focus groups.

1.5 Mapping key organisations

While considering the question of access to the participants, it was important to work out how to secure the collaboration of potential participants of the study and ensure that participants were willing to share their life experiences in a manner that led to reliable data (Flick, 2014, p. 158). During the scoping work, I had informal discussions with Menuka Thapa, the founder of Raksha Nepal, Shova Dangol of SWAN, Bijaya Dhakal of JMMS, and Balakuamari Ale of Biswas Nepal. I was also able to meet a few women who benefited from their work. The dialogue was immensely fruitful as it helped me to clarify the intention of my research while also examining their work. I became more familiar with the underlying problems and challenges that women face in the industry, and the process also served as a trust-building exercise. The organisations showed keen interest in the project and felt that there was a need to analyse and document the outcome of the work they were doing.

Whilst all four organisations mentioned above are documented in this study, Raksha Nepal was selected as a primary route through which to access the women who work in the sex and informal entertainment sector. The decision was mainly based on the strategic location and expertise of the organisation and the scale of its outreach work: Raksha Nepal has established a union, an adult women's school, a shelter for children, and a credit and savings scheme. These multiple branches offered a framework through which to study how they contribute to the process of women's empowerment in the sector. It was also strictly mandated by the DFID ethics committee and the University of Portsmouth that sampling of the participants must be done with the help of local organisations that are active in the field.

Due to the subjective and qualitative nature of the interviews, it was necessary that a proper mechanism was put in place to deal with the safety and security of the participants and the researcher. I also recognised at an early stage that interviewing those who were already in touch with or active within the organisation might result in participants showing bias in favour of the organisation with which they were connected when responding to questions. To minimise such risks, I requested that Raksha Nepal reach out to women who were not directly associated with them, though this did not entirely avoid the limitation. Also, all the participants responded differently to the questions asked, and the overall sample (including the focus group) consisted of women who were not directly associated with Raksha Nepal but who were nonetheless aware of the organisation's activities. The number of interviewees was limited to 21 participants due to the complexity and sensitivity of the subject. It was also, at times, difficult to request that women participate in a study where the average time of the interview was going to be at least an hour.

The main advantage of seeking Raksha Nepal's help was that they had an office right in the heart of Thamel, where most of the women work. This made their presence highly visible, and the field workers of the organisation had developed a good rapport with the women and girls working in the sector, regularly interacting with them irrespective of their affiliation to the organisation. They organised their fortnightly union meetings in the area and ran an adult literacy programme that was designed for the women with whom they worked, but it was also open to others. Due to their strong network, Raksha Nepal was in a position to explain the research to participants and invite them for an interview. The location for the interviews was chosen strategically as the women could easily come to the office before, in between, or after work. Raksha Nepal also provided a secure space for the interviews and a female interpreter who was well versed in Nepali and English and worked as a programme officer with the organisation. The potential participants were already familiar with the staff members of Raksha Nepal, which was an asset as it meant that the interviews could be conducted in a space that was safe for the participants.

1.6 Description of interviewees

The background of each participant in terms of age, caste, religion, and marital status was not known until the time the interview was conducted. The ages of the participants varied from 19 to 51 years, though the majority of the participants were aged between 20 and 28. Of the 21 participants, 15 had experienced child marriage (under the age of 18) and had become mothers before the age of 18 and were no longer living with their husbands, though legally they were not divorced. There were three widows in the sample. None of the participants had had access to good education, with only one participant having attended high school, though she had also eventually dropped out. Child marriage and the Maoist conflict (as explained in Chapters 2 and 3) were the main reasons for not attending school. It was also determined that women of diverse castes (including Brahmins and Dalits) and religions, but particularly Hindus and Buddhists, had found their way into the informal entertainment sector. All women shared experiences of suffering and of poor economic conditions; these were the common denominators among all the participants.

1.7 Research framework

The research was framed by a number of linked themes, which in turn helped me to generate interview questions. The themes outlined below were intended to help participants present their views in the framework of the question.

1.7.1 Early life and migration

Both rural to urban migration and cross-border migration are on the rise in Nepal. The study sought to capture the impact this has on women working in the informal entertainment sector and their early vulnerabilities to violence. This broad line of enquiry underpinned the following narrower questions: Do women working in this sector feel they are more or less vulnerable following their move from their village into a city? Is income the primary motivation for migration? Did they explore other income-generating activities following migration or before joining the informal entertainment sector? This theme was useful to develop an understanding of the beliefs, values, social frameworks, and practical conditions that had shaped the participants' early experiences of violence and whether that had contributed to economic engagement in the sector. Chapters 3 and 4 provide in-depth intersectional analyses of various relevant sociocultural, economic, and political factors relating to these questions.

1.7.2 *How earning an income affects relationships within the home*

Much of the existing literature relating to intra-household bargaining suggests that earning an income increases a woman's bargaining and decision-making powers at home, but others have suggested that the outcome of increased income is context specific. This is discussed in detail in the context of the participants of this study in Chapter 4. The key questions were: Do women have control over their income? How do they spend their money? Does earning an income make women feel confident? And, if they are married, does earning an income introduce tensions due to challenging traditional gender norms and power relations?

1.7.3 *Causes of violence and vulnerability*

Questions were also asked that explored how certain women working in the informal entertainment sector may be more or less vulnerable to particular forms of violence and how this may or may not link to income levels and earning activities. The research sought to identify whether social norms contributed to situations where violence in women's personal lives was normalised (discussed in Chapter 3). Specific questions were also asked in order to ascertain whether some groups (such as partners, police, clients, or business owners) sanction particular forms of violence and not others. Questions included: Do women exercise resilience to violence and, if so, in what ways are they able to do this? What is the role of peer networks (discussed in Chapters 5 and 7) in promoting the well-being of women working in this sector? Does it help them to draw on resources or display greater agency to ensure protection from and responsiveness to violence?

1.7.4 *Nature, type, and conditions of work*

Questions were also asked that sought to gain in-depth information pertaining to the work histories of the participants. The questions that underpinned this part of the interview were: Have they always worked in the informal entertainment sector, and how willing or unwilling were they to talk about it? If they have not, what other jobs had they been engaged in? Why did they leave those jobs to join the informal entertainment industry? What were the main drivers? Does access to women's collective action (peer networks) through cooperatives and unions, support services, and other networks have a significant impact on determining both how empowered a woman feels to exert decision-making power and how vulnerable to violence she feels?

1.7.5 *Aspirations for the future*

Finally, questions were asked regarding the personal aspirations of participants, which included discussing their willingness to stand up against violence, the importance of education, community attitudes, and what changes would make a difference to their lives. The aim of these questions was to understand the outlook of participants regarding their life and if they are optimistic despite the daily challenges that they encounter.

1.8 Chapter structure

In Chapters 2 and 3, I analyse the key factors that contributed to participants making the decision to move to the capital, Kathmandu, and eventually join the sex and informal entertainment industry. Together, these two chapters consider the lives of the participants before they joined the informal entertainment sector. Chapter 2 focuses on the impact of the 10-year Maoist conflict (1996–2006) on the lives of the participants. During the interviews, I found that one-third of the participants' lives had been significantly affected during the insurgency that gripped Nepal. The chapter provides evidence of some of the worst forms of violence that were perpetrated by the rebel forces. The chapter offers a significant contribution to understanding the relationship between migration, violence, and sex work because, as the International Centre for Transitional Justice (ICTJ) report *The Impact of Nepal's Conflict on Women* (Sharma & Young, 2010) underlined, information pertaining to sexual violence against women and girls during the armed conflict in Nepal remains scarce and scattered. The chapter demonstrates how the lack of transitional justice mechanisms has failed the marginalised women who have been further victimised by the conflict. They have faced severe stigmatisation that, coupled with a lack of monetary compensation or rehabilitation programmes, meant that they were left to fend for themselves. Many found their way into the sex and informal entertainment industry as a means to meet their survival needs.

Chapter 3 discusses the beliefs, values, social frameworks, and practical conditions that shaped the violence experienced by the participants in their early lives. A combination of factors including child marriage, dowry, notions of honour, excessive consumption of alcohol, and intimate partner violence (IPV) intersect in ways that lead to abuse. These early experiences of violence have left scars of deep trauma on the lives of the women who were interviewed for this study. In many cases, they were abandoned by their abusive partners. For some of the participants, these circumstances also influenced their decision to join the informal entertainment industry. In this chapter, Heise's (2011) adapted ecology model is used to analyse the data. The framework affirms that VAWG is caused by one or a combination of many factors; such violence can be attributed to genetics or the personal history of the perpetrator or can be situational. The framework is useful as it provides a structure within which to analyse the complex interplay of probabilistic factors that work at the micro, meso, and macro levels, and in turn locates these levels within broader cultural frameworks that can help explain the underlying reasons for the violence experienced by the participants.

In Chapter 4, various theories of empowerment and concepts of power are introduced. These concepts are discussed in relation to women's income, their degree of autonomy, and their ability to make choices. It has been argued that WEE refers to participation in activities that generate an income. However, economic activity does not necessarily equate to empowerment. Empowerment is a holistic concept, denoting a process in which an individual is able to access resources and build agency. Typically, it means increasing decision-making power, building self-efficacy and self-esteem, gaining control of assets, and generating positive outcomes (Kabeer, 2001). Studies on WEE have not looked in detail at what empowerment *means* for those working in the sex and entertainment industry. Thus, many questions remain, for example: What resources are available to women working in this sector? How do they exercise choice and express agency? How can their empowerment be measured? In this chapter, I contribute to addressing some of these questions by applying the concepts of empowerment and power and discussing them in relation to the experiences of the participants. I argue that they use their bodies as a resource and, as they earn an income from it, they are able to gain a certain degree of autonomy with regard to decision-making processes in respect of their own lives. I propose a model as a measure of empowerment for the participants based on the examples discussed in the chapter.

Building on the discussions of the previous chapter, Chapter 5 discusses how the women who participated in this study demonstrate resilience against the various forms of violence that are prevalent in their profession. Resilience means the ability of an individual to withstand, challenge, and overturn the power structures that shape choices, opportunities, and well-being. In this chapter, I outline the various frameworks on resilience and examine how the question of the resilience of sex workers has been explored by other studies. The chapter captures the depth of trauma the participants have experienced and presents a comprehensive analysis of how peer networks help women to further strengthen and develop the characteristics of their resilience. Based on this analysis, I propose a framework that can be used to demonstrate how resilience leads to a process of empowerment for the participants. The framework illustrates how women working in the informal entertainment sector collectively create a model in the form of a peer network, which serves as a protective lens, and through that lens they reconstruct their relationship with the outer world.

Chapter 6 introduces the concept of "positive deviance", which is described as a form of social inquiry "based on the premise that in every community there are certain individuals or groups whose uncommon behaviour and strategies enable them to find better solutions to the same problems facing their peers" (Herington & Fliert, 2018).

In this chapter, I look at the lives of four women: Menuka Thapa of Raksha Nepal, Bijaya Dhakal of Jagariti Mahila Maha Sangh, Balkumari Ale of Biswas Nepal, and Shova Dangol of SWAN, whose extraordinary initiatives have had a transformative impact on the lives of other women working in this sector. I propose a framework in which these four women can be described as "positive deviants", in order to identify the factors that play a significant role in their becoming champions of change, which in turn has positive consequences for other members of the community.

Chapter 7 details the role of peer networks in the context of the broad range of services that they offer by way of creating institutions such as credit and savings schemes, shelter homes for children, and a union. I consider what these services mean for the women who work in the sex and informal entertainment sector, as well as what strength they derive from it. I use a culture-centred approach to address these questions (Basu, 2011, 2017; Basu & Dutta, 2008). In the culture-centred approach, the narratives of the cultural participants (in this case the women working in the sex and informal entertainment industry) are used to reconstitute discourses that contextualise the cultural meanings and structures of their living conditions. These discourses challenge the perception that marginalised communities, including sex workers, are incapable of making informed choices on matters pertaining to their lives. The chapter also examines the role of the union of sex workers at the global level, including the services it provides to the women who work in the sex and informal entertainment sector in Kathmandu.

Before moving on to the conclusion, Chapter 8 reflects on the impact of the COVID-19 pandemic on the lives of women who work in the informal entertainment sector in Nepal. The chapter frames how sex worker groups have responded to the pandemic in the context of the nascent human rights movement of sex workers in Nepal. It documents how sex worker groups can be empowered to further build their survival strategies during a pandemic and can mobilise in a time of crisis to demand basic relief services from the authorities. Based on a recent survey. The chapter also draws attention to the devastating impact of the pandemic –in terms of both livelihood and health – on the sex workers and those engaged in the informal entertainment sector in Nepal.

To conclude, I summarise the findings, identify the remaining gaps in research, and propose a number of policy recommendations. I argue that there is a need for a more pragmatic approach to regulating the informal entertainment industry in Nepal and elsewhere. To safeguard the interests of women working in this sector, it is imperative to protect their human rights and treat them as equal citizens. The industry is strongly connected with the global tourism and hospitality industry, and, as such, governments around the world cannot simply turn a blind eye. Adopting a pro-work model can bring more transparency to the industry, which in turn can protect women from violence, promote better working conditions and their human rights, and assist in tackling human trafficking.

References

Aguettant, J. L., Basnyat, M., & Fredrick, J. (2010). *Trafficking and Exploitation in the Entertainment and Sex Industry in Nepal: A Handbook for Decision Makers.* Terre des Hommes Foundation.

Baltiwala, S. (2013). How sex workers expand feminist concepts of choice and consent. In L. Murthy & M. S. Seshu (Eds.), *The Business of Sex* (pp. 125–147). Zubaan.

Basnyat, I. (2014). Lived experiences of street-based female sex workers in Kathmandu: Implications for the health intervention strategies. *Culture, Health & Sexuality, 16*(9), 1040–1051.

Basu, A. (2011). HIV/AIDS and subaltern autonomous rationality: A call to recenter health communication in marginalized sex worker spaces. *Communication Monographs, 78*(3), 391–408.

Basu, A. (2017). Reba and her insurgent prose: Sex work, HIV/AIDS, and subaltern narratives. *Qualitative Health Research, 27*(10), 1507–1517.

Basu, A., & Dutta, M. J. (2008). Participatory change in a campaign led by sex workers: Connecting resistance to action-oriented agency. *Qualitative Health Research, 18*(1), 106–119.

Bradley, C., & Szablewska, N. (2014). Social justice within transitional justice: The case of human trafficking and sex-work in Cambodia and Myanmar. In N. Szablewska & S. D. Bachmann (Eds.), *Current Issues in Transitional Justice: Towards a More Holistic Approach* (pp. 261–287). Springer.

Bradley, T., Sahariah, S., & Siddiqui, O. (2016). A critical reading of western newspaper narratives of rape in India and their implications for feminist activism. *Continuum: Journal of Media and Cultural Studies, 31*(1), 126–137.

Brooks-Gordon, B. (2006). *The Price of Sex: Prostitution, Policy and Society.* Willan Publishing.

Bryant, C., & Palmer, C. (1975). Massage parlors and "Hand Whores". Some sociological observations. *The Journal of Sex Research, 11*(3), 227–241.

Burke, J. (2013, September 10). Delhi rape: How India's other half lives. *The Guardian.* www.theguardian.com/world/2013/sep/10/delhi-gang-rape-india-women

Busza, J. (2004). Sex work and migration: The dangers of oversimplification. A case study of Vietnamese women in Cambodia. *Health and Human Rights: An International Journal, 7*(2), 231–249.

Caviglia, L. (2017). *Sex Work in Nepal* (South Asia Edition). Routledge.

Ditmore, M. P. (2014). "Caught Between the Tiger and the Crocodile": Cambodian sex workers' experiences of structural and physical violence. *Studies in Gender and Sexuality, 15*(1), 22–3.

Dworkin, A. (1993). Prostitution and male supremacy. *Michigan Journal of Gender and Law, 1*(1), 1–12.

Estébanez, P., Fitch, K., & Nájera, R. (1993). HIV and female sex workers. *Bulletin of the World Health Organization, 71*(3–4), 397–412. World Health Organization. www.who.int/iris/handle/10665/26167

Flick, U. (2014). *An Introduction to Qualitative Research* (Fifth Edition). Sage.

Fortunato, F. (1973). Rubdub: The massage is the message. *Penthouse* (October), 129–134.

Global Network of Sex Work Projects (NSWP). (2014). *Economic Empowerment Programmes for Sex Workers* (Stepping Up, Stepping Out Project: Regional Reports Summary). www.nswp.org/resource/nswp-briefing-papers/briefing-paper-economic-empowerment-sex-workers

Goetz, A., & Sen Gupta, R. (1996). Who takes the credit? Gender, power and control over loan use in rural credit programs in Bangladesh. *World Development, 24*(1), 45–63.

Gutschow, N. & Michales, A. (2012). *Getting Married: Hindu and Buddhist Marriage Rituals Among the Newars of Bhakaapur and Patan, Nepal.* Wiesbaden: Harrassowitz Verlag.

Hahn, K., & Holzscheiter, A. (2013). The ambivalence of advocacy: Representation and contestation in global NGO advocacy for child workers and sex workers. *Global Society, 27*(4), 497–540.

Hakim, C. (2015). Economies of desire: Sexuality and the sex industry in the 21st century. *Economic Affairs, 35*(3), 329–348.

Halley, J., Kotiswaran, P., Shamir, H., & Thomas, C. (2006). From the international to the local in feminist responses to rape, prostitution/sex work, and sex trafficking: Four studies in contemporary governance feminism. *Harvard Journal of Law and Gender, 29*(2), 335–423.

Harman, J., Kaufman, R. W., Menger, L. M., & Shrestha, K. D. (2016). Understanding the experiences and needs of female commercial sex workers in Kathmandu, Nepal. *Health Care for Women International, 37*(8), 872–888.

Heckert, A., & Heckert, D. M. (2002). A new typology of deviance: Integrating normative and reactivist definitions of deviance. *Deviant Behavior, 23*(5), 449–479.

Heise, L. L. (2011). *What Works to Prevent Partner Violence? An Evidence Overview* (STRIVE Working Paper). London School of Hygiene and Tropical Medicine.

Herington, M. J., & van de Fliert, E. (2018). Positive deviance in theory and practice: A conceptual review. *Deviant Behavior, 39*(5), 664–678.

International Covenant on Economic, Social and Cultural Rights (1966). https://www.coe.int/en/web/compass/international-covenant-on-economic-social-and-cultural-rights

Jeffreys, S. (1997). *The Idea of Prostitution.* Spinifex.

Jeffreys, S. (2009). *The Industrial Vagina: The Political Economy of the Global Sex Trade.* Routledge.

Kabeer, N. (Ed.). (2001). *Discussing Women's Empowerment, Theory and Practice* (Sida Studies. Vol. 3). Swedish International Development Cooperation Agency.

Kotiswaran, P. (2011). Born unto brothels: Toward a legal ethnography of sex work in an Indian-red light area. In P. Kotiswaran (Ed.), *Sex Work* (pp. 157–181). Women Unlimited.

Kristvik, E. (2002). *Nepali Sex Workers. Narratives of Violence and Agency.* Lambert.

Liechty, M. (2005). Carnal economics: The commodification of food and sex in Kathmandu. *Cultural Anthropology, 20*(1), 1–38.

Lim, L. L. (1998). *The Sex Sector: The Economic and Social Bases of Prostitution in Southeast Asia.* International Labour Organisation.

MacKinnon, C. A. (1993). Prostitution and civil rights. *Michigan Journal of Gender and Law, 1*(1), 13–31.

Moret, W. (2014). *Economic Strengthening for Female Sex Workers: A Review of the Literature.* United States Agency for International Development (USAID) (USAID Cooperative Agreement No. AID-OAA-LA-13-00001). www.fhi360.org/sites/default/files/media/documents/Economic_Strengthening_for_Female_Sex_Workers.pdf

Murthy, L., & Seshu, M. S. (2013). *The Business of Sex.* Zuban.

O'Connell Davidson, J. (2006). Will the real sex slave please stand up? *Feminist Review, 83*, 4–22.

Onyeneho, N. G. (2009). HIV/AIDS risk factors and economic empowerment needs of female sex workers in Enugu Urban, Nigeria. *Tanzania Journal of Health Research, 11*(3), 126.

Overs, C. (2013). Sex workers and feminists: Personal reflections. In L. Murthy & M. S. Seshu (Eds.), *The Business of Sex* (pp. 81–98). Zuban.

Rajan, R. S. (2011). The prostitution question(s): Female agency, sexuality and work. In P. Kotiswaran (Ed.), *Sex Work* (pp. 118–156). Women Unlimited.

Sagade, J., & Forster, C. (2018). Recognising the human rights of female sex workers in India: Moving from prohibition to decriminalisation and a pro-work model. *Indian Journal of Gender Studies, 25*(1), 26–46.

Sandy, L. (2009). "Behind Closed Doors": Debt-bonded sex workers in Sihanoukville, Cambodia. *The Asia Pacific Journal of Anthropology, 10*(3), 216–230.

Sharma, M., & Young, K. (2010). *Across the Lines: The Impact of Nepal's Conflict on Women.* International Centre for Transnational Justice Advocacy Forum. www.ictj.org/publication/across-lines-impact-nepals-conflict-women

Skeldon, R. (2000). Trafficking: A perspective from Asia. *International Migration, 38*(3), 7–30.

Sullivan, B. (2007). Rape, prostitution and consent. *The Australian and New Zealand Journal of Criminology, 40*(2), 127–142.

Sutherland, K. (2004). Work, sex, and sex-work: Competing feminist discourses on the international sex trade. *Osgoode Hall Law Journal, 42*(1), 139–167.

Szablewska, N., & Bradley, C. (2014a). Social justice within transitional justice: The case of human trafficking and sex-work in Cambodia and Myanmar. In N. Szablewska & S. D. Bachmann (Eds.), *Current Issues in Transitional Justice: Towards a More Holistic Approach* (pp. 261–287). Springer.

Szablewska, N., & Bradley, C. (2014b). The nexus between sex-work and women's empowerment in the context of transitional societies of Southeast Asia. In N. Szablewska & S. D. Bachmann (Eds.), *Current Issues in Transitional Justice: Towards a More Holistic Approach* (pp. 235–260). Springer.

Tablet, T. (2004). *La Grande Beffa.* Soveria Mannelli: Rubbettino Editore.

Thapa, T. M. (2018). *Statement Delivered at the Sixth Periodic Review of Nepal at 71st session of CEDAW committee by the Leader of Nepali Delegation Hon'ble Minister for Women, Children and Senior Citizens Mrs. Tham Maya Thapa.* https://tbinternet.ohchr.org/Treaties/CEDAW/Shared%20Documents/NPL/INT_CEDAW_STA_NPL_32836_E.pdf

Universal Declaration of Human Rights (1948). https://www.un.org/en/about-us/universal-declaration-of-human-rights

Weitzer, R. (2005). New directions in research on prostitution. *Crime, Law and Social Change, 43*(2), 11–35.

Weitzer, R. (2011). Sex trafficking and the sex industry: The need for evidence-based theory and legislation. *Journal of Criminal Law and Criminology, 101*(4), 1337–1370.

Wilson, A. (2004). *The Intimate Economies of Bangkok: Tomboys, Tycoons, and Avon Ladies in the Global City.* University of California Press. ebookcentral.proquest.com/lib/portsmouthebooks/detail.action? docID=471000

2 The impact of Nepal's Maoist conflict on women

2.1 Introduction

In this chapter (and also Chapter 3), I compare and contrast the experiences of the women who participated in my research and identify the key factors that influenced their decisions to move to the Kathmandu Valley and eventually join the informal sex and entertainment industry. Among the most significant findings that emerged from the interviews conducted with the women working in the sex and informal entertainment industry in Kathmandu is how the 10-year-long Maoist conflict also referred as Nepal conflict (1996–2006), led by the Maoist forces – known as the People's Liberation Army (PLA) – against government forces, had devastating consequences on their early lives (UNOHCHR, 2012). From the sample of 21 women interviewed, one-third had been directly affected by the conflict; four women confirmed that they had been abducted, sexually abused, raped, and used as child soldiers during the conflict. Others, who had migrated to Kathmandu when they were very young, said that the conflict was their main reason for leaving their villages. They explained that schoolchildren were regularly abducted by the PLA and coerced to join various ranks in its forces. Recruited girls were used as combatants, scouts, spies, porters, and cooks, and also as "cultural troops" (people who propagate the Maoist ideologies through music and culture).

Studies of the Maoist conflict in Nepal have dealt with the wide-ranging gendered implications of the conflict. They have acknowledged that sexual violence and horrifying atrocities were inflicted on women, and their bodies were used as "tools of war" by both government forces and rebels with impunity (Aryal, 2016, p. 177). A report by the International Centre for Transitional Justice (ICTJ), *Across the Lines, The Impact of Nepal's Conflict on Women* (Sharma & Young, 2010), found that information about sexual violence perpetrated by the rebel forces against women and girls during the armed conflict in Nepal is scarce and scattered. It stressed that while other conflict-related human rights violations such as enforced disappearances, killings, and torture were widely reported and systematically documented, the issue of sexual violence has been largely ignored by international organisations as well as national institutions such as the National Human Rights Commission. It is believed that factors such as cultural stigmatisation, insecurity,

DOI: 10.4324/9781003156796-2

and fear of retaliation from the warring parties discouraged the reporting of sexual violence during the conflict. The silence around sexual violence has meant that the issue is under-researched, which has left most victims and survivors without the necessary psychosocial support, medical assistance, or legal recourse to process their trauma and seek justice (Sharma & Young, 2010, p. 45). One of the key contributions of this volume has been to document cases of sexual violence committed by Maoist forces. Much of this came to light while conducting this research. Doing so is also important because earlier studies have acknowledged that evidence of sexual violence committed by the PLA is scarce (UNOHCHR, 2012). The Transitional Justice Reference Archive (TJRA), a database of approximately 30,000 documents and cases sourced from the monitoring work of the National Human Rights Commission and the Office of the United Nations High Commissioner for Human Rights (OHCHR) in Nepal since May 2005, indicates that most atrocities against women were committed by the security forces. Of over 100 cases catalogued, only 12 list PLA personnel as the alleged perpetrators (TJRC as cited in Aryal, 2016, p. 175). However, Nepalese human rights groups have asserted that though stories of sexual violence committed by the Maoist forces were widespread, the cases were not documented and remain anecdotes (Aryal, 2016, p. 176).

The chapter begins by presenting the background to the 10-year-long conflict between the PLA and government forces. Here, the political and social factors that eventually culminated in the civil conflict between the warring factions are discussed. The next section (2.3) explores the impact of the conflict on women and girls by examining the gendered narratives used by the Maoist forces in order to attract women and girls to join the rank and file of their army. While Maoist propaganda inspired some women, Maoist forces also systematically abducted girls from schools and coerced them to do a variety of jobs. The section following it (2.4) documents the experiences of the women who took part in this study, as they recounted examples of abuses including rape and violence inflicted by the Maoist forces. During the conflict, both the government forces and the PLA targeted women of families alleged to be sympathisers of the opposing group. However, the evidence provided illustrates a contradiction between the wider claims made by Maoists regarding gender equality and the reality of their ruthless treatment of women. The chapter then goes on to explore the cumbersome process of seeking justice and the various measures set up by the government following transition, which were ultimately ineffective in facilitating justice for women. In the conclusion, I summarise the main findings of the chapter and argue that a range of interlocking factors must be considered when analysing the long-term gendered implications of the conflict. It is clear from the interviews and the analysis of them that political instability and a lack of political will are major obstacles that deny the women and girls who were sexually abused during the conflict access to justice and rehabilitation.

2.2 The Maoist conflict (1996–2006)

The 10-year-long Maoist insurgency that gripped Nepal is believed to have displaced 200,000 people and killed 13,000 people (OHCHR report as cited in Bhusal, 2016; Manchanda, 2004b; Shakya, 2011; Valente, 2011). It began in February 1996 when the Maoist Communist Party of Nepal (CPN-Maoist) declared a "People's War" against the government for its inability to address a wide range of social, economic, and political issues. The Maoists believed that the ruling class in Kathmandu, including the monarchy and the government, were corrupt, elitist, and feudal and that only a revolutionary armed struggle could put in place a genuine democratic republic to represent the poor and the peasants (Bhusal, 2016; Thapa & Sijapati, 2005, as cited in Shakya, 2011). In the early years of the conflict, the Maoist movement was repressed by the state through armed police operations including Operation Romeo in 1995 and KiloSera II in 1998 (Thapa & Sijapati, 2005, as cited in Bhusal, 2016).

Despite this, the Maoists were able to establish themselves in the mid-western region of Nepal, especially in the districts of Rolpa, Rukum, Salyan, Jajarkot, and Sindhuli. In the late 1990s, they rapidly expanded their radical movement throughout the country (Shakya, 2011), and by 2001 they controlled 22 of the 75 districts. These districts were underdeveloped, hard to reach, and extremely poor (Bhusal, 2016, p. 137). The Maoist forces attacked government officials and establishments, burned down police stations, and paralysed the machinery of the state, leading to an all-out war with the then Royal Nepal Army (NPA). The government responded by declaring a state of emergency, which resulted in the suspension of a host of civil rights. The CPN (Maoist) was then declared a terrorist organisation, and it was during this period that draconian laws including the Terrorist and Disruptive Activities (TADA) were passed, affording government forces sweeping powers to detain and interrogate anyone suspected of involvement in the conflict.

In February 2005, ex-King Gyanendra reinstated monarchical power through a royal coup, and the main political parties subsequently came together to agitate against the takeover in a Seven-Party Alliance (SPA). This alliance initiated negotiations with the CPN (Maoist), and a twelve-point memorandum of understanding was drafted, in which an agreement was made to fight against the monarchic autocratic rule. In April 2006, Jana Andolan II (the People's Movement) successfully removed the king and reinstated the House of Representatives. The SPA and the Maoists reached a historic six-point agreement on 8 November 2006, signing a comprehensive peace agreement on 21 November 2006 and finally an agreement on the monitoring of arms and armies on 28 November 2006. On 10 April 2008, during the constituent assembly election, the CPN (Maoist) won more seats than any other party, leading to the formation of a coalition government (Bhusal, 2016; Sharma & Young, 2010; Shakya, 2011). However, as a result of the preceding conflict, as many as 200,000 people were estimated to have fled their rural homes, seeking work abroad or migrating to Nepali cities as internally displaced peoples (IDPs).

2.3 State actors and sexual violence during the conflict

A study in 2009 by the Advocacy Forum of Nepal and the ICTJ in 16 districts across the country investigating the impact of the armed conflict on women found that the perpetration of sexual violence including rape was widespread and was committed by both sides: the government forces and the Maoist forces (Bhusal, 2016). The report, which was based on interviews with women from marginalised groups, found that the majority of the alleged perpetrators were state actors or security personnel appointed by the state. Of the 128 cases of sexual violence recorded, 73% were found to have been perpetrated by state security personnel. Among them, more than half (56%) involved multiple perpetrators including incidences of women raped by the security forces and then by Maoists when they came to interrogate the women about what had happened. Many of the allegations accused the armed police force and the state army of torture, which included blindfolding and handcuffing people for weeks and months without any trail. An Amnesty International (2003) report found that state actors (including the police and the army) resorted to methods of torture including rape, electric shock, and mock executions, on both men and women. Most of these crimes were committed during search operations and interrogations by state forces (UNOHCHR, 2012, p. 158), but there were also numerous opportunistic violations (Pokhrel & Sharma, 2016, p. 106). There were a significant number of women combatants among the rebels (UNOHCHR, 2012, p. 153), and those arrested were subjected to rape, threats of rape, torture, and other forms of sexual and physical abuse by the security forces. The 2012 OHRCHR report even noted that there was potentially an environment of "implicit consent" among the higher ranks of the security forces for the use of rape.

As discussed in more detail later in this volume (see Chapter 3), patriarchal norms are deeply entrenched in Nepal and much of the collective and cultural identity among communities is woven around women's sexuality. As such, women and girls who have been victimised through sexual violence are considered not only to have lost their honour but also to have brought shame on their entire community (UNOHCHR, 2012, as cited in Bhusal, 2016, p. 141). Bhusal (2016, p. 142) argued that women and girls were particularly targeted for rape and sexual violence for the purpose of inflicting shame on their family or to show disrespect towards the male members. The atrocities committed against women by the security forces, Bhusal adds, indicates that even sympathisers or those affiliated with the opposing groups were not spared. Women who were not themselves rebels were targeted by the security forces because their husbands or family members had joined the Maoist forces (AF and ICTJ 2010 as cited in Bhusal, 2016). The majority of the reports of sexual violence against women and girls were thought to have happened in Maoist strongholds or near army barracks, but Bhusal's research found reports of cases in all tribes, castes, and religions, and especially in the rural areas and against women of marginalised groups. This is because the Maoists had sympathisers in the rural areas and in communities that were marginalised – geographically, economically, and socially – as most Maoist combatants were recruited from villages (the Maoist indoctrination programmes that targeted women and girls in the rural areas are discussed in the next section). Pokhrel and Sharma (2016) state that there was virtually no reporting of the rape and sexual violence that took place during the war owing in part to sociocultural and economic constraints, but the women were also silenced by the culture of impunity: the final section of this chapter discusses this in more detail. Despite the many cases documented by human rights organisations, only one case of conflict-related rape has been heard in court since the end of the conflict. It was initially unsuccessful but was later taken to the UN Human Rights Committee, following which a member of the state personnel was found guilty of rape and subsequently prosecuted (Bhusal, 2016).

Apart from during search and interrogation operations, many other cases of rape, sexual violence, and torture perpetrated by security personnel against women in detention were reported (Bhusal, 2016, p. 145). It is alleged that the perpetrators were often shielded by higher-ranking officers, who were party to the crime. During the conflict, security forces had the power to detain anyone suspected of being a threat to national security or believed to be a Maoist sympathiser. Testimonies of victims and witnesses reveal that a number of women and girls who were detained were treated brutally, and many were even disappeared (Sharma & Young, 2010, p. 52).

2.4 Maoist propaganda and the gendered implications of the conflict

The Maoist conflict in Nepal was not just a rebellion against the state; it was also characterised as a people's movement to bring about a social revolution. The Maoists believed that an agrarian revolution would not be possible without the participation of women. In order to attract women to join the armed movement, the Maoists ran a calculated campaign and recruitment drive. In their propaganda, they espoused the virtues of women's liberation and equality of opportunity in their ranks, and they promised social reformation programmes to tackle issues including domestic violence, alcohol, gambling, sexual violence, and exploitation (Sharma & Young, 2010; Sharma & Prasain 2004 as cited in Ariño, 2008).

Manchanda (2004a) discusses an article by Hsila Yami, a central committee member and head of the Women's Department of the Communist Party of Nepal. In the article published in a local newspaper, *Kanitpur*, Yami explained that the party recruited women because "women make up the biggest segment of the population in the downtrodden communities". She added, "since women have suffered class and sexual oppression, they have double the capacity to revolt". Manchanda goes on to note that

> When the People's War was initiated in 1996, the CPN (M) leadership made it mandatory to include two women in every unit of 9 to 11 members, especially in the fighting ranks. In the Maoist strongholds, every third guerrilla was a woman. In the new districts where the Maoist influence was spreading, every tenth combatant was a woman.
>
> (Manchanda, 2004a, p. 241)

Furthermore, during the course of the armed conflict, there was speculation that the proportion of women combatants was as high as 40–50% of the total (Manchanda, 2004a). However, the final figures offered by the United Nations Mission in Nepal (UNMIN), after the process of verifying the Maoist combatants, revealed a much lower proportion. According to the United Nations (UN), the PLA was made up of 19,602 combatants, of whom approximately 20%, or 3,846, were women (Ariño, 2008).

Aryal (2016) cited Amitra Thapa – a woman member who joined the Communist Party of Nepal (Marxist) during the early days when the "People's War" was still taking shape – as saying in an interview that the party pledged to bring about a revolution around four social issues: gender, class, ethnicity, and religion. It was seen as a progressive movement that would liberate women from the bondage of domestic servitude. Thapa said, "the old system has suffocated women so much that they wanted to fight for their rights, there was a feeling of revenge, and the way they wanted to fight back was through bullets" (Aryal, 2016, p. 181). Although Thapa and others like her voluntarily joined the rebellion, research into the Maoist programme for women has indicated that there was also coerced recruitment of women and girls, and many of those who joined the PLA were illiterate and less than 15 years old (Manchanda, 2004a).

Shakya (2011) documented how schools became recruitment centres and a battleground for both sides of the warring parties, whereby schoolchildren were indoctrinated through cultural programmes. Children were mobilised by the Maoists to create student unions in schools to influence their peers towards their ideology and to motivate them to become a part of the insurgency. School mobilisation was very effective because it focused on social justice and equal rights without discrimination on the basis of caste or gender. In addition, the propaganda material was designed to ignite revolutionary zeal, including through stories of the heroic sacrifices made by women guerrilla leaders (Gautam et al., 2001, as cited in Manchanda, 2004a). Shakya (2011, p. 560) noted that "recruitment speeches were so moving and powerful that many joined the PLA as they deeply felt they are contributing to social justice". One of the girls from Akhil Nepal Mahila Sangh, the Maoist women's organisation, from Doti commented, "I was fascinated by the Maoists ideology. I was in ninth grade when I left to become a whole timer in the Maoist party" (Shakya, 2011, p. 560).

In large parts of rural Nepal, once girls reached puberty, they were married off by their parents, often to a man who was not the girl's choice. Most often, it would be an older man because this meant paying a smaller dowry. For the parents, marrying their daughter unburdened them of a huge social responsibility. This was one of the reasons why the Maoist recruitment drive had such an impressionable effect on teenage girls: joining the Maoist forces in the forest was akin to acquiring a new social identity because it signalled a break with social traditions related to gender roles. Leve (2007) explains that most girls in rural Nepal undergo a major life change during adolescence. This time in their lives invariably involves leaving their parental home for a place where they will live under the orders of others and will endure hardships and suffering. From the point of view of the would-be girl soldier, the main difference may have been that the Maoist option involved not only a higher degree of physical danger but also greater opportunities for individual expression.

A number of factors enabled the Maoist insurgents to recruit girls and women in large numbers. The conflict saw many men temporarily relocating from villages to Kathmandu and neighbouring India for work and/or fleeing for their safety. It was not common for the entire family to move as women were often required to remain behind to look after the land (Menon & Rodgers, 2015, p. 52). A study by the World Bank (2004) (as cited in Menon & Rodgers, 2015) indicated that the absence of husbands and their income led to a dramatic increase in women's labour in the form of household work and farm work. Pettigrew and Shneiderman (2004) noted that the conflict created insecurity and disturbed the social structure; the migration of men meant that family ties were broken. Women were forced to leave their houses and take on non-traditional roles including tending to agricultural lands. The Maoists moved to exploit the situation and engaged in mass mobilisation by selling an ideology of hope and resurrection. Many women joined the Maoist forces believing that they would be given blanket protection in the event of an unforeseen disaster and from violence perpetrated by their alcoholic husbands. The Maoists' anti-alcohol campaign struck a chord with women and is among the most noted aspects of women's participation in Maoist-associated action (Fajikura, 2003).

Hsila Yami, a Maoist leader, pointed out that the role played by women in the domestic sphere meant that they were much more effective in mobilising the masses, in part because they facilitated access to other members of the family (Ariño, 2008). The Maoist forces introduced a decree instructing every family to send at least one child to their movement. Media reports suggested that many families sent their daughters rather than sons because girls were seen as more "disposable" than boys, thereby reinforcing the special status of the male child in the Nepali social context (Manchanda, 2004a, p. 246). However, the drive to forcibly abduct and recruit children from schools compelled many other schoolgirls to migrate to Kathmandu. This not only disrupted their studies but also often forced them to take up exploitative jobs in the city. My research indicates that many such girls struggled because, without any skills, they could not find work. Three of the participants in this study said they had fled their villages for fear of being abducted from school or because the environment in the village was tense. They took on unskilled labour as domestic maids or in construction, but this work was often low-paid, exploitative, and physically gruelling, and employers were abusive. Like many of the women who took part in this study, they joined the sex and informal entertainment industry because there was scope for earning more and doing so with a relative degree of freedom and flexibility in their working hours. Some of these women had married men who had physically abused them and committed other forms of intimate partner violence (IPV), and some had abandoned them when they became pregnant (discussed further in Chapter 3). For women in such circumstances, the sex and informal entertainment industry seemed like a viable option for survival. The following example illustrates the reality of the working conditions for girls and young women who migrated to Kathmandu.

Participant 2 (age 30, low caste, married but living separately, has one daughter) said she was the fifth of six daughters in her family. She was 17 years old when the Maoist insurgency crippled the village economy. There was no food, and her father, who she described as an alcoholic, was violent towards everyone. She said, "My neighbours told me that in the city I can get good job, good food, and good clothes. So I thought I will be able to help my mother". On arrival in Kathmandu, she worked as a maid for a family of eight: "I worked from five in the morning to midnight. I used to live in their house. They used to give me food and no salary". She added that the family treated her badly and often beat her, and she was later fired because they discovered that she belonged to a low caste.

Another woman, Participant 4 (age 28, low caste, married, has one seven-year-old child), said she migrated to the city when she was 14 years old because Maoists were recruiting children from her school. She said:

> I did not feel safe and came to live in Kathmandu. I had no intention to go to the city and work but was afraid of being abducted by the Maoist. They were coming and writing down names. We feared they would take us away.

On arrival in the city, she lived with her uncle and worked as a domestic maid. She later joined a massage parlour because she was ill-treated by her employer and by her uncle who did not want to keep her indefinitely. She stated that she had "no intention to work".

Likewise, Participant 19 (age 32, upper caste, married but not living with husband, has two children) came to Kathmandu when she was 14 years old years old because there was a risk of her being abducted by the Maoist forces, where it was feared she would become a child solider. Many children like her were forced into the Maoist insurgency because of the PLA recruitment policy of "one house, one person" (Shakya, 2011). If children were not offered voluntarily by their parents, they could be abducted directly from the school. Various respondents and human rights organisations reported that between 100 and 200 students from each school were abducted at a time to become child soldiers (Human Rights Report, 2008 as cited in Shakya, 2011).

The UN has defined child soldiers as "boys and girls under the age of 18, who are enlisted either voluntarily or forcibly in an armed force (government armed forces or armed groups) regardless of the role they play (combatants, scouts, spies, servants, sex slaves)" (Shakya, 2011, p. 559).

Direct participation in the hostilities or the use of a weapon by a child is not a determining factor. Girls used as sex slaves or subjected to forced marriages within an armed force are also considered to be child soldiers.

When applying this definition to the context of Nepal and the Maoist conflict, it is clear that children were used and made into soldiers against their will. My data reveals a number of cases, confirming that children were routinely abducted by the Maoists, used as child soldiers, and, in extreme cases, sexually abused and raped. For example, Participant 3 (age 20, caste Tamang [ethnic], widow, has one daughter) said:

> I was taken by the Maoist when I was six years old. They said that I have to avenge my father's death. I was in the entertainment wing (advocacy) and our job was to influence people with Maoist ideology. I was the dancer. I also used to carry guns and ammunition. I was made to kill a lot of people. Every time they came across someone, they would say he is your father's killer so shoot him. I am not sure how many people I killed. We would walk for days sometimes in the forest sometimes without food. There were over one-hundred women and girls.
>
> When I returned home after the peace agreement was signed between the rebels and the Government in 2006. I wasn't accepted by the society. I was ostracised. They thought I was a rebel. There were families in the village that had a member either in police or in the army who were killed. They blamed me for that. I couldn't have lived in the village. My stepmother mistreated me and said I should stay away from house. I suffered a lot in life.

The interviews confirmed the claims made by other studies that children were routinely used as soldiers. Bhusal (2016, p. 141) explains that one reason why girls like Participant 3 were not accepted back into society is that they were no longer considered honourable as their sexuality was assumed to have been compromised if they had been away from their community with the armed militia. As mentioned above, in the Nepalese context a girl's honour is viewed as a delicate and valuable asset, which must be preserved at all costs. If she is victimised, the honour of the entire family or the village is at stake. This notion of honour or *izzat* revolves around a woman's sexuality and occupies a pivotal place in Nepalese society. Its "defilement" is seen as an affront to her husband's honour, and she risks being socially ostracised if her sexuality is suspected of having been abused or compromised (Pokhrel & Sharma, 2016).

The stigma associated with rape was well known by the Maoist forces; their actions were deliberate and were intended to prevent girls from returning home. In this context, rape can be seen as a weapon of war. In an interview in 1997, while affirming the party's trust in women combatants, Hsila Yami reinforced this view when she said:

> women returning [home] is not a ready option. Sons will be welcomed back with open arms, but for the daughters, can there be a return? When they become guerrillas, the women set themselves free from patriarchal bonds. How can they go back?
>
> (cited in Pettigrew & Shneiderman, 2004)

Pettigrew and Shneiderman also noted that women returning home from the conflict were shunned because of the possible reprisals and harassment of family members by the state forces due to their presence.

The patriarchal system was ever-present, even within the ranks of the PLA, and there were reported tensions among the male and female comrades as recalled by Comrade Parvati, the pseudonym of a writer who identified herself as a central committee member and head of the Women's Department of CPN (Maoist). Pettigrew and Shneiderman (2004) observed that

> male leadership relegates women's issues to women rather than taking them up as central issues, neglects to implement programmes developed by the women's mass front, are unnecessarily overprotective of female cadres, and resort to traditional division of labour by monopolising [...] mental work and relegating women to everyday drudgery work. [...] Married women who show promise are discouraged from taking up positions that would take them away from their husbands. Women active in the Maoist movement frequently experience marginalisation when they have children and [...] many bright aspiring communist women are at risk of being lost in oblivion, even after getting married to the comrades of their choice.
>
> (Pettigrew & Shneiderman, 2004, p. 25)

2.5 The PLA's violent contradictions

As summarised in the introduction to this chapter, studies looking into the gendered implications of the Maoist conflict have highlighted that the role of women in the conflict marked a move away from traditional gendered roles. As the conflict progressed, women increasingly took on various responsibilities within the rank and file of the Maoist army. In the areas of the country that they controlled, the Maoists ran parallel courts and punished men for abusing their wives. They also ran campaigns on alcoholism, which was thought to be one of the major causes of domestic violence. The feeling of rapid justice engendered a sense of security among women and contributed to the reduction in violence within families. Within the rank and file of the Maoist army, a strict code of conduct was enforced, which seemed to offer protection to female combatants, and any offences against women combatants were firmly handled. Both the PLA and the state forces also dealt brutally with anyone suspected of being a spy or whose family member was in the army or in the rebel forces (Thapa, 2016, p. 208).

The following cases illustrate that a pattern of sexual violence was committed against women by the PLA. The statements provided are very similar to the documented cases of violence against women committed by the security forces.

Participant 7 (age 33, lower caste, married but not living with husband, has three children) was just 14 years old when she was abducted by Maoists and kept hostage for three months before she managed to escape: "I was abducted by the Maoists and taken to a jungle. I was abducted because my brother was in the army", she said. When asked if she was sexually assaulted, she responded, "Yes, I wasn't raped. I was harassed both physically and mentally". In response to the interviewer's question "What was their expectation from you?", she recounted the following:

> We were trained to kill people from the army. We also had to carry ammunition as we moved from one village to another. Because my brother was in the army, I was given a gun and bullets to kill army personnel, but I didn't know how to use them. I was very young. Once during a clash, I lied down on the ground, but a bullet hit my leg. I was bleeding and was in a terrible pain, but I still had to trudge along. They simply gave me a pain killer. As a part of the training, I was made to lie on the ground. They would then chop off a branch from a tree, which would fall on my stomach like a thud. We were told this would help build confidence and provide strength to fight the army.

When asked how she escaped, she continued:

> I ran from the village and reached the highway and then took lift in a lorry. There was another girl who was being repeatedly raped. They told me that it was my turn. After hearing this I was very scared and decided to run away. I spent the night in some cattle shed and, in the morning, I managed to get to a bus stop. I didn't have money, so I requested the bus conductor to help me. I had to sleep with the bus driver for the favour.

Participant 14 (age 40, low caste, Hindu but practices Christianity, married, has six children) was abducted by Maoist forces when her youngest daughter was just one month old. She was accused of being a spy. When asked what the Maoist forces had done to her, she responded:

> I was taken in the jungle. I was tortured, stoned, and beaten badly, and made to do a lot of work. When the baby cried, they put mud in her mouth and took her away in a cave or something. I fainted several times. They used to give me food once in 2-3 days. I was sexually abused. I was hanged to a tree and raped repeatedly. Had I not run I wouldn't have been alive.

She was 28 years old when she was abducted in 2004, when the conflict was at it its peak. When asked how she escaped, she showed the bullet marks on her body and said:

> I tried to run away several times, but I didn't want to leave my baby behind. I was badly injured but one day I got an opportunity to run. We came across a village and I was asked to share a room in somebody's house as I had a baby and that would not raise police suspicion. I spotted an opportunity there to run away when that man had gone to the toilet.
>
> It was pitch dark. I ran through the jungle as taking the road was dangerous. In the jungle, I came across a cave and I stayed there for three days hiding. Under the cave down below in the ditch there was a wild animal [...] so, I couldn't move. I was breast feeding. On the third day, I met some villagers who came to the jungle to collect woods. I was very weak. My face was bruised. When they saw me with the baby, they gave me some food and

> helped me get out of the jungle and took me to the village bus stand. There I met a woman [described as a friend], who helped me and took care of me. She sold ten kilograms of millets and gave me the money to buy a bus ticket.
>
> When I got home the family refused to accept me. They said I ran away with another man and brought shame to the family. I decided to leave along with my children. My husband supported me. We managed to go to another village where we worked for a month to earn the bus fare and then come to Kathmandu.

The above cases illustrate the extent of the violence and sexual abuse committed by the Maoist forces, especially against those who were forcibly abducted, or those suspected of being a spy or of being a close relative of someone serving the state army or police. This also shows that notions of gender justice within the rank and file were selective. There seems to have been widespread abuse of women and girls, perhaps at all levels, but certainly at the lower levels of the PLA. And despite making up 20% of the PLA combatants, women were unable to stop the violence. Subodh Pyakurel, a human rights activist, argues that the greater participation of women in the Maoist forces did not ensure that all women fighters were safe (Aryal, 2016), and women at the top levels were powerless to protect women in the lower echelons. A 2012 report by the Office of the High Commission of Human Rights (OHCHR) in Nepal stated that children under the age of 18 were particularly vulnerable, and one-third of the victims of sexual violence were children, many under the age of 15 (UNOHCHR, 2012, p. 172 as cited in Aryal, 2016, p. 189).

Adding to the evidence presented in the above statements, Participant 9 (age 28, upper caste, married but separated, has two children) said:

> When I was around 12–13 years old, I was raped by my teacher. I was blamed by the community as the teacher was a powerful man and enjoyed a higher status in the society. The Maoists, instead, punished me. They took me away and I was kept in captivity for three months. They abused me verbally and even tried to rape me.
>
> After three months, I couldn't take it. The place was around twenty kilometres from the district headquarters. I followed the light of the passing vehicles and walked through the night and arrived at the district headquarters. After that I went home but they came after me. I ran away from there to Kathmandu.

The experiences described in this chapter contribute to a body of scattered work confirming that sexual violence was committed on a large scale by Maoist forces as well as by the state security forces. The impact of the conflict on women was devastating. While during the course of the conflict the Maoists tried to bring about social reforms by taking measures such as allowing the remarriage of widows or breaking taboos around menstruation, such initiatives were not sustained and were abandoned soon after the conflict (Ariño, 2008; Geiser, 2005).

And despite any attempts to address gender inequality, the conflict killed thousands of women, made many widows, and left many more to face extreme social stigmatisation.

Manchanda (2004b) notes that conflict-related displacement often marginalises women further. In the case of Nepal, as mentioned above, there is a greater possibility of women being treated as outcasts for stepping beyond the boundaries of the patriarchal social order. In the post-conflict context, the status of a woman as a "victim", devoid of agency and incapable of representing herself, plays into the state system that is dominated by patriarchy. Under such scenarios, "women are largely seen as non-subjects, enjoying at best secondary citizenship" (Manchanda, 2004b, p. 4179). Bunch (as cited in Aguirre & Pietropaoli, 2008, p. 51) stresses that armed conflict causes additional violations to women's lives but that these are linked to gender-based violence (GBV) and the abuse of women in "normal" patriarchal life. Thus, women were affected by the conflict in Nepal in ways that were different from their male counterparts because of their subordinate position in the pre-conflict society.

2.6 Barriers to justice

In Nepal, the trauma of conflict is still fresh and there is a renewed call to address the issue of the sexual violence that was committed by the warring parties. However, studies have identified the following bottlenecks in Nepal's justice system as primary reasons why women who were caught up in the conflict often refuse to speak out about sexual violence:

- Social stigma and shame, as highlighted above, is a major cause. In general, rape victims do not speak out about their case because of social pressure (Bhusal, 2016).
- The worst affected areas of conflict are those that have an illiterate and extremely poor population. Women like those mentioned above are often not aware of how to access justice. There is no mechanism to educate women about their legal rights or provide legal assistance (Bhusal, 2016).
- Despite Supreme Court guidelines on maintaining the confidentiality of cases related to violence against women, there are no proper laws to protect the identity of a victim of sexual violence. In a traditionally patriarchal society such as Nepal, the breach of women's confidentiality with regard to their sexuality can have enormous negative fallout, and dealing with it can take a serious psychological, emotional, social, and physical toll. Such issues lead to further stigmatisation, and there is a tendency towards victim blaming. Cases of this kind are widely covered by the local media (Danker, Taylor, & Youssef, 2011 as cited in Bhusal, 2016, p. 159).
- The definition of rape in Nepali law that existed during the conflict was narrow in its scope (*Muluki Ain*, chapter 14). The code refers to "sexual intercourse" instead of rape. This type of language creates an understanding that there must be evidence of force and signs of a struggle to prove non-consent

(Pokhrel & Sharma, 2016, p. 114). However, the government has amended the existing law in order to broaden the definition of rape.

Nepal's peace agreement mandated the government to provide relief packages when the compensation-based Interim Relief Programme (IRP) for conflict victims was announced. The measures included NR 100,000 for the nearest kin of those who had been killed or reported missing during the conflict. An additional NR 25,000 was offered to the widows or wives of those killed or reported missing, and education scholarships were provided for their children. However, the guidelines excluded victims of sexual violence and rape (Thapa, 2016, p. 233). According to Aryal (2016, p. 200), experts have said that the government has never sought to investigate accusations of sexual violence and rape, nor has there been a proper documentation of sex crimes during the war.

After years of failed post-conflict talks between all stakeholders to investigate the gross violations of human rights, the Truth and Reconciliation Commission (TRC) and the Commission of Inquiry on the Disappearances (CoID) were formed through the CoID TRC Act by Nepal's parliament on 25 April 2014. Although Section 2 (j) of the TRC recognises rape and sexual violence as a "serious violation of human rights" (Sharma & Pokhrel, 2016; Thapa, 2016, p. 224), Section 26 of the act gives the commission power to mediate between victims and perpetrators, even in the case of rape. Thapa (2016, p. 224) notes that this is in contravention of Article 11 of UN Resolution 1325 to end impunity by abolishing amnesty in cases related to sexual violence and Article 4 of UN Resolution 1820, which urges members not to use blanket amnesty as a tool of reconciliation to shield the perpetrators of sexual violence during the conflict as such acts amount to crimes against humanity.

In 2015, broad amendments were made to the definition of rape to expand its scope in Nepali law. Under the new law, the statute of limitations on the reporting of rape cases has been extended from 35 days to 180 days. The Act to Amend Laws to End Gender Violence and Ensure Gender Equality 2072 has also increased the penalties and prison terms in cases related to domestic and sexual violence. The law has broadened the definition of rape to include "penile penetration of orifices" and "non-penile penetration of vaginas". The new act has also made marital rape a non-bailable crime; it has increased maximum prison terms to five years and the maximum penalty for an acid attack from three to eight years in prison.

Studies in Nepal have identified specific but wide-ranging drivers of GBV including women's legal subordination, economic dependency, cultural obligations, social position, and their lack of autonomy, education, and knowledge of sexuality. This is compounded by men's perceived entitlement to sex, early marriage, women's dearth of family and legal support, and husbands' use of alcohol (see Sharma & Tamang, 2016). When the Maoists began their insurgency, one of their objectives was to initiate a social revolution that would transform the structure of society by emancipating women from their subservient roles. As explained above, some measures to achieve this end were taken, such as running a parallel court to address issues of domestic violence, though these measures were more "rooted in aspiration than in reality" (Sharma & Young, 2010, p. 23), and they were unsuccessful in bringing about sustainable social reform that would strengthen the position of women in society. In some ways, it had an adverse effect on women who had become part of the movement as they were often stigmatised and were not accepted back into their families. Furthermore, despite the enormous contribution made by women during the conflict, they were systematically kept out of the peace-building process, as observed by UN Secretary-General and head of the United Nations Mission in Nepal, Ian Martin, who stated that "at all the political negotiating tables I have seen in Nepal during the peace process, not once have I seen a woman at the table. So far in the peace process, decisions are being made by men for women" (Martin, 2007 as cited in Ariño, 2008, p. 10).

In 2007, Amnesty International also noted that during the course of the negotiations, neither the SPA nor the Maoists included any women on their negotiating teams (Ariño, 2008, p. 10).

2.7 Conclusion

This chapter has drawn attention to the enormous social cost of the conflict on women in Nepal and has highlighted the violence and abuse at the hands of the PLA in particular. This is important because, although all parties of the conflict committed such violence, those committed by Maoist forces are more poorly documented. Moreover, it draws attention to the contradictions between the ideological aims of the insurgency and the outcomes of the conflict. The temporary moves towards increased gender equality that took place as a result of the conflict did not materialise in terms of substantive changes to the law and policy of successive governments. But despite this, some shifts in the role and social status of women did take place that must be considered when analysing the long-term implications of the conflict. For example, the contribution of women in various capacities to the social movement as well as the armed conflict disrupted the prevalent discourse that regarded Hindu Nepali women as weak and powerless. However, on the other hand, most of these women had to return to their families and communities when the conflict ended, and they found themselves immersed once again in a social system and patriarchal order from which they had sought to break away. The chapter also demonstrates that years of political instability and the lack of political will, even after the conflict had ended, have resulted in the denial of justice for women who were affected by the conflict or were victims of sexual abuse. Their cases have not even been properly documented. The women whose interviews are referred to above have evidently been underserved by the mechanisms that have been set up to compensate people who were victimised through sexual violence. This may be because most of these women were very young and/or illiterate at the time the crimes took place and therefore had no route through which to seek legal support.

The lack of access to justice for women in Nepal has highlighted that gender inequalities remain a major issue in the country. The conflict evidently exacerbated many of the difficulties faced by women, and, as the interviews also illustrated, women were used as instruments of violence and coercion by the Maoist forces. But the conflict also provided a possibility for women to redefine their status. For this reason, the Maoists had the sympathy and the support of women as some of their political demands were seen as legitimate attempts to improve social justice. These included inheritance rights for women; abolishing exploitation based on caste and ethnicity; special protections for orphans, disabled persons, and the elderly; and the provision of employment opportunities for all, as well as forgiving rural agricultural debt, redistributing land "to the tiller", and other more familiar Marxist policies (Karki & Seddon, 2003 as cited in Leve, 2007). Their firebrand advocacy promised to bring about lasting prosperity based on equality and justice, free from gender discrimination, and it caught the imagination of the youth. Many joined voluntarily in the hope that by being part of the armed struggle they could forge a new social identity.

However, when the peace agreement was signed between the government and the Maoists, many of the top commanders in the Maoist forces came to occupy powerful positions in the police and the army, and they abandoned the objectives of the movement, which were to reframe social, gender, and economic relations. Subsequently, the women who had served in the Maoist army, especially those at the lower ranks, were detached from the peace-building process. As shown above, women who had paid a heavy price in supporting the Maoists during the conflict were simply abandoned to their fate. Many of these women had forfeited their childhood or had been violently tormented and raped by Maoist forces, and when they returned to their communities, they were not accepted by their families. They have had multiple experiences of violence and betrayal that did not end with the conflict; some have since been subjected to further exploitation and violence by men they trusted and even married, as Chapter 3 demonstrates. It was clear during the interview process that the pain and trauma inflicted by the Maoists had left deep scars that remain fresh in the minds of the women who took part in the study. This raises the question of how these women deal with this trauma in their daily lives, particularly in the absence of justice. It is also unclear whether their violent past makes them stronger and more resilient when confronting the abuse and violence that underpins the sex and informal entertainment industry. I explore these questions with reference to various frameworks of empowerment and resilience in Chapters 4 and 5 in order to better understand how women working in this sector develop their survival strategies and reconstruct new relationships amidst the chaos and uncertainty of their lives.

References

Aguirre, D., & Pietropaoli, I. (2008). Gender equality, development and transitional justice: The case of Nepal. *The International Journal of Transitional Justice*, *2*(3), 356–377.

Amnesty International (2003). Amnesty International Report 2003 – Nepal. Available at: https://www.refworld.org/docid/3edb47dc1c.htm

Ariño, M. V. (2008). Nepal: A gender view of the armed conflict and the peace process. *Peacebuilding Papers (Quaderns de Construcció de Pau)*, *4*, 4–17. School for a Culture of Peace (Escola de Cultura de Pau). www.ceipaz.org/images/contenido/Nepal_%20a%20gender%20view%20armed%20conflict_peace%20process.pdf

Aryal, M. (2016). Truth, silence and justice: The Maoists' view. In M. Sharma & S. Tamang (Eds.), *A Difficult Transition: The Nepal Papers* (pp. 174–204). Zuban.

Bhusal, B. M. (2016). Prosecutorial process in armed conflicts and states of emergency. In M. Sharma & S. Tamang (Eds.), *A Difficult Transition: The Nepal Papers* (pp. 135–173). Zuban.

Danker, M., Taylor, T., & Youssef, M. (2011). *Confidentiality and the Legal Process: Leveraging Legislation and Policy to Protect Nepal's Most Vulnerable Victims.* Washington DC: Georgetown University Law Centre.

Fujikura, T. (2003). The role of collective imagination in the Maoist conflict in Nepal. *Himalaya: The Journal of the Association for Nepal and Himalayan Studies*, *23*, 7.

Gautam, S., Banskota, A. & Manchanda, R. (2001). Where there are no men: Women in the Maoist insurgency in Nepal. In Rita Manchanda (Ed.), *Women, War and Peace in South Asia* (pp. 214–251). New Delhi: Sage.

Geiser, A. (2005). *Social Exclusion and Conflict Transformation in Nepal: Women, Dalit and Ethnic Groups, FAST Country Risk Profile Nepal.* Swiss Peace Foundation. https://gsdrc.org/document-library/social-exclusion-and-conflict-transformation-in-nepal-women-dalit-and-ethnic-groups/

Karki, A., & Seddon, D. (2003). *The People's War in Nepal: Left Perspectives.* Helhi: Adroit Publishers.

Leve, L. (2007). "Failed Development" and rural revolution in Nepal: Rethinking subaltern consciousness and women's empowerment. *Anthropological Quarterly*, *80*(1), 127–172.

Manchanda, R. (2004a). Gender conflict and displacement contesting "infantilisation" of forced migrant women. *Economic and Political Weekly*, *39*(37), 11–17.

Manchanda, R. (2004b). Maoist insurgency in Nepal: Radicalising gender narratives. South Asia Forum for Human Rights, Nepal. *Cultural Dynamics*, *16*(2/3), 237–258.

Menon, N., & Rodgers, Y. (2015). *War and Women's Work: Evidence from the Conflict in Nepal.* Mimeo.

Pettigrew, J., & Shneiderman, S. (2004). Women and the Maobadi: Ideology and agency in Nepal's Maoist movement. *Himal Southasian*, *17*(1), 19–29.

Pokhrel, D., & Sharma, M. (2016). Impunity for conflict-related sexual violence in Nepal. In M. Sharma & S. Tamang (Eds.), *A Difficult Transition: The Nepal Papers* (pp. 96–105). Zuban.

Shakya, A. (2011). Experiences of children in armed conflict in Nepal. *Children and Youth Service Review*, *33*(4), 557–663.

Sharma, M., & Prasain, D. (2004) Gender dimensions of the People's War. Some reflections on the experiences of rural women. In M. Hutt (Ed.), *Himalayan 'People's War'. Nepal's Maoist Rebellion.* London: Hurst & Company.

Sharma, M. & Tamang, S. (2016). *A Difficult Transition: The Nepal Papers.* Zuban.

Sharma, M., & Young, K. (2010). *Across the Lines: The Impact of Nepal's Conflict on Women.* International Centre for Transnational Justice Advocacy Forum. www.ictj.org/publication/across-lines-impact-nepals-conflict-women

Thapa, R. (2016). After the war: Transitional justice in Nepal. In M. Sharma & S. Tamang (Eds.), *A Difficult Transition: The Nepal Papers* (pp. 205–255). Zuban.

Thapa, D., & Sijapati, B. (2005). *A Kingdom Under Siege: Nepal's Maoist Insurgency.* London, UK: Zed Books.

UNOHCHR (2012). *Nepal Conflict Report, 2012.* Geneva: United Nations. ohchr.org/Documents/Countries/NP/OHCHR_Nepal_Conflict_Report2012.pdf

Valente, C. (2011). *What Did the Maoists Ever Do for Us? Education and Marriage of Women Exposed to Civil Conflict in Nepal* (World Bank Policy Research Working Paper WPS5741). documents.worldbank.org/curated/en/292931468062633909/pdf/WPS5741.pdf

World Bank. 2004. Social change in conflict-affected areas of Nepal. *Social Development Notes: Conflict Prevention & Reconstruction 15*, 1–4.

3 Social norms, masculinity, and violence

3.1 Introduction

Chapter 2 discussed the 10-year-long Maoist conflict and its implications for violence against women and girls (VAWG) in Nepal. It highlighted how the conflict triggered the migration of women from their villages to the relative safety of urban areas, particularly the capital, Kathmandu. It discussed how women and girls were abducted by the Maoist forces and how sexual abuse and rape were perpetuated by both the warring parties during the conflict. In order to understand the relationship between earning an income and experiencing violence among women engaged in the sex and informal entertainment industry, I considered the backgrounds of the participants and analysed their situations with regard to key variables including child marriage, intimate partner violence (IPV), education level, and caste. The interviews revealed that one or a combination of these factors has had severe consequences on the lives of the interviewees and contributed to their decision to migrate to Kathmandu. Upon migrating, the women found themselves in precarious situations that eventually created circumstances forcing them to enter the sex and informal entertainment industry.

This study consisted of 21 qualitative interviews and two focus groups of eight and seven women, respectively. Out of the 21 interviewees, 15 women were reported to have married under the age of 18, three married between ages 18 and 21, two were unmarried, and only one woman married after 21 at the age of 26. The data shows that child marriage was a key contributing factor. As such, this chapter examines how child marriage and IPV severely traumatised the lives of women who were interviewed for this study. These factors are important because, as later chapters reveal, violence experienced through marriage at a young age is, in many cases, responsible for pushing women into the informal entertainment industry. However, their early experiences of violence also led to the creation of coping mechanisms for dealing with violence in the workplace. "Coping mechanisms" refer to the ability of participants to show resilience and manage external and internal stress by finding ways to deal with them. In the context of this study, it also means the manifestation of inner strength to negotiate their way through the risks and violence that characterise the sex and informal entertainment industry. For some participants, their experience of violence at a young age made them

DOI: 10.4324/9781003156796-3

strong and even more determined to resist potential violence: they experienced worse, and so they were less afraid of being hurt if they resisted. They asserted that their choice to join the sex and informal entertainment industry was made in extreme situations: it was needed for survival.

Based on the participants' interviews, the common causes of violence and the factors that shaped them began to emerge. Social norms around child marriage and dowries and the experience of IPV were found to have been the main causes of suffering among the interviewees.

3.2 Child marriage and dowry

According to a Human Rights Watch (HRW) report in 2016, Nepal has the third-highest rate of child marriage in Asia after Bangladesh and India. The study pointed out that 37% of Nepali women between ages 20 and 24 were married by the age of 18, and 10% were married by the age of 15 (Pandey, 2017). According to Nepal's 2011 national census, approximately 75% of the married women surveyed were married before their twentieth birthday, and over 100,000 girls were given away in marriage before reaching 10 years old (National Population and Housing Census, 2011 as cited in Centre for Reproductive Rights, 2016).

In another study, Pandey (2017) analysed a sample of 9,783 women between the ages of 15 and 49 from the 2011 Nepal Demographic and Health Survey (NDHS) and found that, on average, Nepalese women were married at the age of 17 and gave birth to their first child before the age of 20. Nearly one in three women were married before their sixteenth birthday and 78% of women were married before the age of 20 – Nepal's legal marriage age. The same study noted that nearly half of the women (48%) had no formal education (Pandey, 2017, p. 243).

According to the reports of a number of key development donors, the social and cultural values surrounding women's sexuality, dowry, and patriarchy in Nepal remain the key drivers for early marriage (see e.g. Human Rights Watch, 2016; UNFPA et.al, 2016). This is compounded by the ineffective implementation of existing legal provisions that ban child marriage, as well as barriers to accessing legal remedies (UNFPA, 2016 et.al). Furthermore, in Nepal's context (as well as in South Asia more generally), cultural norms put a high value on women's virginity before marriage as this constitutes a sign of purity. There is an underlying belief that delaying the marriage of a girl could increase the cost of a dowry and also increase the chances of premarital sex, which would then bring shame and dishonour to the family (Raj, 2010; Warner, 2004 as cited in Pandey, 2017).

Nepal is a diverse society with over 60 ethnic groups differentiated by language, dialect, religion, and region of residence (Choe, Thapa, & Misra, 2005). Studies on child marriage have indicated that the customs and culture of marriage vary considerably across ethnic groups and regions and, as such, the prevalence of child marriage also varies significantly among Nepal's many ethnicities, religions, and caste groups. A HRW (2016) study, for example, found that among the disadvantaged Dalit caste in Nepal's Terai region (plains bordering India), the rate of marriage before the age of 19 is 87% and it is 65% in the hills region. The rates of child marriage are also higher among people who have spent fewer years in education, and higher among Muslims and Hindus when compared to Buddhists and Christians. Pandey's study (2017), which examined marriage and caste dynamics, found that high caste Madhesi women (a community inhabiting the Terai plains region of Nepal with strong cultural links to the bordering Indian states of Bihar and Uttar Pradesh) were 51% more likely to marry before the age of 16 than high caste Hindu women of other communities in Nepal. Low caste Hindu women were 45% more likely to marry before 16 years of age compared to other low caste communities in the country (Pandey 2017, p. 245). In another study, Aryal (2007) found that variables such as education, caste, socio-economic status, year-of-birth cohort, and age at menarche were significant determinants of female age at first marriage in Nepal. The age of marriage varied significantly across communities based on societal and cultural factors.

Child marriage can have severe physical and psychological health implications for an adolescent girl, which can include serious pregnancy-related issues such as miscarriage or maternal mortality (Aryal, 2007). Women and girls subjected to child marriage are likely to face slavery-like practices including servile marriages, sexual slavery, child servitude, child trafficking, and forced labour. For example, a 51-year-old participant (Participant 18) in this study was a mother of six and was married at the age of 11. She is Chettri (higher caste) and her husband, who worked in the police, was 27 at the time of marriage. She no longer lives with her husband. The following is an excerpt from her interview:

Interviewer: Why did you get married when you were so young?

Participant 18: My grandparents believed that it is good to marry off daughters before their menstruation.

Interviewer: What age did you become pregnant for the first time?

Participant 18: I was pregnant for the first time when I was thirteen, but it was a miscarriage.

Interviewer: Why aren't you living with your husband?

Participant 18: He married another woman, when the youngest child was six months old. I raised all the children on my own.

Interviewer: Did your husband treat you properly?

Participant 18: No because I didn't bring any dowry. My in-laws used to beat me. My husband used to come once a year during the festival [October-November].

The participant later moved to Kathmandu but faced further harassment. Her husband refused to support her, and she had no place to sleep. She suspected that her husband worked as a "pimp" for men seeking prostitutes. Later, when her husband had lost his job, she became a sex worker in order to feed her children.

Participant 13, a 32-year-old Brahmin woman (upper caste) who was married at the age of 15 to a man of the same caste who was 12 years older, offered another example. The following is an excerpt from her interview:

Participant 13: I was forced to marry by my parents because of dowry. We were from a very poor family. A delayed marriage would have meant more dowry.
Interviewer: Did you pay dowry?
Participant 13: No, not in my case. He was a lot older to me. This was his second marriage. He said he would not take dowry, so my parents married me off. He had land, so they thought it was a great offer.

The participant moved to Kathmandu five years after her marriage. But she explained that her husband abandoned her and their children while she was pregnant:

> My husband remarried, sold all the property and abandoned me. I wasn't aware that he had sold everything. I was pregnant with the fourth child. I had one friend who was working in a dance bar in Kathmandu. She asked me to come. It was important for me to look for a job so that I could feed my children.

Closely connected to the issue of child marriage is the economics of a dowry, which is the primary motivating factor for parents to marry off their daughters at a young age. This study (as shown in the examples above) found that some of the participants were married at a young age to much older men, some of whom had been married before, because that meant the parents had to pay little to no dowry. In such cases, the young age of the girl compensated for the lack of marital gift-giving. To put this in context, it is important to consider the problem of a dowry in South Asia and Nepal before moving on to discuss the consequences of child marriage in the lives of the participants.

Researchers have struggled to provide a precise definition for a dowry because it has undergone a distinct transformation over time and can mean different practices of marital gift-giving (Bradley, Subramaniam, & Tomalin, 2009, p. 1). But along with child marriage, a dowry in South Asia has been identified as an oppressive practice (Bradley, Subramaniam, & Tomalin, 2009). This is partly because it became so institutionalised and embedded in some South Asian cultural systems that families of bridegrooms started extorting astronomical material gifts and cash from the bride's family. Although the practice itself is not violent – it was traditionally seen as an inheritance that women received on the death of their husband as they lacked inheritance rights that were equal to those of men – there has been significant documentation of dowry-related abuse of women. In India, a dowry was outlawed in 1961 through the enactment of the Dowry Prohibition Act, but it continues to be the centre of negotiations between the two families in the process of arranged marriages. In extreme cases, incidents have been reported in which the families of girls have faced dowry-related harassment resulting in "dowry-death" or "bride-burning" (Bradley, Subramaniam, & Tomalin, 2009).

Similarly, in Nepal a dowry is a common practice, particularly in the country's Terai region, which shares an unregulated border with the Indian states of Uttar Pradesh and Bihar. The Terrai region comprises 46% of Nepal's population (Karki, 2014). This is despite the practice of paying a dowry being illegal in Nepal with penalties of up to NR 10,000 and prison sentences of up to three years. Additionally, a 2015 act to amend a number of laws in Nepal in order to promote gender equality and end gender-based violence (GBV) stipulates that any psychological abuse of women, including asking for a dowry, or humiliating, physical torturing, and shunning women for not providing a dowry is a punishable offence (Human Rights Watch, 2016, p. 28). Yet, a dowry remains common in Terrai, and the high price of dowries has significantly contributed to GBV in the region.

As previously mentioned, the economic basis for a dowry is associated with the inheritance system. In both India and Nepal, the practice of a dowry came into existence in order to give women economic and financial security after their marriage. The 2007 Interim Constitution stated that sons and daughters are equally entitled to ancestral property, but the demand for larger dowries remains due to "the general rise in prices and the current obsession with gold and silver, the prices of which are rising almost every day" (Karki, 2014, p. 21). The 2016 HRW report found:

> sporadic incidents of killing or attempted killing of brides over dowry disputes, despite efforts to eradicate the practice. Activists claimed that in Dhanusa district, for example, the cost of a dowry had increased over the past several years from the cost of a cow (NRs 25,000 or $250) to between NRs 400,000 and NRs two million ($4,000 to $20,000), demanded in cash. In some cases, as part of a pre-dowry agreement, the bride's family will pay the tuition fee for the bridegroom to pursue academic study. Activists reported that many men left the country to work abroad to earn money to pay for family members' dowries, which left the men's wives more vulnerable to abuse.
>
> (HRW, 2016, p. 29)

The same report noted that a dowry is just one of the factors influencing child marriage in Nepal, but culturally girls are often seen as a "burden" and as someone who is destined to move to someone else's family after marriage, meaning investment in her education is not considered necessary. This perception means families often give preference to the needs of boys over those of girls, and in some cases the abject poverty and social circumstances of the family also compel girls to marry young.

The cases of the two participants in the study discussed above (Participants 18 and 13) illustrate the helplessness of poor families that have an obligation to marry off their daughters. It is important in such circumstances, however, that the girl marries within the same caste, especially if she is a Brahmin (upper caste). Although poverty remains an underlying factor for deprivation, it nonetheless interacts with the cultural norms and values that construct the social hierarchy in Nepalese society. The social structure recognises Brahmins as superior and as being situated at the top of the hierarchy. The differentiation between Brahmins and lower castes at the social level is the principle through which the "pollution and purity ideology" operates (Cameron, 1998). This is based on the belief that Brahmins, as a superior caste, must not dilute their pure status by marrying men or women from a lower caste. Social norms dictate that the purity of caste and sex (a woman is considered to be pure) must be strictly preserved and protected and, as such, it is important for upper-caste women to marry a man of the same caste. However, a 2014 United Nations Development Programme (UNDP) looking at masculinity and GBV in Nepal suggested that lower education groups and lower economic classes (not castes) typically hold more traditional views on masculinity, including with regard to polygamy. This is supported by the research conducted for this volume, which found that husbands routinely abandon their wives or marry multiple times. The UNDP study also found that "People from the 15–20 and above 50 age groups hold stronger beliefs in the traditional notions of masculinities and homophobia. Caste and ethnicity do not appear to impact perceptions of masculinities" (UNDP, 2014, p. 10).

Returning to the participants' experiences, in both of the aforementioned cases the economics of a dowry played an important role in their parents' decision to marry off their daughters early. Their purity (i.e. their virginity) and young age were the two factors that were seen as compensation for the lack of a dowry in a marriage to a man who was far older. One of the participants was married to a man who had already married once, which also contributed to the payment of a dowry not being required. But despite this, once married she was ill-treated by her in-laws for not bringing a sufficient dowry. The other participant never had any decision-making power within her marriage. She says she was ill-treated by her mother-in-law and was later abandoned by her husband who sold off all his property. "I was not given any personal space and forced to do household work. I was abused if they thought I wasn't doing it right". This shows how GBV can manifest in many forms. As noted, the legal provisions that have been put in place have not ended the dowry: laws alone cannot bring about a significant change in the face of economic drivers and social and cultural norms that sanction the practice. Instead, improving the lives of women requires the long-term transformation of social and cultural norms relating to gender, including with regard to masculinity.

3.3 Intimate partner violence

GBV remains a pervasive global challenge, and women marrying at an early age are associated with the most widespread form of violence perpetrated against women: IPV (Atteraya, Gnawali, & Song, 2014). At least 35% of women worldwide have experienced non-partner sexual violence or physical and/or sexual IPV. South Asia has the highest regional prevalence, with at least 43% of women having experienced physical and/or sexual violence at the hands of their partner. Abuse by an intimate partner has profound consequences for the health and well-being of women, families, and communities, and also for development outcomes globally. Preventing violence requires understanding its root causes and situational triggers, and it is recognised that VAWG is largely a manifestation of unequal gender relations and the imbalance of power between men and women (Aryal, 2007).

In Nepal, which ranks 108 out of 152 countries on the Human Development Report (HDR) Gender Inequality Index, IPV has become a major public and human rights issue (Ghimire & Samuels, 2017). A 2017 study based on the NDHS shows that 33% of married women aged 15–49 have experienced IPV and 17% have experienced IPV in the past 12 months (Ghimire & Samuels, 2017, p. 5). Another study looking at the consequences of sexual violence within marriage among young girls between the ages of 15 and 24 years old in two districts of Nepal (Dang and Tanahu) found that nearly 50% of women had experienced forced sex in their marriage (Puri et al., 2011 as cited in Pandey, 2017). A larger study carried out in four districts of Nepal (Dolkha, Sindupalchowk, Dang, and Kapilvastu) that interviewed 1,296 married women aged between 15 and 25 years found that 46% had experienced sexual abuse and 25% had experienced physical abuse from their husbands (Dulal, Lamichhane, Puri, & Taman, 2011).

Consistent with the above data, the data collected for this research suggests that most of the women had suffered severe IPV at the hands of their husbands. This is significant because it shows that the consequences of domestic violence and IPV can be far reaching, as many respondents for this study ultimately engaged in the sex and informal entertainment industry as a result of violence at home and/or abandonment by their husbands, many of whom generally resorted to violence after consuming alcohol. No study, to my knowledge, has explored the nature and patterns of IPV faced by women who work in the sex and informal entertainment industry in Nepal. Studies in the South Asian context (see e.g. Aryal, 2007; Ghimire & Samuels, 2017) have shown that there is a link between IPV and early marriage, and two studies (one from Nepal and one from India) have shown that girls who marry under the age of 18 are at higher risk of experiencing IPV compared to those who marry later (Atteraya, Gnawali, & Song, 2014; Hokama, Jimba, Oshiro, & Poudyal, 2011). One objective of the research presented in this volume, as indicated earlier, is to determine the factors that have contributed to creating the circumstances that lead women to work in the sex and informal entertainment industry in Nepal.

The interview conducted with Participant 1 (age 41, upper caste, married but not living with husband, has three children) illustrated how various factors – ranging from deeply rooted social and cultural norms that legitimise patriarchy to male dominance and notions of honour (*izzat*) – can come together to increase the risk of IPV:

> I was married in April 1990 when I was 14 years old and was studying in standard ten [high school]. I come from a Brahmin family. My father is a

> priest and commands a lot of respect in the society. My husband approached my father for my hand in marriage. He was very reluctant for a number of reasons: I was too young, going to school; we are Brahmins (upper caste), and the boy was alcoholic and was known to have a bad character. He pressurised my father and threatened to kidnap me or marry me forcefully. My father married me off taking into consideration his and family's reputation and honour.

The above example shows that social influences can create circumstances in which families marry their daughters off at a young age in order to uphold the honour of the family, which outweighs other considerations, including the education and safety of the girl child. In *On the Age of the Auspicious*, Cameron (1998) argues that honour as a social concept is articulated through various structures and that girls in the family, in particular, are seen as the flag bearers of the family's honour. In her study with the Bhalara community in Western Nepal, she found that the notion of *izzat* has a strong association with the women in the family, pointing out that the *izzat* is not necessarily behaviour but is a "nexus of ideas separated from behaviour" (Cameron, 1998, p. 137). There is a widely prevalent view, as mentioned above, that a person's sexual conduct can greatly damage the reputation of the family and community. In Nepal (and in other parts of South Asia), upholding honour is the responsibility of both the woman and the household, which serves to maintain caste hierarchies (Joshi, 2001; Laurie, Poudel, Richardson, & Townsend, 2016).

Participant 1 also shared the following:

> my husband started beating me weeks after our marriage. It became more frequent and severe, sometimes he would trash me with a table, as days passed. He would usually beat me when he is drunk. No one came – including my husband's parents, his four brothers and two sisters – ever came forward to protect me. [...] I was still studying. I would wake up at dawn and cook food for the entire family. In our culture, the daughter-in-law is not expected to eat food before serving the husband's parents, so I used to go to school on an empty stomach. If I ate, my in-laws wouldn't. They expected me to do all household work and were not at all happy that I was leaving for school every morning. Eight months into the marriage, my husband's parents asked me and my husband to leave the house due to frequent beatings that they witnessed and tensions thereof.

The participant continued to endure violence while pregnant with her first child. She recalled:

> my husband kicked me very hard and beat me ruthlessly. I came to know that day that he remarried someone else. So, after a few days when the time of delivery came, I was all alone in the hospital. In the Kathmandu Maternity Hospital, known as Prasuti Griha, Thapathali, I gave birth to a dead child.

> The doctors suspected that the baby succumbed when my husband kicked me in my stomach.

Despite this incident, the participant remained in the marriage. Her husband returned and asked for forgiveness, but the violence soon resumed. She gave birth to a second son, again in the absence of her husband who had left home and did not return for five years. When asked why she became pregnant again and did not separate from her husband, she said:

> The *izzat* of my father and my in-laws were important. My father is still a respected man in the community; divorce or separation is not accepted. I had nowhere to go. My husband still had four unmarried brothers and two sisters. The presence of elder daughter-in-law is very important for any social functions so the family's *izzat* was tied with me. Plus, if my children had to study, they needed a father. Otherwise, their life would be doomed. In school, they ask for the father's name.

The above example is illustrative of a common trend in South Asian societies in which a married woman is expected to do all the household work in her husband's family home, and the parents and sisters of her husband sometimes become the key drivers of IPV or, as in the above example, they become silent observers. Family members complain to their sons and brothers that their wives are lazy, disobedient, not bringing enough dowry to the household, and so on (Ghimire & Samuels, 2017).

Social norms around masculinity, femininity, male guardianship of women, and polygamy have a strong influence on the behaviour and choices of men in Nepal, as well as on IPV (Ghimire & Samuels, 2017). There is a social acceptance of domestic violence, and it is sometimes seen as a man's right to control women. It is also largely accepted that a woman must be subservient and submissive in marital relationships. Moreover, low social status and women's lack of decision-making power, lack of access to resources and information, and shame related to speaking out about certain abuses can put women at further risk of experiencing violence.

Gender-based violence is a broad term, and it is often used to refer to any form of violence perpetrated against women or girls, though the factors and circumstances under which violence occurs can be strikingly different. Heise (2011) argues that the broad term underscores what each of the abuses has in common: namely, they are grounded in the fundamental devaluation of women and girls. It makes more sense, then, to look at the specific nature of violence in relation to this rather than to address the full spectrum of violence captured under the acronym VAWG (Heise, 2011, p. 2). Based on a study carried out in two districts of Nepal, Ghimire and Samuels (2017) note that the perception of what constitutes IPV varies among different age groups of boys and depending on their exposure to information and communication technology. While wife-beating is still very common among older men, extra-marital affairs, polygamy, sexual coercion, controlling mobility and social interactions, crimes such as acid attacks due to suspicion and jealously, and cyberbullying were identified as "new" forms of violence (i.e. more prevalent among younger generations of men).

Ghimire and Samuels (2017) also analysed the broad reasons why, in the context of Nepal, men and boys who marry child brides, or who themselves marry young, tend to be more likely to commit IPV against the women and girls they marry. They argue that because after their marriage girls might have to give up their studies, boys may still attend school. While at school they meet other girls, who tend to become more important to them than their wives. Also, in some cases, arranged marriages take place between boys and girls who are both very young, and they do not see each other for some time after their childhood wedding ceremonies. But because of social obligations, the boy has to accept the girl into his family or he could be fined up to NR 200,000 (USD 200) if they do not complete their *Gauna* (obligations connected with child marriages) and fulfil their other social obligations. In such cases, tensions arise as young women and girls often find themselves living with husbands who can barely tolerate their presence and who berate them and inflict violence on them for interfering with their relationships with other women. Men who migrate to other cities or countries also tend be more violent towards their wives because, according to Ghimire and Samuels, they get used to a whole new lifestyle, which influences their attitude. Exposure to modern attitudes can then lead to conflict as their wives remain within the confines of the household and are not exposed to these different practices. This creates incompatibility between them, leading to tensions that result in husbands inflicting violence on their wives, having extra-marital affairs, or simply abandoning them (Ghimire & Samuels, 2017).

Participant 2 (age 30, low caste, married but not living with husband, has one child), who married at the age of 26, was one of the interviewees who had been abandoned by her husband. She told me that she was three months pregnant when her husband went to Qatar for work, "He kept in touch for a few months and then stopped all connections [...] he had come to Nepal but never met my son". In some instances, boys marry early because of family needs. When a mother dies young, for example, another woman is needed to take care of the house, leading a son to marry early. This has sometimes left boys feeling frustrated with their marriage. When they become adults, they take that frustration out on their wives in the form of violence and also resort to polygamy and extra-marital affairs.

Participant 17 (age 33, high caste, not living with husband, has two children) was married to a 20-year-old man when she was just 15 years old. She now works in the informal entertainment industry. They moved to the city when her father-in-law passed away and this was when the problems began. The following is an excerpt from the interview conducted with her:

Participant 17: We had an ancestral house in Kathmandu. The bad days started after my father-in-law's death. My husband was the only son, and he became astray after his death. He refused to take care and would disappear for days.

Interviewer: Was your husband supportive of your work?
Participant 17: No, never. He didn't care. I had to look after my children, educate them and feed them so I had no other choice.
Interviewer: Does your husband work?
Participant 17: Yes, he worked as a contractor.
Interviewer: Did he contribute to the household income?
Participant 17: Never, he used to entertain himself with other women and blow the money.

Participant 2 (age 30, low caste, not living with husband, has one child) says she migrated to Kathmandu because of poverty and the Maoist conflict. Her parents had six daughters, and her father was an alcoholic. She said "He [her father] never earned, there was no food to eat, and my father used to beat my mother and all of us". When she moved to the city, she took a job in a massage parlour where she met her future husband. The following is an excerpt from her interview:

Interviewer: How did you meet your husband?
Participant 2: He used to come there as a customer. He encouraged me to leave the job and promised to marry me. I too wanted to get out of the profession.
Interviewer: How long were you married?
Participant 2: There was a problem with caste. He left me when I was pregnant ... I was five months pregnant. I was married for about two years. He was fine, but when he realised my caste, he tortured me mentally.

Studies indicate that at the household level, the risk factors for IPV against married women across all castes and classes tend to be higher if she is economically dependent on her husband and his family. Women's lack of economic independence means that the difficulties they face without a husband's financial support outweigh the violence they experience from their husband (Ghimire & Samuels, 2017). But it has also been observed that women who are employed were vulnerable to violence too and were 28% more likely to experience IPV than those who were unemployed (Ghimire & Samuels, 2017; Dulal, Lamichhane, Puri, & Tamang, 2011). My research found that participants who had migrated to Kathmandu before marriage and were earning an income had experienced high levels of IPV. Earning an income did not necessarily lead to reduced violence. A number of participants disclosed that they were subjected to extreme physical violence when their husbands, who refused to work themselves, forcibly sought to take their money. For example, Participant 5 (age 27, upper caste, married, has one daughter) had migrated to Kathmandu because of the turmoil in her village during the Maoist conflict. She worked as a dishwasher in a hotel and then at a construction site before marrying the man of her choice when she was just 20 years old. It was an inter-caste marriage, and soon after marrying she quit her job and stayed at home to raise their daughter who was born within a year of their marriage. After four years, tension began to rise in the relationship;

her husband's behaviour began to change and he was no longer contributing to the household income. The following is taken from the interview conducted with her:

Interviewer: What triggered behaviour change in your husband?
Participant 5: I suspect he was having another affair.
Interviewer: Did he beat you?
Participant 5: Yes, it was quite regular usually at night.

In order to care for her daughter, Participant 5 found a job in a furniture shop but eventually joined a massage parlour because "the pay [in the furniture shop] was very less, and I had to manage all the expenses including my daughter's school fees. My husband was not at all contributing". The domestic violence perpetrated by her husband eventually pushed her out of her home.

> It is one of the major causes. It is very expensive to live in Kathmandu and if the husband is not working, it is difficult to survive after paying all the bills and fees for children's education. All the responsibilities fall on women. On top of that there is domestic violence, so women have to fend for themselves and have to take jobs for survival.

Similarly, Participant 9 (age 28, upper-caste Brahmin, not living with husband, has one daughter) gave examples of the extreme nature of the violence she had faced at the hands of her husband. She was 16 years old when she married a man who was 10 years older. She worked in a cabin restaurant, and her husband had been a frequent customer. In the interview, she described the violence he had perpetrated against her:

Interviewer: You are separated from your husband; can I ask what happened to the relationship?
Participant 9: He was already married, which I didn't know. He was alright for a year. He said I never have to work in a cabin bar. I still had to earn, and he used to take away everything. I was pregnant, and my first baby died. I was never taken to his house. Also, it was an inter-caste marriage. I was a Brahmin, and he was a *janajati* [lower caste].
Interviewer: What other violence did you face at home?
Participant 9: I suffered so much that I can't even explain. He used to lock me up and go away for days and he would beat me up. I went without food for a number of days.
Interviewer: Did you have control over the money you earned?
Participant 9: No, my husband took away everything.
Interviewer: When did you actually separate?
Participant 9: My husband had never taken me to the in-law's house. I discovered he had another wife and had two children. Once he was very violent after I gave birth. I was frequently beaten up. I even used to faint. Sometimes

he wouldn't come back home. Once I and the baby were without food and I went out looking for him and found out that he had another wife.

It is evident from the above examples that early and child marriage leave women and girls particularly vulnerable to IPV, which can then be triggered or exacerbated by factors such as alcohol consumption, extra-marital affairs, and polygamy, and this in turn can result in men abandoning their wives, especially in the case of inter-caste marriages or when women become pregnant.

3.4 Alcohol and domestic violence

Several studies from developing countries report alcohol use as a significant precipitating factor in domestic violence (see e.g. Puri, Shah, & Tamang, 2010). Participant 4 (age 28, low caste, married, has one child) described her husband as an alcoholic and said that he beat her regularly. She described having no control over her sexuality and said that her husband had not been present at the birth of her child. Her husband's attitude towards her worsened when he discovered that she had started working in a massage parlour. When asked if she had control over the money she earned, Participant 4 responded: "I practically ran the house and gave him money whenever he asked for it. He would spend the money drinking". The relationship between alcohol consumption and IPV was also identified in a community-based cross-sectional study of the urban poor in Kathmandu (225 participants) and the general population of Nepal (680 participants), which found an IPV prevalence of 33.8% among the urban poor compared with 19.9% across the country in general (Hokama, Jimba, Oshiro, Poudel, & Poudyal, 2011, p. 2081). The report found that, although there was a higher overall prevalence in urban areas, the husband's level of alcohol consumption and his (lower) socio-economic status were correlated with incidences of IPV in both sample populations. Additional risk factors for IPV in the general population were early marriage and the husband's lower level of education.

Pandey (2014) points out that the husbands' characteristics are important predictors of IPV and refers to studies that have consistently linked husbands' alcohol consumption to IPV (e.g. Abbey et al., 2009 as cited in Pandey, 2014), noting that part of the reason may be that excessive alcohol consumption reduces inhibitions and clouds judgement. George and Stoner (2000) have argued, however, that the perpetration of violence is premeditated and that men are more likely to act violently when drunk only because they think that they will be forgiven for their violent behaviour. As Pandey (2014) also acknowledged, poverty and the associated stress are also key contributors to domestic violence. Other studies have also found that a husband's higher level of education serves as a protective factor against violence (Ackerson & Subramanian, 2008). Pandey's own study (2014), which is based on Nepal's 2011 Demographic Survey Data, analysed variables such as property ownership, education level, age difference between husbands and wives, and years in marriage, alongside relationship variables including husband's excessive control over his wife, humiliation in front of others, and the autonomy of household decisions. The study concluded that those who consumed excessive alcohol were 74% more likely to commit sexual violence against their wives than those who did not, while husbands having secondary or higher education served as a protective factor against physical and sexual IPV. In terms of other indicators, the study reinforced the results of existing research, which reported that child marriage remained a social norm in Nepal and that 59% of Nepali women were married before the age of 18, and this group was most vulnerable to sexual violence at the hands of intimate partners.

3.5 Analysis

In this section, I analyse the key factors that contributed to violence against the participants of this study before they joined the sex and informal entertainment industry. I apply Heise's (1998) ecological model, which is used to analyse IPV, the most common form of violence perpetrated against women. It states that developing a clear understanding of the causes o VAWG is necessary before undertaking any design or evaluation of programmes that aim to reduce such violence. The ecological model provides a platform for conceptualising the causes of violence as probabilistic rather than deterministic (Gupta & Samuels, 2017). It affirms that VAWG can be the result of one key factor or a combination of many factors. As outlined above, the risk factors relating to violence perpetrated against the participants of this study emerged at multiple levels, with the following factors playing a particularly important role:

1. **Individual Level:** The main risk factor was a woman's (or girl's) age at the time of marriage. In most cases the participants were married while still girls and were below the legal marriageable age. Age differences between husband and wife (usually the husband being considerably older), a husband having a poor level of education, and a husband consuming excessive amounts of alcohol were also potential triggers or predictors of violence.
2. **Relationship Level:** Factors within the relationship include a husband's tendency to control and humiliate his wife and a wife's lack of voice in the relationship.
3. **Community Level:** Sustaining customs that promote child marriage and women being stigmatised for not conforming to social norms.
4. **Societal Level:** Norms supporting men's dominance over women and accepting violence as a means to resolve conflicts.

(Heise, 1998; Pandey, 2014)

The ecological model is an appropriate approach in the context of examining Nepal's sex and informal entertainment industry as studies on human trafficking have indicated that many women describe situations that compel them to enter the sex trade, either voluntarily or by force or deception, because of ubiquitous social inequalities and dire economic circumstances (Gurung, 2014). Many women reported having migrated to Kathmandu from rural areas to escape conflict, poverty, domestic violence, and other family-related stressors in their communities and that sex work represented the only means to financially support themselves and their families (Harman, Kaufman, Menger, & Shrestha, 2016). Heise's (2011) revised conceptual framework of IPV identifies that childhood violence, social attitudes such as acceptance of wife-beating, low social support, and economic factors such as women's (un)employment increase women's risk of violence. Other factors such as social norms, gender hierarchy, and cultural factors can increase the likelihood of men perpetuating IPV.

Since this study only interviewed women who were engaged in the sex and informal entertainment industry and had experienced violence, it is difficult to identify the specific causes of violence as there is no control group. In light of this, I identify the apparent risk factors, including those suggested by the participants themselves, and use secondary data and the existing literature to analyse the extent to which these risks are generally associated with increased vulnerability. Nonetheless, it is clear that at the individual level, child marriage was the most significant risk factor for experiencing violence. In this study, 71% of women interviewed married before the age of 15, and 85% of women were married before 21 years of age. Only one participant was older (26 years old) when she married, and she too was abandoned by her husband after he went abroad for work. Studies have shown that child marriage can adversely affect girls in a number of ways as it reduces their ability to make informed decisions and to have control over their sexual and reproductive rights and increases the risk of forced sex, leading to early pregnancy and pregnancy-related complications (see Pandey, 2017).

In the data set of this study, the women engaged in the sex and informal entertainment industry who married before the age of 15 had all done so through arranged marriages. It was the interplay of social-level factors such as the caste of the girl, notions of linking male honour to women's bodily purity, the correlation between adolescent age and dowry, and poverty that influenced their parents' decision to marry their daughters at a very early age. However, for the girls who were economically engaged after migration to Kathmandu and had married a partner of their choice, they did so based on factors including falling in love, the assurance of a better life by their partners, or feeling a sense of security. Although these women were economically active, the nature of their work exposed them to exploitative and vulnerable situations, and, as previously discussed (see Chapter 2), some of them had experienced intense violence during the Maoist conflict.

Against this backdrop of trauma, it is perhaps unsurprising that the participants described being attracted to men who they thought might provide emotional comfort or security. In a review essay that considered the kinship ties of prostitution, Stinchcombe (1994) argued that it is difficult for women working in the sex industry to experience conjugal love, which is attributed to a lack of commitment on the part of the man and his kinship group to possible children. In this industry, it is very common for men to pretend to love a commercial sex worker, but in reality, most men are unprepared to make kinship commitments. The rituals of sex work are characterised by low commitment, "entertainment", and commerce: the industry is associated with "fun", and it overlaps with recreational drugs and alcohol use, night life, and sexually significant theatre (Stinchcombe, 1994, p. 856). The indulgence that some men shower upon women in the sex and informal entertainment industry is often temporary; as clients, they are aware of the steady supply of new faces that enter the industry as older women retire at a certain age. This lack of commitment implies exploitation and is antithetical to the social norms relating to kinship. Men who frequent sex and informal entertainment spaces are aware of the vulnerability of the women who work there: they are often perceived as women who have no shame or lack honour and therefore have no claim to rights in kinship ties.

The other key factor is the woman's level of education. None of the participants in the study had completed high school. Research in 18 of the 20 countries with the highest rates of child marriage has shown that a girl's level of education is the strongest predictor of her age of marriage (Human Rights Watch, 2016). Around the world, girls with more education are less likely to marry as children; for example, girls with little or no education are up to six times more likely to marry early than girls with secondary schooling. Studies have shown that education (of both girls and husbands) could serve as a potent protective factor against domestic violence (Pandey, 2014; Puri, Shah, & Tamang, 2010; UNFPA et.al, 2016). Other studies, however, have noted that the effect of women's education on their experience of physical violence is mixed; in some studies, educated women were found to be less likely to experience physical violence (Ackerson & Subramanian, 2008; Agarwal & Panda, 2005), whereas in other studies this relationship was not found to be significant (Dulal, Lamichhane, Puri, Tamang & Shah, 2011). In Nepal, however, political factors such as the 10-year long Maoist conflict deprived a large number of girls in rural areas of a school education. Moreover, schools themselves (as pointed out in Chapter 2) became a focal point for promoting the Maoist ideology and recruiting, and in some cases abducting, young girls.

The participants in this study said that they were forced to discontinue their studies and move to Kathmandu. Other factors that hampered their access to education were poverty, migration, and early marriage. Some participants suggested that better education was the main factor that could have made a huge difference in their lives. For example, Participant 3 (age 20, Buddhist [Tamang], widow, has one child) was abducted by Maoist forces and now works in a massage parlour. She said: "My life would have been better if I had basic education. If there as was no war I would probably be studying in a university". Likewise, Participant 8 (age 48, upper caste, widow, has four children) said her lack of basic education was a hindrance to getting a job in a hospital. She later worked in a spa that was a conduit for sex work. The 48-year-old widow and mother of four children said that social and cultural norms result in the education of boys being prioritised within families, which puts women at a disadvantage:

> in the village, no one sends their daughter to school because they think she eventually will go to someone else's house. They think it is a waste of money. It is the society that stops women from realising her full potential.

Pandey (2014, p. 815) notes that husbands' tendencies to control the behaviour of their wives or to humiliate them in front of others were strong signs of the co-occurrence of physical or sexual abuse. This finding is consistent with other studies that have reported that men who were jealous and who mistrusted their wives were more likely to be violent against them (Garcia-Moreno et al., 2006 as cited in Pandey, 2014, p. 815). Pandey identifies humiliation (i.e. husbands mistreating wives in front of others) in particular as one of the strongest predictors of both physical and sexual violence. Her study documented that husbands who humiliate their wives are also likely to subject them to physical (70%) and sexual violence (46%). Moreover, of the women who reported spousal control, many were also physically (44%) and sexually (28%) abused.

Spousal control and humiliation were reported by the participants of this study. However, one of the limitations of the study is that the male partners or husbands of the women were not interviewed because most of the women who had experienced severe levels of violence were no longer living with their husband. That said, since the approach of this research was to prioritise the voices of women by using qualitative methods to record their experiences of violence, the descriptions of the patterns of violence and abusive behaviours were described from their perspective. Some of the patterns of violence that were described are summarised as follows:

- It was "normal" for men to beat their wives.
- It was common for husbands to abandon their wives, even at the advanced stages of pregnancy.
- Husbands indulged in polygamy and promiscuous behaviour.
- Husbands stopped any form of contact with their wives, especially after going abroad.
- Husbands quit their job and often resorted to violence against their wives to extort money.
- Sex was seen as an entitlement.
- There was a general imbalance of power.
- There were accounts of husbands exercising control over their wives, including humiliation.
- Husbands were mostly addicted to alcohol.

Regarding how much control women have over the money they earn, Participant 16 (age 51, upper caste [Chettri], married but not living with husband, has six children) who worked in a cabin restaurant said, "My husband used to take away the money. He used to beat me up. He used to bring other women and made them pregnant, and he asked me money for abortion". None of the husbands of the participants were well educated, and most were themselves very young. Their behaviour was shaped by prevailing notions of masculinity, characterised by an assumed entitlement to power and privilege over women. Also, the husbands had experienced a loss of kinship ties because, like the women, most of them had migrated to cities due to economic circumstances, which absolved them of marital responsibilities.

The reasons behind the violence listed above have emerged throughout the existing literature relating to the causes of VAWG in the South Asian context, and although the participants in this study contend with many of these risk factors, they are also employed in professions that make them particularly vulnerable to violence and exploitation. For example, some of the women met their husbands at work, and such marriages are governed by fragile trust as men might continue to frequent places where sex work and informal entertainment are conducted and may meet other women engaged in sex work. Men who meet and marry women in this context may also be conscious of the lower social status of their wives as women who work (or have worked) in the sex and entertainment industry. Since both partners in the relationships discussed by the participants lead vulnerable lives in the context of urban poverty, protective factors – such as wealth, women's education, employment, property ownership, and autonomy in intra-household decisions as identified by other studies (see Babu & Kar, 2010; Acharya, Koenig, & Stephenson, 2010; Dulal, Lamichhane, Puri, & Tamang, 2011; Maitra, Marinshaw, Martin, & Tsui, 1999; Agarwal & Panda, 2005) – that might minimise the risk of physical and sexual violence are lacking, especially in the ecosystem of the highly exploitative and high-risk sex and informal entertainment industry.

A study in Nairobi, Kenya (Ngugi et al., 2012) explored why some women enter into commercial sex work while other women in the same socio-economic environment do not. To address this question, respondent-driven sampling principles were adopted to recruit and collect data from 161 female sex workers and 159 women from the same age group who never engaged in commercial sex in Kibera, a large informal settlement in Nairobi. The study indicated that basic kinship measures, including a low number of family members seen during adolescence and thereafter, not having a male guardian while growing up, earlier times of ending relationships with both male and female guardians, and low educational attainment, were associated with engaging in commercial sex work in Kibera. By far the most important predictor of entering sex work was not having any male guardian, such as a father, uncle, or older brother, during childhood.

In the context of Nepal, as this chapter (see also Chapter 4) shows, joining the sex and informal entertainment industry happens for multiple reasons. Participants' kinship ties were often disrupted owing to political factors, including abduction by Maoist forces, which often led to not being accepted by their own family members following their return due to the perception that the honour of the family had been compromised. But loss of kinship ties was never the sole reason for joining the informal entertainment industry. The participants were not asked specifically about how they felt about losing their kinship ties, but through what they chose to share it was evident that the detachment from their immediate communities meant that they worried less about shame and honour when deciding to join the sex and informal entertainment industry. However, the participants were asked if life was better after migration, and responses were mixed. Some participants responded positively, including Participant 5 who said, "yes, it is better after years of struggle. I am earning good income and there are better opportunities for children", while another participant who lost her husband said life in the village while her husband was alive had been better.

3.6 Conclusion

This chapter has built on Chapter 2 on the Maoist conflict to examine the social norms and cultural factors that, along with trauma and violence in the early lives of the participants, may increase vulnerability to violence. From the data collected in this study, it is clear that women's decisions to enter the sector were driven by factors that are embedded in the social, cultural, and patriarchal norms that have been instrumental in reinforcing the subordinated status of women and normalising violence against them. Added to this are political factors, including the failure of the government to facilitate transitional justice on behalf of the already marginalised women and girls who were directly affected by the Maoist conflict. Analysing the background of the participants and understanding their early experiences of violence are critical steps towards understanding if and how these contribute to developing the strength and the resilience to deal with the trauma, challenges, and abuses that they encounter on a regular basis when they work in the informal entertainment industry. In the following chapters, I shift focus to empowerment and resilience, rather than risk and vulnerability, in order to reveal whether the participants perceive their lives to be better now than in the past and whether they feel their work liberates them from the deeply entrenched social norms and values that limit their agency as women. I also consider their aspirations for the future, and whether they feel empowered to achieve them.

References

Abbey, A. (2011). Alcohol's role in sexual violence perpetration: Theoretical explanations, existing evidence and future directions. *Drug and Alcohol Review*, *30*(5), 481–489.

Acharya, R., Koenig, M. A., & Stephenson, R. (2010). Domestic violence and early childhood mortality in Rural India: Evidence from prospective data. *International Journal of Epidemiology*, *39*(3), 825–833.

Ackerson, L. K., & Subramanian, S. V. (2008). State gender inequality, socioeconomic status and intimate partner violence (IPV) in India: A multilevel analysis. *Australian Journal of Social Issues*, *43*(1), 81–102.

Agarwal, B., & Panda, P. (2005). Marital violence, human development and women's property status in India. *World Development*, *33*(5), 823–850.

Aryal, T. R. (2007). Age at first marriage in Nepal: Differentials and determinants. *Journal of Biosocial Science*, *39*(5), 693–706.

Atteraya, M. S., Gnawali, S., & Han Song, I. (2014). Factors associated with intimate partner violence against married women in Nepal. *Journal of Interpersonal Violence*, *30*(7), 1226–1246.

Babu, B. V., & Kar, S. K. (2010). Domestic violence in Eastern India: Factors associated with victimization and perpetration. *Public Health*, *124*(3), 136–148.

Bradley, T., Subramaniam M., & Tomalin, E. (2009). *Dowry: Bridging the Gap between Theory and Practice*. Zed Books.

Cameron, M. (1998). *On the Edge of the Auspicious*. University of Illinois Press.

Choe, M. K., Thapa, S., & Mishra, V. (2005). Early marriage and early motherhood in Nepal. *Journal of Biosocial Science*, *37*(2), 143–162.

Dulal, B., Lamichhane, P., Puri, M., & Tamang, J. (2011). Women's status and violence against young married women in Rural Nepal. *BMC Women's Health*, *11*(19), 2–9.

Garcia-Moreno, C., Jansen, H. A., & Ellsberg, M. et al. (2006) Prevalence of intimate partner violence: Findings from the WHO multi-country study on women's health and domestic violence. *Lancet*, *368*, 1260–1269.

George, W. H., & Stoner, S. A. (2000). Understanding acute alcohol effects on sexual behavior. *Annual Review of Sex Research*, *11*, 92–124.

Ghimire, A., & Samuels, F. (2017). *Understanding Intimate Partner Violence. Prevalence, Drivers, Challenges*. ODI.

Gupta, T., & Samuels, F. (2017). *Literature Review of Male Perpetrators of Intimate Partner Violence in South Asia*: Final review. London: Overseas Development Institute.

Gurung, S. H. (2014). Sex trafficking and the sex trade industry: The processes and experiences of Nepali women. *Journal of Intercultural Studies*, *35*(2), 163–181.

Harman, J., Kaufman, R. W., Menger, L. M., & Shrestha, K. D. (2016). Understanding the experiences and needs of female commercial sex workers in Kathmandu, Nepal. *Health Care for Women International*, *37*(8), 872–888.

Heise, L. L. (1998). Violence against women: An integrated, ecological framework. *Violence Against Women*, *4*(3), 262–290.

Heise, L. L. (2011). *What Works to Prevent Partner Violence? An Evidence Overview* (STRIVE Working Paper). London School of Hygiene and Tropical Medicine.

Hokama, T., Jimba, M., Oshiro, A., Poudyal, A. K., & Poudel, K. C. (2011). Intimate partner violence among general and urban poor populations in Kathmandu, Nepal. *Journal of Interpersonal Violence*, *26*(10), 2073–2092.

Human Rights Watch. (2016). *"Our Time to Sing and Play": Child Marriage in Nepal*. www.hrw.org/sites/default/files/report_pdf /nepal0816_web.pdf

Joshi, S. (2001). "Cheli-Beti" discourses of trafficking and constructions of gender, citizenship and nation in modern Nepal. *Journal of South Asian Studies*, *24*(1), 157–175.

Karki, S. (2014). *A Study on Dowry Related Violence in Nepal*. INSEC. www.inseconline.org/pics/ 1409727203.pdf

Laurie, N., Poudel, M., Richardson, D., & Townsend, J. (2016). Women and citizenship post-trafficking: The case of Nepal. *The Sociological Review*, *64*(2), 329–348.

Maitra, K., Marinshaw, R., Martin, S. L., & Tsui, A. O. (1999). Domestic violence in Northern India. *American Journal of Epidemiology*, *150*(4), 417–426.

Ngugi, E., Benoit, C., Hallgrimsdottir, H., Jansson, M., & Roth, E. A. (2012). Partners and clients of female sex workers in an informal urban settlement in Nairobi, Kenya. *Culture, Health & Sexuality*, *14*(1), 17–30.

Pandey, S. (2014). Persistent nature of child marriage among women even when it is illegal: The case of Nepal. *Children and Youth Services Review*, *73*, 242–247.

Pandey, S. (2017). Persistent nature of child marriage among women even when it is illegal: The case of Nepal. *Children and Youth Services Review*, *73*, 242–247.

Puri, M., Shah, I., & Tamang, J. (2010). Exploring the nature and reasons for sexual violence within marriage among young women in Nepal. *Journal of Interpersonal Violence, 25*(10), 1873–1892.

Puri, M., Tamang, J., & Shah, I. (2011). Suffering in silence: Consequences of sexual violence within marriage among young women in Nepal. *BMC Public Health, 11*(1), 1–10.

Raj, A. (2010). When the mother is a child: The impact of child marriage on the health and human rights of girls. *Archives of Disease in Childhood, 95*(11), 931–935.

Stinchcombe, L. (1994). Review: Prostitution, kinship, and illegitimate work. *Contemporary Sociology, 23*(6), 855–859.

UNDP. (2014). *Nepali Masculinities & Gender Violence*. www.np.undp.org/content/nepal/en/home/operations/projects/closed-projects/poverty-reduction1/avrscs/publications.html

United Nation Population Fund (UNFPA) et al. . (2016). *Ending Impunity for Child Marriage in Nepal: A Review of Normative and Implementation Gaps.* Centre for Reproductive Rights. Retrieved from: https://nepal.unfpa.org/en/publications/ending-impunity-child-marriage-nepal

Warner, E. (2004). Behind the wedding veil: Child marriage as a form of trafficking in girls. *American University Journal of Gender, Social Policy and the Law, 12*, 233–271.

4 Women and empowerment in Nepal's sex and informal entertainment industry

4.1 Introduction

This chapter argues that the women who took part in the research have undergone a dramatic shift in the day-to-day structure of their lives, during which they have moved from conventional family units towards new, all-women, peer networks. I discuss how earning an income, even within an industry that is as exploitative as the sex and informal entertainment sector, represents a transformative moment for women. In part, this is because they have been able to leave behind violent husbands and/or destructive family and community contexts. The income they have been able to access has enabled them to take control of their lives and build resilience while connecting with other women who share a similar background in order to challenge the ongoing violence that they endure. Income, then, has enabled them to gain a greater degree of agency.

The term "agency" refers to the capacity of individuals to act independently and to make their own free choices (Kabeer, 1999). However, income alone has not empowered the participants. There are other factors at play, and the support of peer networks – associations of women working in the informal entertainment sector – appears to be the most significant. The organisations reviewed and mapped for this research were set up by women who had previously worked in the sector (discussed further in Chapter 7 on "Positive Deviance"). And through these organisations, they have been able to mobilise other women and girls working in the sector, offering them vital support to build resilience to cope with the violence, stigma, and discrimination that characterise their daily lives (see also Chapter 5). In this chapter, I look at the concepts of empowerment, autonomy, and power and examine how they play out in the lives of the participants and how they gain voice and agency. These concepts are applied in this chapter, and they are further discussed in Chapter 6, which considers the ways in which women build their resilience to violence. I revisit these concepts once again in Chapter 7 where I further illustrate how the various branches of peer network organisations help women to campaign for work-related rights.

This chapter is structured as follows. In the first section (4.2), I discuss the meaning of the term empowerment and the different theories on empowerment proposed by various scholars. These theories look at the different conditions and

DOI: 10.4324/9781003156796-4

trajectories through which an individual might be able to make choices for their growth and development. It is argued that for true empowerment to take place, an individual must have access to certain resources and be in a requisite enabling environment to be able to make decisions and choices and realise their goals. I use various concepts of empowerment to unpack and contextualise how my participants exercise choice, gain decision-making capabilities, and take control over their income, thereby expressing their agency.

Following this, I go on to address the concept of power and how it relates to theories of empowerment. The process of empowerment entails a power struggle, and for women in particular it involves confronting and challenging barriers at every step. Such barriers impede their decision-making capabilities and their economic potential at the individual, social, community, and political levels. Power in the context of empowerment has a number of dimensions: it refers to autonomy over making decisions (power to); control over personal decisions (power over); individual characteristics – self-esteem, confidence, and resilience – (power within); and the ability to collectively assert one's position and rights by being part of a community or group (power with). Understanding the concept of power is particularly important to this study as it reveals how the participants continuously gain and redefine power relations at various stages of their lives, which plays a pivotal role in the process of empowerment.

Later in the chapter, I illustrate how the participants of the study gained and now express their agency using the data collected during the qualitative interviews. I analyse case studies to see how the different concepts of power and agency play out in their lives. The section (4.5) focuses in particular on how the positive role of income in their lives enables them to express agency at the individual and household levels. In the conclusion, I summarise the concepts discussed in this chapter in relation to the case studies of the participants. I illustrate this with the aid of a diagram that shows how the women who took part in the study exercise choice and make use of the available resources in order to move forward in their lives. I point out how the concepts of power are enacted as women begin to take control of their lives and gain decision-making capabilities. The concepts of empowerment and power are discussed further in Chapter 5, where I explain how the participants exhibit resilience and what factors enable them to do so.

4.2 The meaning of empowerment

This section critically reflects on what empowerment might mean and what it might look like for the women who participated in the study. The terms "empowerment" and "agency" have been assigned various meanings, but definitions are typically linked to an individual's growth and development. Empowerment is widely seen as a process where people have the freedom to act and the ability to make choices, which in turn leads to an outcome (Alsop, Bertelsen, & Holland, 2006; Datta & Kornberg, 2002). Kabeer (1999) equates empowerment with people's ability to make life choices. She sees it as a process whereby people who were previously denied (or simply did not have) the option of making choices due to such factors as poverty or social suppression can, over time, acquire such ability. Kabeer (1999, p. 437), however, makes it clear that the question of choice arises only when an individual's survival needs have first been met, defining survival needs as "strategic life choices". The ability to exercise choice can be thought of in terms of three interrelated dimensions: *resources* (preconditions) that form the conditions under which choices are made; *agency*, which is at the heart of the process through which choices are made; and *achievements*, which are the outcomes of choices (Kabeer, 1999, p. 438).

Boender, Malhotra, and Schuler (2002, p. 8) noted that *resources* in empowerment theory can also be treated as catalysts for empowerment or conditions under which empowerment is likely to occur. They argue that it may be more useful to think of resources as "enabling factors", as potentially critical inputs to foster an empowerment process rather than as part of empowerment itself. Becker and Mahmud (2012) point out that for women, in particular, access to resources defines the path of the empowerment process. They argue that access to and control over material, human, and social resources that a woman acquires through interaction with multitudes of domains in her life (such as the family, the market, and the community) creates conditions that could either support or hinder her growth. For example, in Chapter 3, we saw that a bad marriage, lack of access to household wealth, and the ill treatment of a woman by her in-laws played a significant role in determining her life situation. This chapter demonstrates how such circumstances in turn shape the opportunities and choices available to her.

The second dimension that influences an individual's ability to make a choice is *agency*. Agency is an actor's or a group's ability to make purposeful choices (Samman & Santos, 2009, p. 3). A number of authors have argued that an individual's or a group's ability to express agency meaningfully depends on factors ranging from access to material assets and education to social status or identity. It is also shaped by psychological factors such as self-esteem, self-confidence, the ability to imagine and aspire to a better future, and by people's collective assets and capabilities such as voice, organisational representation, and identity (Narayan, 2002, 2005; Alsop & Heinsohn, 2005; Petesch, Smulovitz, & Walton, 2005, as cited by Samman & Santos, 2009). Chen and Mahmud (1995) include in their definition of agency relational factors such as changes in self-perception on the part of the woman, changes in the perception of the woman by others, and cognitive faculty, including changes in contractual agreements and bargaining power in various types of relationships. This point is further demonstrated in Chapter 5 on resilience in this volume where it is seen that participants' self-perception undergoes a transformative change when they come in contact with peer networks.

Kabeer (1999) argues that agency also encompasses motivation and purpose that an individual brings to an activity. For example, understanding agency requires an assessment of what motivates an individual to do certain jobs, what is the purpose of earning an income, and what is the end goal. More recent studies (Donald et al., 2017) point out that understanding an individual's ability to set goals based on their preferences is a key dimension in measuring an individual's agency. However, a person's preferences are largely determined by the resources that are available to them. For example, a woman's ability to find a job depends on her skills and qualifications (which in this context are understood as resources). So, the ability to set goals based on her personal preferences can translate into the meaningful exercise of agency only when she is fully conscious of the outcome and the consequences of her decision. A number of women in this study appear to be acting with agency as they consistently maintain their motivation and purpose for working in the informal entertainment and sex sector, which is driven by their desire to provide a better future for their children beyond simply providing for their survival needs.

The descriptions cited above highlight an important feature of empowerment: it can be both a process and an outcome (see Bird, Luttrell, Quiroz, & Scrutton, 2009, p. 5). As an outcome, it can mean the ability to act freely and make choices, or that there is increased participation of previously excluded groups in development activities. This can be brought about through various political processes, including affirmative action, or through a quota system that ensures marginalised groups are represented in critical roles. For example, one third of positions in all of Nepal's state institutions, including the legislature, are reserved for women (The Diplomat, 2016). Some stress that the transformative approach that relies on participation alone is meaningless unless there is also an outcome, which means that demanding the rights of marginalised groups is not enough; it must be action oriented so that they can actually reap economic and social benefits. Such achievements are seen as an outcome of empowerment (Malhotra Schuler & Boender, 2002). An emphasis on outcome also means gaining control over decisions and resources which improves people's lives (Longwe, 1991, as cited by Luttrell et al., 2009). This can be facilitated by a robust mechanism for the distribution of wealth and welfare benefits especially targeted at the poor (Luttrell, Quiroz, Scrutton, & Bird, 2009, p. 5). However, achieving the outcome in the long term means improving the social and strategic position of women in society (achievements), and this enhanced status should be visible at all levels and domains of society (discussed in the next section), which is not necessarily the case (Malhotra et al., 2002).

Malhotra et al. (2002, p. 9) note that specific indicators of empowerment are always context specific and whether any empowerment indicator or form of agency (such as exercising control over decisions or resources) amounts to meaningful empowerment in a given context will be an empirical question, and there will always be situations when a particular indicator does not signify empowerment. The authors further argue that empowerment as a concept itself is an iterative process and not an end in itself. The reason agency is significant is because there are many examples in the literature whereby a woman might have access to resources but might not have any control over them. This is particularly true in many societies with a strong patriarchal setup in which a woman may be married into a wealthy household, but she does not have financial autonomy nor is she allowed to work. Similarly, in both India and Nepal, changes in legal statutes that ostensibly provide women with greater opportunities to participate in the political process or seek to protect women from the negative outcomes of a dowry have not resulted in improving the situation of the vast majority of women. Thus, while resources – economic, social, and political – are often critical in ensuring that women are empowered, they are not always sufficient (Malhotra et al., 2002). The research conducted for this volume illustrates how, in the context of women working in the informal entertainment industry, access to resources can bring about empowerment only when women collectively come together to recognise the potential for them to do so and find ways to effectively utilise the resources in their own interests.

While it is clear that both empowerment and agency are necessary if a person is to live a free life, these intrinsic values are linked to an individual's capacity to make choices based on the circumstances and resources at hand. Agency – the freedom to be able to achieve whatever the individual has reason to value in life – therefore, is considered an important end in itself, and it is seen as a crucial part of development (Sen, 1985, p. 206 as cited in Samman & Santos, 2009). This concept is the foundation of Sen's capability approach (Sen, 1985a), which emphasises that by expanding the capacity of the poor and the marginalised, they can achieve a better quality of life. This approach has been instrumental in designing development policies aimed at reducing poverty and has been incorporated by the Human Development Report (HDR) (World Bank, 2001) as well as the *Voices of the Poor* study (cited in Narayan, 2000). It has also been endorsed by other researchers to develop a conceptual framework for understanding empowerment, which in this context is defined as the capacity of an individual or a group to make effective *choices* and transform them into *actions* (see Samman & Santos, 2009). The process of transforming choices into actions can be understood as an interaction between two building blocks: agency and opportunity structure.

4.3 Alsop and Heinsohn's agency and opportunity structure

In this section, I discuss agency and "opportunity structure" in order to familiarise the reader with the two concepts as they are used later in the chapter as part of the suggested framework for the measurement of empowerment demonstrated among the participants.

"Opportunity structure" broadly refers to the institutional, social, and political context made up of formal and informal rules, which in turn creates the environment that enables actors to operate and translate their choices into action (Alsop & Heinsohn, 2005). Agency and opportunity structure are thought to correlate with the degree of empowerment a person or a group experiences. Degrees of empowerment (DOE) can be measured by assessing: "(1) whether a person has the opportunity to make a choice, (2) whether a person actually uses the opportunity to choose, and (3) once the choice is made, whether it brings the desired outcome" (Alsop & Heinsohn, 2005, p. 7).

Alsop and Heinsohn (2005) point out that the apparent relationship between empowerment and development outcomes that has been observed – and that underpins the claim that there is an instrumental purpose to empowering people – is largely based on anecdotal evidence. They contend that robust data that demonstrates a clear association between empowerment and development outcomes is hard to find as most studies rely on intermediary indicators of empowerment. For this reason, the link, and particularly the causal relationship, between empowerment and development remains a hypothesis: more empirical studies are therefore needed to establish how and to what extent investing in empowerment shapes development outcomes (Alsop & Heinsohn, 2005, p. 6). In their framework for measuring empowerment, Alsop and Heinsohn look at the indicators of agency (in terms of the capacity to make meaningful choices) in the context of asset endowments. The assets can be psychological, informational, organisational, material, social, financial, or human. But while human assets (such as skills and literacy) can be directly measured, it is difficult to quantify psychological assets (such as the capacity to envision) or social assets (such as social capital). However, any of these assets or a combination of them can potentially help actors to make choices and translate them into action. In Chapter 5, I consider how psychological assets in particular can interact with resources to enhance agency.

In addition to agency and opportunity structure, Alsop and Heinsohn conceptualise three domains and levels that essentially cut across the lives of all individuals. The domains and levels are conceptualised in such a way in order to rationalise the complexities that are inherent in the measurement of empowerment. This is necessary because an actor may feel, and indeed be, empowered in one particular domain but not in another. The authors illustrate this through an example of an Indian woman who may experience a form of empowerment when exercising choice over domestic resources within the household, but at the same time she might experience a different form of empowerment when trying to access a loan from a bank. Her experiences will also vary depending on where she is operating from, be it her home, within her village, or in a nearby city. To deal with such complexities in the process of measuring empowerment, Alsop and Heinsohn (2005, p. 11) state that it is important to conceptualise three domains and three levels that operate in a person's life. Levels are defined as the administrative boundaries of the state such as the council, district, or national level. Mapping the domains and levels can also help in identifying the gaps and formulate effective points for empowerment.

The diagram shows the various factors that interact within a person's life and how at each domain they might experience a different degree of empowerment. Alsop and Heinsohn stress that a certain degree of empowerment at one level does not necessarily reflect the same degree of empowerment at other levels.

For example, social norms can largely influence the choices made by an individual or a social group. The author cites an example of an Indian household where a son might be given preferential treatment over a daughter, but if the family belongs to a higher caste, she might experience a higher degree of empowerment compared to women of low caste. In this study, we see in Chapter 6 that a sex worker is likely to experience a higher degree of empowerment when

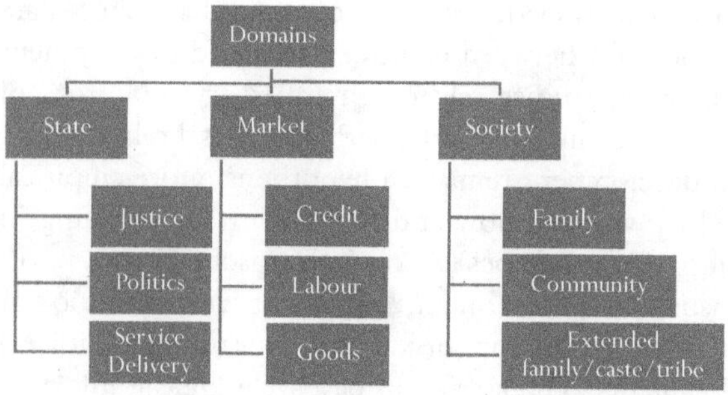

Figure 4.1 The domain structure, as proposed by Alsop and Heinsohn (2005).

she is linked with a non-governmental organisation (NGO) and works as a peer worker. Equally, the degree of empowerment in one domain may well correlate with a similar degree of empowerment in another domain. For example – as will become evident later in this study – the participants are severely disempowered at the social level because of the stigma attached to their job, and they also feel disempowered in the market and, when faced with violence, while accessing justice (Alsop & Heinsohn, 2005, p. 12).

The above framework is relevant when examining the different degrees of empowerment of the participants in this study. The following sections and chapters critically explore how the participants of this study express choice, show resilience, and make use of informal opportunity structures presented through the peer networks. The data suggests that networks set up by women leaders, described as "positive deviants" in this study (see Chapter 6 for further discussion of this concept) due to their uncommon behaviour and strategies, enable them to find better solutions to the same problems faced by their peers. They create an enabling environment that helps other actors to also realise their potential, which in turn allows them to optimise the use of the available resources. The study analyses how the various domains and levels in which they operate contribute to their empowerment or offer them some opportunities for growth.

4.4 Power and empowerment: Ibrahim and Alkire's power indicators

Understanding the concept of power is particularly important to this study as it reveals how the participants continuously gain and redefine power relations at various stages of their lives, which plays a pivotal role in the process of empowerment. In this section, I discuss four internationally comparable "power" indicators proposed by Ibrahim and Alkire (2007) for measuring agency, which I apply to the analysis of the experiences of empowerment among the participants in this research.

A number of authors conceptualise empowerment as an enhancement of power in the sense that the individual should have control over their destiny or the ability to make effective changes, even when such changes are opposed by a certain group (Oakley, 2001 as cited in Ibrahim & Alkire, 2007). Uphoff (2005, as cited in Ibrahim & Alkire, 2007, p. 384) discusses "power resources", arguing that power can be effective only when resources (material, social, human, and institutional) are made available for the poor and the marginalised. Oakley (2001) differentiates between two types of power: in one, the poor gain power and become empowered without altering the power dynamics, while in the other, the gains made by the poor inevitably result in a reduction in the power of others (i.e. the more powerful become less dominant). So, in this conception, the process of empowerment entails a power struggle, and for women in particular it involves challenging and confronting barriers at every step. Such barriers impede women's decision-making capabilities and economic potential at the individual, social, community, and political levels.

Alkire and Ibrahim (2007, p. 388) argue that the criteria for selecting indicators for measuring empowerment should take into account five points. First, the chosen indicators are relevant to the lives of the poor. Second, they should be internationally comparable. Third, the indicators need to assess both instrumental and intrinsic aspects of empowerment, which means a person's decisions are based on what he or she values and that the person feels motivated in exercising agency. Fourth, the indicator allows for the changes in agency over a period of time to be identified. Fifth, the chosen indicators have been previously tested for measuring empowerment and found to be adequate for research purposes. So, drawing on Rowlands (1998) typology (i.e. "power over", "power to", "power with", and "power within"), Alkire and Ibrahim proposed four indicators for measuring empowerment and agency in individual and household surveys. They used the same types of power but made adjustments to their definitions as follows: "power over" (Rowland's "ability to resist manipulation" became "*control over personal decisions*"), "power to" ("creating new possibilities" became "*autonomy and household decision-making*"), "power with" ("acting in a group" became "*changing aspects in one's life*"), and "power from within" ("enhancing self-respect and self-acceptance" became "*changing aspects in one's life at community level*").

By asking similar questions to those suggested by Alkire and Ibrahim, the research presented in this volume seeks to better understand how these power indicators appear in the lives of the participants. The subsequent sections and chapters demonstrate how they are actualised in their lives and the impact of this actualisation. Below, I explain how these indicators are framed in this context.

Indicator 1: "Power over/control": control over personal decisions

This indicator reflects control over personal decisions and considers the extent to which an individual challenges power relations and patriarchal social hierarchies (Alsop et al., 2006, p. 21, as cited by Ibrahim & Alkire, 2007, p. 389). To measure this indicator, the participants of this study were asked the following questions:

- What is your income mainly spent on?
- Who decides?

As discussed later in the chapter, one of the first things that emerged while analysing the role of income in the lives of the participants is that they all have full control over the money they earn and all other aspects of their personal lives.

Indicator 2: "Power to/choice": household decision-making

The "power to" indicator is used to determine how autonomous an individual is while making decisions within the household and within the domains that they operate. In the context of women working in the informal entertainment sector and sex work, the domain of their economic activity is the market.

"Choice" is usually denied to women in the traditional Nepalese social setup, more especially when they are not earning an income. The ability to make household decisions addresses two levels of empowerment (Ibrahim & Alkire, 2007 p. 389): the *existence* of choice and the *use* of choice. In this study, questions were asked regarding how and where the participants chose to spend their income, including:

- How important is it for you to earn an income?
- Do you send some of your income to your pre-migration home?

From their responses, it was clear that they have a say over household life and decision-making even in cases where the women are still living with their husbands or partners.

As per the literature, the "power to" is seen as an important indicator of power relations because the household serves as the "fundamental building block of the society as the place where an individual confronts basic livelihood concerns, norms, values, power and privilege" (Narayan et al., 2000b, p. 219). A number of studies in the 1990s (e.g. Hashemi, Riley, & Schuler, 1996; Jejeebhoy, 2000; Kishor, 2000) used "decision-making within household" as a key indicator of women's agency and empowerment. These studies were set in a variety of different contexts and yielded mixed results. In general, they tended to show that agency and empowerment are difficult to measure as they have multifaceted dimensions. As discussed, a woman might enjoy relative empowerment in one domain (e.g. in the home) but that might not translate into other domains of her life (e.g. the market). Hence, different indicators show different results depending on the sociocultural context that defines the position of women in a given society.

For example, Hashemi, Riley, and Schuler's (1996) study in Bangladesh, which looked at women's empowerment using eight indicators (mobility, economic security, the ability to make small purchases, the ability to make larger purchases, involvement in major household decisions, relative freedom from domination within the family, political and legal awareness, and involvement in political campaigning and protests) found that involvement in a credit programme made a significant difference to women's overall level of empowerment. But another widely quoted study by Goetz and Sen

Gupta (1996) that looked into credit programmes in Bangladesh questioned whether credit or loans to women necessarily enhance their decision-making power within the family or if they even give her control over the money she borrows. The authors argued that the high demand for loans and the propensity to repay cannot be construed as signs of empowerment and control. While credit is an important tool for women's economic empowerment (WEE), for households where the loan amount is diverted for other purposes and controlled by male relatives, it might not empower women at all. On the other hand, women who transfer their loan to their husbands might enjoy relatively higher status, but the important thing to bear in mind is that the context matters. There have been instances where delays or women's inability to access loans have resulted in tensions and violence within the household. The study by Goetz and Sen Gupta (1996) found that few women had full control over the money they borrowed, and most had no idea how the loan money was being spent. Goetz and Sen Gupta (1996, p. 53) also indicated that a range of other factors, such as gendered division of labour, gender inequality in terms of control over economic activities, and the consequent gendered differences in consumption patterns, affect the way credit is used.

It must be emphasised here that even though the examples above relate to the household setting, they are relevant to this study because they help to highlight the importance of income in the lives of the participants and to better understand if their income enables them to enjoy greater status or respect within their families or households. It appears that the women who took part in the study are largely content with what they earn and their ability to lead a life without violence within the household. In many cases, their family members are not aware of their profession, but the fact that they are sending money home has contributed to earning a greater degree of respect within the family.

Ibrahim and Alkire (2007) point out that "income" is the single most widely used indicator of empowerment, but they caution against using income as the sole indicator of empowerment, especially in the case of households headed by a single woman. To address this, further questions are asked about community perceptions of women, given their unique position as deviant from the norm due to their profession and background, and as single mothers. Although marginalised, the position of the women who participated in this study afforded them more control over all aspects of decision-making. Thus, while they are severely stigmatised by the community, they are also less restricted in their mobility by social structures. This is because they are detached from their immediate communities and earn a living in a more heterogeneous context in the urban district of Thamel where identities of caste, religion, and community can become blurred (Liechty, 2005). Some of the barriers that they face, such as discrimination in marketplaces, are not necessarily due to stigmatisation but instead are shared common experiences of all women in Nepal. However, as later chapters will demonstrate, the participants remain undeterred by community attitudes towards them and show resilience on many fronts. To analyse the "power to" dimension in the context of this study, the following questions were asked:

- Have you always earned income in the same way?
- Has it increased/decreased over time, or is it likely to increase in the future? Please give details.
- How important is it that you earn an income? What difference does earning an income make in your life?
- How does your family feel about you earning an income?
- How does the wider community feel about you earning an income?
- Rate how supportive you feel the community is towards women earning an income? Give a number from 1 to 5 (5 being very unsupportive).
- Do you feel any tensions with family members as a result of earning an income?

Indicator 3: "Power from within/change": changing aspects in one's life (individual level)

Ibrahim and Alkire (2007, p. 394) describe power from within as the "ability to induce change in one's life, thus enhancing one's own self-acceptance". This indicator is used to assess the willingness of an individual to change different aspects of their life and whether the change they want to see is consistent with their values. It also captures the extent to which a person is able to action the change in the domain in which they wish to act as an agent of change.

This indicator is particularly significant in respect of the women working in this sector because they experience "power from within" in their interactions with peer networks in the domain of their work specifically. They make a conscious decision to be a part of such groups and to network with or work in NGOs, and they receive support through them in a number of ways. This then contributes to building their inner resilience and ability to envision a better future. For example, one of the changes the women who participated in the study generally wanted to see is a better future for their children. In order to action this, they reach out to NGOs (described in more detail in Chapters 6 and 7) that provide shelter and education for the children of women engaged in this sector. The questions that were asked to assess this indicator (changing aspect of one's life) included:

- Do you think that since earning an income you feel more or less confident?
- If you feel more confident as a result of earning an income, has it resulted in changes in how you think about other aspects of your life (e.g. stronger views about the role of women and how they should be treated)?
- What change would make the biggest difference to your life?
- How do you see the future?

Indicator 4:"Power with/community": changing aspects in communal life (communal level)

This indicator measures the ability of people to change things collectively and how the participants of this study collectively experience empowerment. This is addressed in detail in Chapters 5 and 7, which discuss unions and how the association with them enables the participants to speak with one voice against violence and assert their basic rights. Although Ibrahim and Alkire (2007) used this indicator in the context of household settings, for the women engaged in the informal entertainment and sex industry, the indicator is useful in understanding how women perceive violence and how they have come to accept their own position in the community amidst the high level of stigma and violence they face in their daily lives. It is observed in subsequent chapters that "power with" enables these women to demand justice for the violence that has been perpetrated, not just for themselves but for other women inside and outside their community. The questions that were asked regarding "power with" are

- How does the wider community feel about you earning an income?
- As a result of earning an income, are you more or less likely to challenge violence that you or your friends experience?
- How common do you think it is for women to experience forms of harm (physical and psychological)? (For example, psychological harm may include bullying or having her earnings taken against her will.)
- Have levels of violence increased (for you and/or for other women you know)?

4.5 Gaining and expressing agency

Having outlined how the four dimensions of power are used as proposed indicators or measures of agency, I now use this concept as a foundation for discussing how the participants of this study gain and express agency.

All the women who participated in this study asserted that earning an income and the ability to control it has had a significant and positive impact on their lives. Although these women admit that their engagement with the informal entertainment industry is characterised by stigma, abuse, and violence, they feel that their association with the industry has enabled them to establish new ties with other women and groups and that they have been able to draw on the resources found in each other (power with). As discussed earlier, Kabeer (1999) defines agency as the process by which an individual is able to define one's goals and act on them. Acting on individual goals means taking certain actions and using the outcome of those actions to shape one's strategic needs and objectives. Kabeer says that the manner in which people perceive their needs and interests is largely shaped by individual histories and everyday realities. Individual past experiences in turn create situations or "vantage points" that become the platform from which an individual operationalises certain dimensions of their agency in making choices pertaining to their lives. In this study, for example, the individual circumstances of the respondents were found to create situations that resulted in their choice of a highly vulnerable profession in sex work and informal entertainment.

Although the women interviewed in this study have experienced multiple levels of violence in their personal lives, in most cases their decision to enter the industry was not their first choice. Some of the women had worked as domestic maids, in factories, or on construction sites before eventually migrating to the sex and informal entertainment industry, often because the income is relatively high, which enabled them to cover their daily expenses and to better provide for their children. Most women categorically stated that their children's education and well-being is the most important priority in their life. Table 4.1 illustrates some of the key reasons why the participants chose to enter into sex work and informal entertainment.

The above descriptions show how the lives of the participants were constrained by factors that were not under their control, but for them the sex and informal entertainment industry presented itself as a choice that enabled them to earn an income and provide for their families. From the perspective of Sen's capability approach, it can be argued that women working in the informal entertainment industry use their bodies as a resource to convert the opportunities provided by the market into a living. It must be noted that, at this stage, they do not have access to any other resources. Their actions can be seen as necessary for "basic functioning", which Sen describes as a subset of all capabilities that a person is capable of achieving. It refers to the freedom to do some basic things that are necessary for survival and to avoid or escape poverty. The relevance of basic capabilities is "not so much in ranking living standards, but in deciding on a cut-off point for the purpose of assessing poverty and deprivation" (Sen, 1987, p. 109). Hence, while the notion of capabilities refers to a very broad range of capabilities; basic capabilities refer to the freedom to do those things that are necessary to keep oneself out of poverty.

As described above, obtaining a full understanding of agency requires considering its manifestations in different domains and levels of life (Samman & Santos, 2009, p. 67). "Levels" here refer to the societal structures in which a person is embedded. For a woman engaged in the informal entertainment industry, she is an economic actor, and her domain of operation is the market, which is one area that significantly spans her life (Alsop, Bertelsen, & Holland, 2006, as cited in Samman & Santos, 2009, p. 6).

In the foregoing section, I discussed how various domains and the factors within each of them can interact within a person's life to engender different levels or experiences of empowerment. In the context of women in the informal entertainment industry, it is the market in which they work that provides a space for both economic activity and social interactions, and within this domain they have a degree of autonomy. They are also a unique group when compared to the general population of women in Nepal as once they become part of the informal entertainment sector their identity becomes intertwined with it. For the women who took part in this study, their identity is also shaped by the dynamics of urban life and the constantly evolving economic realities that characterise Thamel, the business centre, where they work and even form their own communities.

Table 4.1 Reasons for women joining the informal entertainment industry

Participant	*Reasons for joining the sex and informal entertainment industry*
Participant 1: Age 41, three children, upper caste (Brahmin)	"My husband was very violent and later abandoned me. Other jobs were not profitable. I used to cycle twenty kilometres to sell vegetables, but the business never picked up. Children were starving; they couldn't go to school. I was struggling to make ends meets. Then a friend told me about sex work. Purely out of desperation I worked as a contract sex worker for a year and I'm not ashamed of it. I couldn't let my children starve. After one year, I saved enough to start another business. I used to import clothes from the Indian border and sell them in Kathmandu. I made around 15,000 rupees. After that I occasionally worked as a contract sex worker".
Participant 2: Age 30, one child, lower caste (Dalit), separated	"I worked as a servant in a family of eight. I worked from 5 am to 12 pm. I used to live with the family. They gave me food but no salary. They used to beat me up. I was treated badly. Then one day they came to know about my caste and fired me. When I used to go buy vegetables for the family, I used to meet a lady who always wore good clothes. One day, she asked me where I worked. That lady worked in the Thamel. She said to me that I am young and can get better jobs. Through her I joined a massage parlour. First few days they asked me to do cleaning work. One day they asked me to massage the customers. Then they told me that I cannot earn money by massaging alone but need to go beyond that".
Participant 5: Age 27, one child, born high caste Hindu but practices Christianity, married but not living with husband	"I needed money to run the house and educate my daughter. I am not educated. I cannot get a job where I can earn rupees 15,000-20,000. It is very expensive to live in Kathmandu especially when your husband does not do anything. On top of that there is domestic violence, so women must fend for themselves and must take up jobs for survival [...] I worked as a domestic maid and at a construction site. Those jobs didn't pay much, and it was physically taxing. I couldn't go back to work as a labourer as I was weak after the childbirth. I asked around and I joined a massage parlour initially as a cleaner. Later, I realized that my nature of job was different. For the sake of money, I joined mainstream sex work".

(*Continued*)

Table 4.1 (Continued)

Participant	*Reasons for joining the sex and informal entertainment industry*
Participant 6: Age 23, upper caste, not married	"After coming from abroad, I came to Kathmandu looking for a job. My family situation was bad, my mom was very ill. Since I am not educated, I couldn't find a job either in the city or in my village, eventually I joined a dance bar. I was introduced [to this sector] by my friends, who said I could be earning more that way and would be able to look after the family. I was forced to work as a sex worker as I had no alternative. I have breast cancer and I couldn't find other jobs"
Participant 15: Age 28, has three children, lower caste, lives with husband	"Earlier I worked as a maid and in the carpet factory. The work was physically challenging. It was dusty. It was difficult to breathe, and a lot of people had TB. Compared to that, sex work is better".
Participant 17: Age 23, has two children, married but lives alone	"The bad days started after the death of my father-in-law. My husband became astray and refused to take care of the family. I was initially working in a beauty parlour of a hotel but was never really doing any work of a beautician. I was asked to clean [the premises]. Later I joined the entertainment industry purely to earn money as I was being exploited anyways"

In this context, the market offers an informal opportunity to make a choice to be a part of an evidently thriving industry, which ensures a decent income, even if it is in the face of undercurrents of violence and harassment. The participants in the study expressed that despite the negative image associated with their profession, at the individual level, they have been able to create a new identity for themselves as the income they earn from this activity gives them a degree of autonomy. They can make decisions pertaining to their lives, which, when seen through the lens of power (as described by Ibrahim & Alkire, 2007), can be seen as "power over". Domains or dimensions are the multiple areas of life in which a person may exercise agency such as decisions on how to spend money, deciding whether to participate in the labour market or not and, if so, in which type of job (Samman & Santos, 2009, p. 6). The informal entertainment sector provides a micro-environment in which the participants are able to redefine their identities as single women in control of decision-making and free from the control of other family members. They consistently maintain that it is income alone, irrespective of the source, that has given them the power and voice to reject their oppressive and abusive past.

All participants clearly stated that their children's future is their most important priority and that they are willing to invest in their education and welfare. Participant 9 (age 28, upper-caste Brahmin, not living with husband, has one child), for example, stated, "I don't have any desires. I want my children to grow up well and be happy in their lives. I would look at their success as a benefit of my struggles and I would be contented". She justifies her work and says it was the best choice she could make in order to provide for her family. "Yes, I work in the entertainment industry, but I am also an independent woman and do not have to beg". Similarly, Participant 5 asserted that they have a right to earn a living, which the informal entertainment industry gives them access to, and she questioned what has been done by the government to provide alternative skills or employment for people like her:

> Yes, I am earning money by giving pleasure. Yes, I get abused, exploited but those who question me I want to say – Can you help? Can government help? Has anyone ever helped? If government can give a job, I will quit. I too don't want to do this job.

In this study, the participants expressed agency on a number of fronts. Through their income they harbour hope for a better future. One of the immediate benefits of having an income is their ability to take control of the household decision-making and divert their resources towards supporting their children and, in some cases, their extended family. For many of the participants, it is the first time that they have been able to exercise agency in this manner, and with time, they have learnt the skills to enhance their bargaining power at their place of work. They see earning an income as an empowering process when compared to the servitude of domestic maids or the physical exploitation of construction work. Wilson (2004) made a related point, arguing that many women who are working in this sector do not always see their work as exploitative as it provides an opportunity to earn an income that allows for more flexible transactions and ongoing negotiation.

However, the participants of this study do contend that the informal entertainment industry is exploitative in nature but also argue that women can stand up to it and find ways to cope with it. They also find support in doing so through peer networks (see Chapter 7). On the other hand, the forms of work that might otherwise be available to them, including selling vegetables at marketplaces, make women equally vulnerable to harassment from the police and male competitors, and the participants assert that informal marketplaces remain unfavourable places for women to operate within. The following case studies illustrate many of the findings discussed above.

4.5.1 Case study 1

Participant 8 (age 48, upper caste, widow, has three children) worked in a spa that also acted as a conduit for sex work for 15 years after the death of her husband. "I was young and had four children to look after", she says. After migrating to Kathmandu as a child, she worked as a domestic maid where she was mistreated. She fled, and after getting married at the age of 14, she worked in a carpet factory. During the interview she said:

> First, I worked in a carpet factory. I only worked there just for a month. I was only fourteen and it was a very difficult job. I learnt how to make the yarn for the carpet on a spinning wheel. Then I had a chest problem; there was dust everywhere, even in food and water. I earned sixty rupees for five kilograms of spun wool for which I worked day and night.
>
> After that I had to work in a place where I had to collect sand from a riverbank. It was illegally done. I had to carry the sand to the place of construction. It was hard labour, and I worked there for five years. I earned around five hundred rupees. I did it on my own. I sneaked in and collected sand and smuggled it. The job was not sustainable and physically challenging. It was too tough. Sometimes I used to go deep in marshy land and there was a fear of police. My friends told me that if I work in the entertainment industry I could earn much more, and it will not be a physically demanding work. They said I could also earn tips. After that I joined the entertainment sector in a spa centre but was earning through sex work.

The participant came in contact with the NGO Raksha Nepal while she was looking for support to leave the industry. Raksha Nepal provided shelter for her children. She said:

> This is the forum where I can socialise and learn new things like the way I am speaking with you. Here, there are people from a similar profession. [...] I left it [informal entertainment industry] because I felt stigmatised by the society. Though I raised my children from the income I earned by working as a sex worker, I never earned respect. Now I am relaxed as children are educated which was my dream. Now I earn for myself.

The participant now works as a vegetable seller; she claimed that the level of harassment that she faced while selling vegetables was equally bad:

> While selling the vegetables, I face a lot of harassment from police. They extort money from us. Sometimes they become violent and throw away the vegetables as you are not allowed to sell on the road. They also took me to the custody once. So, I feel that I should change my job.

When asked was the level of violence the same, less, or more compared to the entertainment industry, she replied:

> there is not much difference, but the violence is of a different kind. There they [authorities] abused us and said why don't you do other jobs. While selling vegetables the municipality and the police shoos us away. It's still a violence.

She added:

> It is not safe as most of the vegetable vendors are women. When it rains, we get wet, and men look on us. We cannot stay long, especially, in the evening.

> Vegetables rot due to rain and we suffer losses. Government hasn't provided us a safe place to sell vegetables.

When asked if the levels of violence had increased for her or other women at her place of work, she replied: "A lot depends on the women but in the entertainment industry it is still the same. Violence will always be there. It is about improving the safety at workplace, which hasn't happened".

As discussed above, the participants were asked questions about income generation in order to ascertain how income enables them to gain autonomy over decision-making. Questions were also asked regarding how income is spent and if there are tensions with family members as a result of earning an income. There were other specific questions about the importance of income in their lives and the attitude of the community towards a woman (in general) earning an income. The answers were subjective in nature and the perspectives of the women varied, but all of them affirmed that income was a positive force in their lives. The women also demonstrated autonomy over decisions and choice, which is seen as an important indicator of agency (Ibrahim & Alkire, 2007, p. 389).

The participants said that income was a significant factor that enabled them to make strategic life choices, including the decision to escape from highly abusive and violent marriages. It gave them the confidence to lead their lives on their own terms without the presence of a husband or other men in their lives. Although they continue to face violence at work, they have created coping mechanisms by organising in groups that enable them to stand up collectively against extreme violence. All the respondents said that their income was mostly spent on meeting basic needs such as food, medicine, rent, and their children's school fees. However, 11 of the women stated that they had been able to realise the dream of educating their children. Participant 1, for example, said, "I am able to earn and feed my children. Earlier many times my children have gone without food for days. This has certainly changed".

As discussed earlier, Ibrahim and Alkire (2007) defined the phenomenon of control over personal decisions as "power over" and the exercise of autonomy as "power to". All the participants claim that they have total control over decisions regarding how they spend their money. However, this degree of autonomy was denied to them whenever they were in a relationship with a man, either through marriage or otherwise. But now, as independent women, they do not face any social constraint on this, even from outside the household. Their association with peer groups (as discussed later) further encourages them to assert their autonomy in all aspects of their lives. Ibrahim and Alkire argue that the ability to make decisions does not really mean that women enjoy autonomy. Rather, "power to" as an indicator questions the extent to which a person feels their actions in each domain are motivated by fear of punishment or, conversely, hope for reward. It then asks the extent to which the same action was motivated by a desire to avoid shame or to gain praise. Finally, it asks to what extent the action was motivated by their consonance with the respondent's interests and values (Ibrahim & Alkire, 2007, p. 392).

When considered in the context of the above-proposed indicators, it appears that the decisions made by the participants were not driven by any reward, as such, but instead were motivated by concern for their own and their children's well-being. The fear/reward component also does not apply directly as the households are run solely by the women themselves who are mostly single mothers. The shame/praise component remains irrelevant in this context, but it becomes abundantly clear that they have hopes for a better life, which keeps them motivated. The "power with" and "power to" components, however, resonate more in the following case study. I refer here to the same example cited in Chapter 3, which showed how social norms can contribute to domestic violence. I do so in order to elaborate further on the experience of Participant 1 after she migrated to Kathmandu, giving examples of her personal struggles and how she tackled them.

4.5.2 *Case study 2*

Participant 1 (age 41, upper caste [Brahmin], separated, has three children) gave the following account of her experience:

> My in-laws expected me to do all the housework and were not happy with my going to school. Eight months into our married life my in-laws asked my husband and me to leave the house because they no longer wanted to witness his beatings. We moved to Kathmandu in December 1990 where we didn't know anyone except a cousin. We stayed in a *dharmsala* [guest house] and then my cousin found a place on the outskirts of the city near the airport. My husband had no money, so the cousin paid the rent. Meanwhile, I became pregnant and at the very advanced stage of my pregnancy my husband kicked me very hard and beat me ruthlessly. I came to know that day that he remarried someone else. I later gave birth to a stillborn.
>
> The doctors thought the child died because of the violence I suffered. I had to restart my life. I started working in a candy factory. My job was to wrap candies. I earned forty rupees a day and rented a room for twelve hundred rupees. I lived like this for three years until I was seventeen. Then my husband returned one day and pleaded for us to live together again. He was sorry for what he did and promised he would be a good man. I became pregnant again and gave birth to a baby boy in 1994. The beatings resumed in June 1995. I was sent home to be with my in-laws and help with the farming. In 2001, my husband returned, and I became pregnant again.
>
> I stayed with him because of the *izzat* of my father and in-laws. I had nowhere to go, and I thought life would be harder for my children without a father. Poverty, though, hit hard, so I returned to Kathmandu in search of work. I stayed with my sister-in-law, but she didn't give us any food. I used to cycle two kilometres a day selling vegetables, but business was bad. Then a friend told me about sex work. Purely out of desperation I worked as a contract sex worker for a year, and I am not ashamed of it. I couldn't let my children starve. I made three thousand rupees a day and slept with at least

> three men every day. Some customers were violent: they would beat me and not pay. Police harassment was huge. After one year I had earned enough to start a new business. I used to import clothes from the Indian border and sell them. I made around fifteen thousand rupees a year. I did occasional contract sex work and lived like this for about five years.
>
> In 2009, a friend told me about Raksha Nepal and their cooperative. The chairperson asked about my life and then introduced me to the savings scheme. I took out a loan and opened my own restaurant bar in Thamel. The business did well, and I paid off my loan and then opened another guest house. Today, I employ seven women. My children are doing well. The eldest is studying engineering, the second son management, and my daughter is in school and wants to be a lawyer.

In the context of this study, the decision to enter the informal entertainment industry can be seen as a strategic life choice since it is taken against a set of extreme circumstances that the women found themselves in. It is strategic because their individual stories talk about dispossession and betrayal (abandoned by husbands, fired by employers) coupled with a desperate need to find an alternative source of income. For some women, income was needed to provide for children who remained exposed to high levels of risk regarding their health. Thus, the income that they earned enabled them to have a degree of autonomy and power. For example, the ability to spend money on looking after their children can be seen as a transformative power, which has come from their income.

While the education and well-being of their children are their main priority when earning an income, one of the immediate benefits that emerges from doing so is that the women largely feel more confident. This sense of empowerment can be seen as what Kabeer describes as a "shift in consciousness", whereby the women have not only taken control of their lives, but they have also been able to overturn dominant masculine and patriarchal norms that have kept them and other women in a situation of subordination. Kabeer (1999, p. 440) also argues that for critical consciousness to emerge, an alternative option must be available, and it is through choosing between these options that people move from a position of unquestioning acceptance of the social order to a critical perspective on it. Table 4.2 shows how some of the participants responded when asked about the importance of income in their lives.

4.6 Conclusion

The literature on empowerment has stressed that empowerment as a concept cannot happen unless women themselves are conscious of their subordinated position and take steps to challenge it (Malhotra, 2002). Stromquist (1993, as cited in Malhotra et al., 2002), for example, says that it involves women's understanding of their conditions of subordination and the causes of such conditions at both micro and macro levels of society. It involves understanding the self and the need to make choices that may go against cultural and social expectations.

Table 4.2 Importance of income to participants

Participant	*Importance of Income*
Participant 1: Age 41, has three children, belongs to upper caste (Brahmin), not living with husband	"Income is everything. Today if I am alive and if my children are going to school, it is because of earning an income. I suffered when I had no income. I had no say in anything. Now I am independent and a confident person. If you have no income even your children don't become yours. Today, if my children wish to have a fruit, I can buy for them. Earlier I didn't have money to buy clothes, now I can afford clothes for myself and my children. I can go to my village whenever I feel like. I stay in a rented house. Income helps me pay the rent. I don't have to worry about my landlord throwing me out".
Participant 2: Age 30, has one child, belongs to lower caste, not living with husband	"I feel very confident I have the capacity to win in life under any circumstances. My daughter doesn't know about my work but one day when she asks, I will not shy away from telling the truth. I am proud to be standing on my own feet. If I don't tell the truth now, someone else will tell her".
Participant 4: Age 28, has one child, belongs to lower caste, married	"Income makes me feel confident. I can provide good education to my son. I can take up any challenge. For me husband is needed purely for child's sake [...] when he grows up and understands a bit, I can think of separating".
Participant 6: Age 23, lower caste, unmarried	"Income has made me very confident. Had I not worked, my family would have married me off and there is no guarantee that I would be happy. Now I am twenty-three, not married. Though in this profession, I am contributing to changing peoples' lives [she also works as outreach worker advocating the use of condoms]. I might not be educated. I am self-dependent. I wish I was educated but I thank my parents for giving me the opportunity to earn for myself".
Participant 9: Age 28, one child, belongs to upper caste, not living with husband	"It is important for me to earn an income so that my child can have a good and decent life. I don't want her to get into this profession at all".
Participant 12: Age 25, has one child, upper caste, widow	"Husband passed away so as a single mum and a sole bread earner it is very important for me to earn".

In this study, the women who participated use the opportunities provided by the informal entertainment industry as a vehicle to move forward in life. Given the lack of available jobs and the limited individual skills they possess, they realised that it was the best option available to meet their daily needs. They see that the prospect of a better life lies in investing in their children's education as they see their future aspirations tied to the well-being of their children. The women demonstrated strength by breaking away from abusive and oppressive relationships and in exercising a choice to enter the sex and informal entertainment sector. Some of the participants then made a further choice to send their children to school, thereby making the most of an element of the opportunity structure from which they themselves could not benefit. In Nepal, there are state schools where rules do not prohibit girls from enrolling, so the participants confronted what Alsop and Heinsohn (2005, p. 7) describe as "traditional notions of an informal-social-element of the opportunity structure" that prevented girls from gaining an education and realising their own potential. Some of the participants believed that education, which had been denied to them, would have made a significant difference in their lives.

In Section 4.2, I discuss one of the ways to measure degrees of empowerment. According to Kabeer (1999), empowerment is underpinned by the ability to make first-order decisions that result in desired outcomes and incorporates three interrelated dimensions: resources, agency, and achievements. Empowerment is conceptualised as a process of change whereby one moves from disempowerment to empowerment, which is achieved by expanding people's ability to make first-order decisions that result in desired outcomes. Kabeer, however, does not provide concrete operationalisation of these three dimensions (Leder, 2016, p. 7). Furthermore, none of the empowerment literature reviewed discusses how the concepts of empowerment and power can be applied in the context of women who are engaged in the sex and informal entertainment industry globally. The indicators of agency, as suggested by Alsop and Heinsohn (2005), are asset based, which can be psychological, informational, organisational, material, social, financial, or human. The participants of this study certainly possess the ability to envision a better future (which is a form of a psychological asset), and as the two case studies show, they make use of the informal opportunity structure offered by peer networks to enhance their lives. The remaining chapters will discuss in detail how such opportunities are optimised. However, based on the concepts and examples discussed so far, I propose the following model as a measure of empowerment for the participants of this study.

From the two case studies above, we see that after making the first-order choice of entering the informal entertainment industry to earn an income, the women make further use of choice in enlisting the help of peer networks (existence of choice). In the first case study, the participant made use of a peer network and the NGO Raksha Nepal to learn new skills, build community relationships, and secure a safe place for her children (making use of the existence choice). She left the informal entertainment industry after her children were educated and moved into another profession (achievement of choice). In the second case study, the participant had access to a credit scheme run by the NGO Raksha Nepal (existence of choice), which she used to take out a loan (use of choice) and was finally able to set up her own business (achievement of choice).

As illustrated in the diagram, the informal entertainment industry is seen as a choice that the participants undertake for survival (as conceptualised in Sen's [1987] capability approach). It is part of a transformative process whereby the

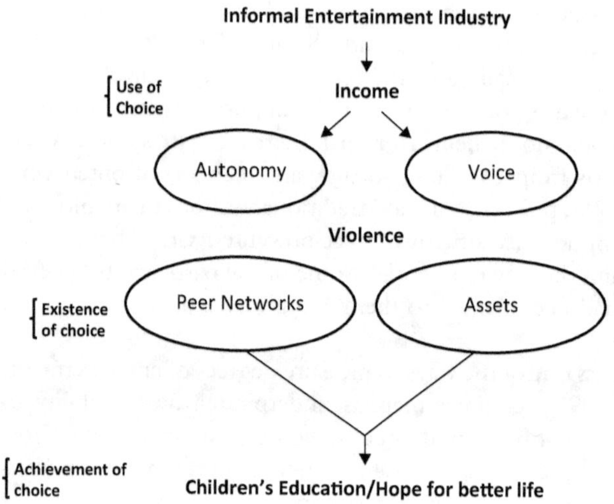

Figure 4.2 "The Use-Existence-Achievement Model of Choice" to measure empowerment.

body becomes the resource for earning an income, which, in turn, provides a degree of autonomy and agency over household decisions as well as those pertaining to the participants' personal lives. In the context of this chapter, the participants experience both "power over" and "power to". The case studies show that the participants use peer networks and individual assets to strengthen their voice and agency and use them to achieve their immediate goals. The violence component, however, remains constant. They acknowledge that exiting the profession abruptly is not a choice they can exercise easily since they have mouths to feed, but they can mitigate the impact of violence by being part of a social group and then taking collective action (see Chapters 7 and 8). In this chapter, the focus has been on income and how it enables the participants to gain autonomy within the personal sphere while operating in the market domain. In Chapter 5, I examine how the participants demonstrate resilience and experience "power within" and "power with" in their empowerment process.

References

Alkire, S., & Ibrahim, S. (2007). Agency and empowerment: A proposal for internationally comparable indicators. *Oxford Development Studies*, *35*(4), 379–403.

Alsop, R., Bertelsen, M., & Holland, J. (2006). *Empowerment in Practice from Analysis to Implementation: A World Bank Learning Module.* World Bank Institute. siteresources.worldbank.org/WBI/Resources/EmpowermentLearningModulebody.pdf

Becker, S., Mahmud, S., & Shah, M. N. (2012). Measurement of women's empowerment in rural Bangladesh. *World Development*, *40*(3), 610–619.

Bird, K., Luttrell, C., Quiroz, S., & Scrutton, C. (2009). *Understanding and Operationalising Empowerment* (Overseas Development Institute Working Paper 308). ODI.

Chen, M., & Mahmud, S. (1995). *Assessing Change in Women's Lives: A Conceptual Framework* (BRAC-ICDDR, B. Joint Research Project Working Paper No. 2). BRAC.

Datta, R., & Kornberg, J. (2002). *Women in Developing Countries: Assessing Strategies for Empowerment*. Lynne Rienner Publishers.

Donald, A., Koolwal, G., Annan, J., Falb, K., & Goldstein, M. (2017) *Measuring Women's Agency* (Policy Research Working Paper 8148). World Bank Group. http://hdl.handle.net/10986/27955

Goetz, A., & Sen Gupta, R. (1996). Who takes the credit? Gender, power and control over loan use in rural credit programs in Bangladesh. *World Development*, *24*(1), 45–63.

Hashemi, S. M., Riley, A. P., & Schuler, S. R. (1996). Rural credit programs and women's empowerment in Bangladesh, *World Development*, *24*, 635–653.

Jejeebhoy, S. J. (2000). Women's autonomy in rural India: Its dimensions, determinants, and the influence of context. In G. Sen & H. Presser (Eds.), *Women's Empowerment and Demographic Processes: Moving Beyond Cairo*. Oxford University Press.

Kabeer, N. (1999). Resources, agency, achievements: Reflections on the measurement of women's empowerment. *Development and Change*, *30*(3), 435–464.

Kishor, S. (2000). Empowerment of women in Egypt and links to the survival and health of their infants. In G. Sen & H. Presser (Eds.), *Women's Empowerment and Demographic Processes: Moving Beyond Cairo*. Oxford University Press.

Leder, S. (2016). *Linking Women's Empowerment and Resilience. Research Program on Water, Land and Ecosystems: Literature Review*. International Water Management Institute. cgspace.cgiar.org/handle/10568/72489

Liechty, M. (2005). Carnal economies: The commodification of food and sex in Kathmandu. *Cultural Anthropology*, *20*(1), 1–38.

Malhotra, A., Schuler, S. R., & Boender, C. (2002). *Measuring Women's Empowerment as a Variable in International Development*. The World Bank.

Narayan, D. (2000). *Voices of the Poor: Can Anyone Hear Us?* Oxford University Press.

Rowlands, J. (1998). A word of the times, but what does it mean? Empowerment in the discourse and practice of development. In H. Afshar (Ed.), *Women and Empowerment: Illustrations from the Third World* (pp. 11–34). London: Macmillan.

Samman, M., & Santos, E. M. (2009). *Agency and Empowerment: A Review of Concepts, Indicators and Empirical Evidence*. Oxford Poverty & Human Development Initiative (OPHI). www.ophi.org.uk/wp-content/uploads/OPHI-RP10a.pdf

Sen, A. (1985). Well-being, agency and freedom: The Dewey lectures 1984. *The Journal of Philosophy*, *82*(4), 169–221.

Sen, A. (1987). The standard of living. In G. Hawthorn (Ed.), *The Standard of Living*. Cambridge University Press.

Stromquist, N. (1993). Praktische und Theoretische Grundlagen für Empowerment. *Nord-Sued Aktuell*, *7*(2), 259–266.

Wilson, A. (2004). *The Intimate Economies of Bangkok: Tomboys, Tycoons, and Avon Ladies in the Global City*. University of California Press. ebookcentral.proquest.com/lib/portsmouthebooks/detail.action? docID=471000.

5 Resilience of women in Nepal's sex and informal entertainment industry

5.1 Introduction

In Chapter 4, I discussed the various theories around empowerment and demonstrated how the participants in my research gained and expressed agency. As noted in the literature, the term empowerment is complex and has multiple interpretations, and its meaning depends on the socio-economic context of the individual. Since it is a process, it is also largely dependent on one's perspective on one's situation and the willingness of an individual to set goals and achieve them. The process of achieving women's empowerment in particular is closely linked with other crucial factors such as power relations and autonomy in decision-making, which in turn have a direct bearing on a woman's ability to make choices and translate those choices into a desired outcome. The process, thus, is dependent on socio-economic, cultural, and political factors, and it is also contingent on the extent to which these factors facilitate an enabling environment for women to realise their individual potential or, conversely, impede the process of their growth by creating social and economic barriers.

Embedded in the concept of empowerment is the resilience of an individual to withstand, challenge, and overturn the power structures that shape choices, opportunities, and well-being. The participants in my research took a strategic decision to step out of the cycle of poverty and subjugation by joining the informal entertainment industry as a last resort to earn an income. For many of them, the decision, though risky, has been empowering in the sense that for the first time they were able to take control of their lives at both the personal and the household levels. Undoubtedly, however, the process of negotiating this part of their life journey and coping with the outcomes of being in extremely vulnerable situations also requires a degree of resilience. That said, the link between empowerment and other relevant concepts such as resilience remains relatively unexplored with regard to the informal entertainment sector (see e.g. Leder, 2016). For this reason, in this chapter I examine the various concepts of resilience and explore how it links with women working in the sex and informal entertainment industry. I discuss how the research participants showed resilience both at the individual level by exhibiting inner strength (through characteristics and behaviours such as determination and perseverance) and at the community

DOI: 10.4324/9781003156796-5

level through the help of peer networks that played a critical role in redefining their lives. I discuss this with reference to the concepts of power addressed in Chapter 4 to show how the participants experience "power with" and "power within" in ways that support the process of their empowerment.

5.2 The concepts and frameworks of resilience

Like empowerment, resilience is a complex concept; it is a context-specific and highly dynamic process (Allison, Armitage, Béné, Charles, & Johnson, 2012), and many indicators and dimensions are required to represent it (Carpenter & Brock, 2004, as cited in Allison, Armitage, Béné, Charles, & Johnson 2012, p. 6). Brodsky and Cattaneo (2013) use the "Transconceptual Model of Empowerment and Resilience" (TMER) to argue that both empowerment and resilience are iterative processes whereby people who are in a disadvantaged situation take action to change their lives. They state that to be resilient, the agent must have the power to adapt, withstand, and resist. However, the actions that a person resorts to in order to alter their life situation depend on the context and the resources available. In underlining the difference between resilience and empowerment, the authors define resilience as an internal process, whereas empowerment is enacted socially; it is aimed at external change to relationships, situations, power dynamics, or context.

In recent years, a growing body of literature has focused on psychological resilience, and the scope of such studies is expanding to incorporate the voices of marginalised groups and populations that have been affected by issues such as migration. Carabine, Graber, and Pichon (2015, p. 5), for example, have defined psychological resilience as a "dynamic psychosocial process through which individuals exposed to sustained adversity or potentially traumatic events experience positive psychological adaptation over time". They stress that "resilience is not a box to tick; it is an ongoing process of meaning-making and growth in which the only reliable constant is the mutually dependent capacity of the individual and their environment for change" (Carabine, Graber, & Pichon, 2015, p. 8). The environment for change refers to the complex interaction of multiple mechanisms including personal relationships, cultures, economies, and neurobiology in which an individual is embedded. Resilience, therefore, means identifying such mechanisms that drive change and understanding their relationships so that an individual can negotiate ways to respond to adversity immediately and over time (Carabine, Graber, & Pichon, 2015).

Such studies state that for resilience to occur there must be a challenge to overcome, and studies on psychological resilience seek to identify and understand processes that allow individuals to cope with abuse, prolonged conflict, or, as in the context of this research, the ability to psychologically withstand past traumas and ongoing violence, which is ever-present in the lives of the participants. Some studies see resilience as a dynamic process that varies over time, and that is dependent on life contexts (see e.g. Best, Garmezy, & Masten, 1990; Luthar & Zigler, 1991, as cited in Holroyd, Tang, Wong, & Yuen, 2014). It can also be considered a part of development that can be enhanced, rather than being a static trait that a person either does or does not possess (Born, Jackson, & Jacob, 1997). In the context of women in the sex and informal entertainment industry, widely referred as "sex workers" (Holroyd, Tang, Wong, & Yuen 2014), a positive psychology and resilience framework has been used to better understand how sex workers cope with work-related stress and violence that often characterise their work. Positive psychology focuses on positive aspects such as the strengths and virtues of an individual to capture the full spectrum of human experiences (Aspinwall & Tedeschi, 2010; Gable & Haidt, 2005; Mann, 2001; Wood & Tarrier, 2010, as cited in Holroyd, Tang, Wong, & Yuen, 2014).

Holroyd, Tang, Wong, and Yuen (2014) found that sex workers in their study suffered from a high degree of trauma, stigma, and psychological distress and experienced high levels of emotional burnout (Vanwesenbeeck, 2005), which is consistent with this study. It is also in line with the findings of Lau, Ho, Tsui, Wong, and Yang (2010), which showed that 53.9% of female sex workers had probable depression, and Gorry, Reilly, and Roen's (2010) observations that sex workers tend to have negative views about themselves and are overcome by a sense of guilt and shame when work-related thoughts come to mind. There are other occupational risk factors such as uncertainty about business, competition for clients, exposure to verbal abuse, physical violence, and risks of being raped or robbed by clients (Holroyd, Wong, Gray, & Ling, 2008, as cited in Holroyd, Tang, Wong, & Yuen, 2014), all of which make the business of sex psychologically distressing and can drastically contribute to lowering the self-esteem and confidence of the workers. The participants of this study shared similar experiences, and this chapter will discuss in detail how they go about building resilience to such situations.

> In the context of Hong Kong, Holroyd, Tang, Wong, and Yuen (2014) studied resilience by identifying the everyday challenges that female sex workers encountered and how these affected their psychological functioning. In the study, the authorsasked open-ended questions drawn from the literature on positive psychology, resilience, and the model of stress and coping (Lazarus & Folkman, 1984). The questions were in the following domains: the impacts of working in the sex industry, self-assessed psychological health, social relationships, sexual health practices, and coping strategies used.
>
> (Holroyd, Tang, Wong, & Yuen, 2014, p. 1234)

The authors then used grounded theory (a methodological tool for qualitative data analysis and a theoretical sampling process based on categories developed from ongoing data analysis) to analyse the transcripts, and from the analysis of interviews with sex workers, four main themes emerged:

1. the challenges,
2. the emotional journey as a sex worker,

3. the resilience processes and
4. coping with challenges as a reflection of resilience.

(Holroyd, Tang, Wong, & Yuen, 2014, p. 1235)

In terms of challenges, most of the sex workers who took part in the study found it emotionally difficult to see themselves as part of the sex industry. It took them time to adjust to their work environment as they "experienced a number of difficult situations such as threats to their physical health, violence and public stigma. These stressors led to self-reported fear, sadness, loneliness, and anger" (Holroyd, Tang, Wong, & Yuen, 2014, p. 1238). They also reported facing abuse and stigma from their clients and the police. Although they felt angry and hurt by these negative factors, they found ways to deal with these emotions by internalising them and considering them as a part of their work, thereby showing inner strength.

In the above-mentioned study, the participants demonstrated resilience by drawing on their inner strength and through exhibiting optimism, self-belief, and determination, and expressing agency at various levels. These factors allowed the participants to neutralise their negative emotions and keep themselves in a different frame of mind when they found themselves with an abusive client or caught in an unsafe situation. This is, however, not easy as a woman's sense of self can be subsumed under her sex worker role, negatively impacting on her psychological well-being (Coy, 2009; Gorry, Reilly, & Roen, 2010; Sanders, 2004). To overcome the challenges that they face in their daily lives, sex workers tend to adopt a range of strategies such as standing up for their rights, self-regulating their emotions, accepting their responsibilities to look after their children and family and the limitations (such as lack of psychosocial support) to overcoming stressors and associated mood disturbances. Based on the above findings, Holroyd, Tang, Wong, and Yuen (2014) conclude that strength-based intervention is a crucial part of enhancing the psychological health of sex workers because resilience, in this context, is manifested through a process in which individuals use their internal strength to adjust while interacting with the outer environment where they work. They argue that the strength-based approach to intervention encourages women in sex work to develop greater self-efficacy and self-esteem as well as independence.

My research found that peer networks (discussed in detail in later sections) play a crucial role in the development of a number of strength-based interventions that are aimed at boosting resilience assets such as the self-esteem, dignity, and positivity of the women working in the sex and informal entertainment sector. These strengths often act as coping mechanism against adversities or violence, which they experience on a regular basis.

Burnes, Long, and Schept (2012) are critical of using a resilience-based lens to study the negative aspects of sex work (i.e. "sex work pathology") but leave out strengths and resilience factors, such as the ability to seek and receive emotional assistance and having autonomy in decision-making (O'Neill, 2010, as cited in Burnes, Long, & Schept, 2012). The researchers argue that engaging in sex work does not mean that they are mentally incompetent or cannot do other jobs; such conceptions of sex workers can further exacerbate existing issues as they are then labelled as mentally unsuitable and/or morally deviant. It also creates adversarial relationships between sex workers and legal bodies, which often mandate that sex work should be illegal because of its perceived detriment to and deviance within society. Burnes, Long, and Schept point to resilience-based research conducted by the Sex Worker Education and Advocacy Taskforce (SWEAT, 2005), which conducted a study of 17 workers with the aim of understanding how they cope with the negative aspects of their work. The participants in that study recognised the value of taking regular breaks, going for a walk, personal religious beliefs, and engaging in leisure activities outside of work to help them deal with the stigma and isolation of their work environments (SWEAT, 2005, as cited in Burnes, Long, & Schept, 2012, p. 138). A number of participants in my research had embraced Christianity, which had been introduced to them by "missionaries". They asserted that they had found spiritual comfort and mental peace by associating themselves with faith-based activities such as attending church services.

Researchers into resilience have also documented a link between resilience factors, such as positive emotions, and the ability to recover from stressful life events (Fredrickson & Tugade, 2004). But psychologists using a strength-based model have shifted the focus from the individual, and have instead used a collectivist, community-based perspective, which means that the concerned community (in this case the women in the sex and informal entertainment industry) collectively create a model of resilience, which then serves as a protective lens through which they reconstruct their relationship with the outer world. This point will be illustrated later in this chapter with reference to the importance of peer networks in the lives of the participants. One of the frameworks used to analyse the resilience of the participants is the "protective model" of resilience suggested by Fergus and Zimmerman (2005). Discussing how promotive factors – inner qualities such as self-esteem, optimism, self-belief, and determination, which help in expressing agency at various levels – can help reduce risk, Fergus and Zimmerman prescribe three models of resilience: compensatory, protective, and challenge, with promotive factors. The models (see Table 5.1 for a summary of the salient features of each) have been described in the context of studying adolescents. I borrow the concept to outline how protective factors influence outcomes for the participants of this study.

The foregoing framework emphasises that resilience can reduce risk factors through protective factors that operate on two levels: assets and resources. Assets are the positive factors that reside within the individual, such as competence, coping skills, and self-efficacy, whilst resources are positive factors that help a person overcome risk, but they are external to the individual. Although Fergus and Zimmerman used the framework in the context of adolescents, it can be modified (as explained later) to understand how the participants of this study exhibit resilience. It is clear from the previous chapters that the participants do show tremendous resilience during their childhood/adolescent years to cope with traumatic experiences by relying on their inner strength. As discussed in

Table 5.1 Models of resilience

Compensatory	*Protective*	*Challenge*
The compensatory model is defined as when a promotive factor counteracts or operates in the opposite direction to a risk factor. A compensatory model therefore involves a direct effect of a promotive factor on an outcome. For example, youth living in poverty are more likely to commit violent behaviour than youth not living in poverty, but adult monitoring of behaviour may help compensate for the negative effects of poverty.	In the protective factor model, assets or resources moderate or reduce the effects of the risk of a negative outcome. For example, parental support reducing the effect of poverty on violent behaviour.	In this model, the association between a risk factor and an outcome is curvilinear. This suggests that exposure to low levels and high levels of a risk factor are associated with negative outcomes, but moderate levels of the risk are related to less negative (or less positive) outcomes. For example, repeated exposure to moderate levels of risk prepares adolescents to better handle stressors in the future.

Source: Fergus and Zimmerman (2015, p. 200).

the following sections, peer networks become their "resource" for facilitating protective mechanisms to deal with the daily violence encountered in their work and beyond.

5.3 Assessing resilience

In comparison to the studies described above that looked at the resilience of sex workers purely with respect to the challenges that characterise their work, my research documents the journey of the participants into the sex and informal entertainment industry from their early lives (as discussed in Chapters 2 and 3). This allows me to look at how the participants exhibit resilience under different circumstances. The research shows that "resilience may be differentially affected in different stages of their lives by entrenched patterns of coping, physiological stress responses and other social relationships" (Carabine, Graber, & Pichon, 2015, p. 5).

It has been argued that moderate prior adversity might give individuals the strength to cope with later traumas as they develop resources, relationships, and effective coping skills. Resilience research makes it clear that change and adaptation are always possible. The participants were asked questions about their reasons for migration, the memories of which run deep among them. This is important because the participants show a great degree of resilience in their ability to cope with the dramatic changes in their circumstances. They state that since they have experienced terrible things early in life, such past experience gives them the strength to cope with the challenges they face both at work and on a personal level. Questions were also asked regarding their personal lives, particularly the age of marriage, if they were still married, and if not, what happened to the relationship. Since most participants interviewed for this study were single women, the nature of these questions allowed women to talk about the violence they suffered at the hands of their husbands or partners, which in most cases resulted in separation. It is deduced from their responses that their decision to join the sex and informal entertainment industry was in itself an act of resilience; they accept their limitations as women with little or no resources or skills necessary to earn a decent livelihood or raise their children (Holroyd, Tang, Wong, & Yuen, 2014). The literature on resilience points out that to move forward, irrespective of the risk involved, for the sake of survival and in doing so changing the status quo of suffering and adversity is an act of resilience (Brodsky & Cattaneo, 2013).

The questions asked also addressed two more areas: the personal safety of the participants in relation to their income-generating activities, and experiences of harm and violence. These questions revealed insights into the specific nature of the violence that the participants face and had faced in the past. Participants were asked about the type of violence, about perpetrators, and about the support they sought during times of distress. Discussing the emotional journey of the participants as sex workers in turn opened up a space for them to discuss coping strategies and what enabled them to show resilience in order to tackle oppressive situations.

In terms of documenting the resilience of women working in the sex and informal entertainment industry, this study interviewed a range of women working as both street-based sex workers and those operating from indoor centres such as cabin restaurants, "duet" restaurants, and massage parlours. Burnes, Long, and Schept (2012) have argued that the location and organisational aspects of sex work have critical implications for understanding the psychology of sex work in terms of how the workers cope with the work environment and the embedded work-related violence that underpins the profession. They recommend that researchers focusing on the resilience of sex workers need to include the entire gamut of sex workers in their research, rather than focusing solely on the participants who are most convenient or accessible, in order to understand how location can help to nurture the strengths of women in the wider informal entertainment sector and protect them from job-related stress and hazards. Notably, the locations, as a determinant of the environment and organisational facets of sex work, have been explored by limited studies carried out in Western countries. This study has included participants who work (or have worked) as street-based sex workers, and women working in massage parlours, cabin restaurants (*dhori*), or dance bars. The two focus groups conducted comprised of women of varied age groups working in different forms of the sex and informal entertainment industry. Doing so allowed the study to consider how resilience factors are enhanced through the ability to seek help through peer networks. This helps to address the gap between how external resilience factors (such as the availability of social support or the ability to ask for help) affect women in this industry.

A resilience-based lens highlights that little is known about why some individuals enter sex work and others do not and that there are many possible reasons for an individual to make this choice. The responses of the participants help to weave together context-specific resilient processes (Canvin et al., 2009, as cited in Graber, Pichon, & Carabine, 2015), which further enables the researcher to look at different intersections where women have been able to cope with extremely challenging situations by exhibiting inner strength. Documenting context-specific resilience processes is useful as it shows that resilient qualities develop over time, and this contributes to building "constellations of strengths and protective processes that are particularly adaptive in the face of a given risk" (Graber, Pichon, & Carabine, 2015, p. 13). For example, association with non-governmental organisations (NGOs) helps the participants to develop resilience through the protective mechanisms that such organisations put in place. It also acts as a reminder that violence and abuse are pervasive across the social-ecological spectrum and that it is not limited to sex work alone; it impacts the lives of all women. The participants of my study assert this point when they explain that, whilst they may be at the margins of society, they feel in general that violence against women is a common phenomenon. For example, a number of participants said that they face harassment on public transport, which they say is experienced by all women. Participant 7 (age 33, upper caste, separated, has two children) said:

> patriarchy is one of the main causes why women suffer. [...] violence is everywhere at home or at office and women of all backgrounds experience it. I think any act that humiliates a person is violence. Beating and hurling abuses are some common forms of harm for most women in Nepal.

5.4 Resilience in the face of trauma

All the participants described negative experiences associated with work, which they said often takes a toll on their psychological health. Almost all the participants also referred to being confronted by daily abuse, stigma, and harassment at the hands of the police, on public transport, and by the community at large. These experiences create emotional trauma, as there is always a fear of being spotted by a client. Below are the accounts of three women who work in a dance bar, a massage parlour, and as a street-based worker, respectively.

Participant 9 (age 28, upper caste [Brahmin], not living with husband, has one child), who works in a dance bar described her situation as follows:

> I am expected to drink with the customers and entertain them. My job is to entice the customers and make them consume alcohol. I need to keep them engaged and even let them touch me. I am paid a commission based on a number of drinks that a customer purchased. That is how we make money. Let me tell you, in our profession apart from sex, there is all other sorts of physical harassment.

> The other problem is that we can't work without fear of police. Also, as a woman I face a lot of harassment while traveling in a bus. There is some sort of daily harassment like someone trying to pinch me or touch me. I do resist but then what else can you do. Police helps women who are privileged and powerful. They only harass women who are working in this sector.

Her experiences are echoed by Participant 16 (age 23Buddhist [Lama], married but not living with husband, has two children) who says:

> There is uncertainty about payment. We are forced to drink alcohol and if we don't drink, we are treated badly. And then men humiliate you. They call you by [bad names] and feel that they can do whatever they want.

Another woman, who works in a massage parlour, stated "I faced a lot of violence: physical, sexual, and verbal. A big percentage of customers look for sex. It is a part of the package. Since prostitution is illegal it is provided in massage parlours".

Participant 14 (age 40, lower caste, husband living abroad, has three children), who was abducted, tortured, and raped by the Maoist forces and now works as a street-based sex worker, says that police harassment is high for those who operate on the street:

> Many men who are from the police come in plain clothes and take my services but later they refuse to pay saying that they are policemen. Since we operate from an open space, police harassment is a major problem. If we do not listen to them, they even take us into custody.

She adds that for the street-based sex worker, the level of violence from clients can be as high as three to four times a week. "Sometimes people lock us inside a room and leave without paying. They beat us, abuse us", she says. Her past trauma of being raped as a child still flashes in her mind and her experiences of daily violence has left her a "broken person". She says it is having an adverse psychological effect on her. "My mind is always disturbed; I tend to forget things; I am often depressed". But despite her sufferings, she is proud of the fact that she makes her own living and feels confident. "Yes, I am happy that I am not dependent on others. At the end of day, I earn it".

Some of the women who participated in the research described how the community lets them down when violence occurs. "It is our character that is questioned", said Participant 9, whose landlord attempted to rape her. Some also mentioned that it is difficult for single mothers to rent a house. Participant 6 (age 23, not married) said of the general attitude of the community that

> They straightaway question our character, and it is women in the family that are wary about letting homes to single women. [...] the women who

> are in this profession are never respected. They are abused, stigmatised, and oppressed and these factors even drive many girls to commit suicide, as there is not much support for them. The society has failed them. People think women who are in this sector are weak and that they will never raise their voice hence they can control and intimidate them.

Against the odds, women still demonstrate considerable inner strength and resilience when dealing with their daily suffering. Their resilience manifests in two ways: one is through the protective mechanism that is built around them through the peer networks (discussed in the next section), and the other is strength-based resilience that they draw from within, referred to as "assets" by Fergus and Zimmerman (2005).

Participant 7 (age 33, Dalit [lower caste], married but not living with husband, has three children) says that "Women face violence and get exploited because they are poor, not educated and not aware of their rights [...] There were times when my children went to bed without food, but income has changed things".

When asked more specifically about what equality means for her, she says, "man is born out of women. Women should and can do what men can do, I don't see any difference". She adds that her hope for a better future for her daughter keeps her going, "I will make sure her life is better". When asked what can make the biggest difference in her life, she says, "if I can get a good job, it will be good".

Their hopes for a good future make women resilient and give them the strength to move forward. In the emotional journeys of the participants as sex workers, we see how women exhibit their personal strength (assets). In the next section, I discuss how the resilience of the participants is further enhanced through peer networks.

5.5 The role of peer networks in building resilience

In this study, it is noted that the high level of violence has taught the women engaged in the informal entertainment industry to be more resolute in accepting the challenges of life both in their personal lives and on the work front. Their inner transformation and sense of confidence are boosted not just through their income alone, but also through membership of organisations and groups that allow the women to come together and provide solidarity to one another on a personal level and also to collectively raise their grievances against issues such as police harassment. The majority of the women in this study mentioned that they are part of the autonomous organisation Raksha Nepal, an NGO that works with women engaged in the sex and informal entertainment industry in the Thamel area.

Raksha Nepal provides critical peer support that enables women to build resilience to violence. Its mission is to empower women working in dance bars, cabin restaurants, "duet" restaurants, and massage parlours. It rescues minor girls (those under the age of 18) from brothels and massage parlours and brings them to their shelter. It provides psychosocial counselling as well as healing through yoga and meditation to women and girls who have suffered trauma. It also provides legal support and skills development courses in organic farming, driving, massage therapy, and housekeeping for those seeking alternative employment. It runs a shelter for children of sex workers and ensures that such children go to a proper school.

Raksha Nepal's skills development programme is also open to street-based and brothel-based sex workers who might want to learn new skills in order to change their profession. Its chairperson, Menuka Thapa, says that "since money is the biggest source of empowerment for women, so from the very beginning, I taught women to save money. In 2008, we set up a credit and saving co-operative with the savings of sex workers".

Many former sex workers have started their own businesses with the support of this scheme. In 2015, it formed a union of women working in the informal entertainment industry. Through the union, the organisation tries to protect the rights of women engaged in sex work and those employed in massage parlours, duet restaurants (which feature live music shows), dance bars, and cabin restaurants (where customers are served by waitresses in tiny individual rooms) (discussed in more detail in Chapter 7).

The individual and focus-group interviews found that women draw on the resources found in each other, and this in turn gives women the much-needed confidence to cope with the enormous challenges both on a personal level and at their place of work. Many of the outreach workers who volunteer for or work in an organisation like Raksha Nepal are themselves engaged in the informal entertainment sector. They, in turn, become outreach workers; their transformation and confidence then become motivating factors for other women to join the peer networks.

Table 5.2 illustrates the varied levels of support that women have received from a peer network like Raksha Nepal. In terms of psychological resilience theory, the support that is generated by organisations can be analysed in terms of a protective mechanism that can help an individual to respond effectively to adverse situations (Carabine, Graber, & Pichon, 2015). However, it must be noted that when analysing resilience, the term "mechanism" is used to emphasise the point that resilience is a process and that no single factor on its own, however powerful, can bring about a defining and adaptive outcome (Graber et al., 2015). As shown in Table 5.2, Raksha Nepal facilitates external intervention that is designed to reduce the impact of risk, reduce or break negative chain reactions, strengthen confidence levels, and open up new opportunities (Carabine, Graber, & Pichon, 2015). In the typology of the mechanisms of the resilience process, Fergus and Zimmerman (2005) see peer networks such as Raksha Nepal as external resources that help in strengthening the inner strength (assets) of the members, thereby enabling the participants to be resilient in different capacities.

Table 5.2 The levels of support that women have received from a peer network

Participant	*Reasons for joining peer network*	*Benefits/resources*	*Resilience*
Participant 2: Age 30, has one child, lower caste, separated	"I learnt about Raksha Nepal from a field worker. I then met Menuka Thapa and told her that I need help to educate my daughter. She advised me to admit her in the Raksha shelter home. I also became associated with Raksha as there was high level of violence in the entertainment industry and I needed support to deal with it".	"I undertook vocational trainings and learnt stitching and tailoring for nine months. I then took a loan of 150,000 rupees and started my own tailoring business and employed two girls. I earned around 15,000 per month. I am now paying back the loan".	"I have the capacity to win in life under any circumstance. My daughter doesn't know about my work, but I will not shy away from telling the truth. I am proud to be standing on my own feet. If I don't tell the truth, someone else will tell her, but I am very confident woman now".
Participant 3: Age 20, has one child, Buddhist, widow	"I joined as an outreach worker".	"The violence I faced in the hands of Maoists and then whilst working in the entertainment industry took a toll on my life. Raksha Nepal provided me psychological therapy and it has given me a lot of hope to live".	"I am beginning to look at the life in a positive way. I am learning tailoring, so I hope to open a shop one day".
Participant 8: Age 48, has four children, upper caste, widow	"I came to know about Raksha Nepal through word of mouth. I came with my friend. I met an employee here, I spent around one hour to learn what Raksha does".	"I liked that women could talk about their problems. I took up sewing as a part of skill development programme. For the first time in life, I acquired a skill and I really enjoyed sitting behind the sewing machine".	"Through my association I have learnt that literacy and early marriage are the main cause of women's problem. I have learnt not be supressed by men".

(*Continued*)

Table 5.2 (Continued)

Participant	*Reasons for joining peer network*	*Benefits/resources*	*Resilience*
Participant 6: Age 23, not married	"I am associated with three organisations Raksha Nepal, FADE Nepal and JMMS. They taught me how to move forward in life".	"Peer networks gives us a voice to talk openly about our problems. I learnt about the importance of using condoms; they tell about all health risks and teach us where to go, where to seek support, they tell us not to go to the client's house etc.".	"Earlier I was afraid of everything around me: the police, society, people. But now things are different. You see I can speak confidently. People might abuse me but that is momentary, but I know that I am standing on my feet. I am not begging. I don't care what society thinks of me. Society is made by us. Society does not provide me food or shelter".
Participant 9: Age 28, has one child, upper caste, married but not living with husband	"I joined it hoping that collectively we will be able to secure a better future for our children".	"I voluntarily work as an outreach worker and meet women who are working in the sector. I tell them about our work. During meetings, we organise ourselves into groups, discuss our problems and look for solutions to our problem".	"I am confident that my future will be better than my past. I am connected with an organisation like Raksha Nepal that has done much more than what my family could have done. There have been days when I went without food, I hope I will never have to see such days. I have learnt to live with dignity".
Participant 17: Age 33, has two children, lower caste, abandoned by husband	"I came to know about Raksha Nepal from my friend. She told me about the support and counselling that Raksha Nepal could provide".	"Meeting Raksha Nepal was transformative. I took beautician courses, which was specifically helpful as most of it was work-oriented training. I was later able to start my own beauty parlour".	"I have attended workshops on gender, leadership, and entrepreneurship. As a woman, I am committed to help women and want to employ women from this sector in my parlour".

The resilience of the participants is further realised when they are backed by resources provided by the peer network. Resilience models stress the importance of the ecological context, and that external factors such as peer networks, in addition to the above-mentioned attributes, may help women to respond more effectively to social, health, and occupational risks (Fergus & Zimmerman, 2005). The social support that Raksha Nepal provides to the women and girls working in the informal entertainment industry is persistently identified in the resilience literature as "a protective mechanism because mentoring relationships, supportive friends and trust that women find amongst peers promote resilience in the face of neglect, abuse, low socioeconomic status and other challenges" (Carabine, Graber, & Pichon, 2015).

So, in the context of the participants of this study, I argue that their resilience can be seen through the lens of a protective model. In this model, assets or resources play a role in moderating or reducing the negative outcomes of risk.

5.6 Linking resilience with power and agency

Leder (2016) notes that perspectives on empowerment vary considerably as it is viewed as a "highly contextualized, multi-dimensional process", so it is important to understand subjectivities and the respective influencing factors in specific contexts, as well as how they interlink (Leder, 2016, p. 3). So, taking Kabeer's definition into account – which underlines the relationship of material, social, and human resources, the decision-making process, and well-being outcomes – it is imperative to examine which dimensions of empowerment influence resilience to bring about a transformative change in the lives of the participants (Kabeer, 1999).

In this study, as discussed in Chapter 4, the participants were seen to exhibit a considerable degree of autonomy and to gain decision-making abilities within

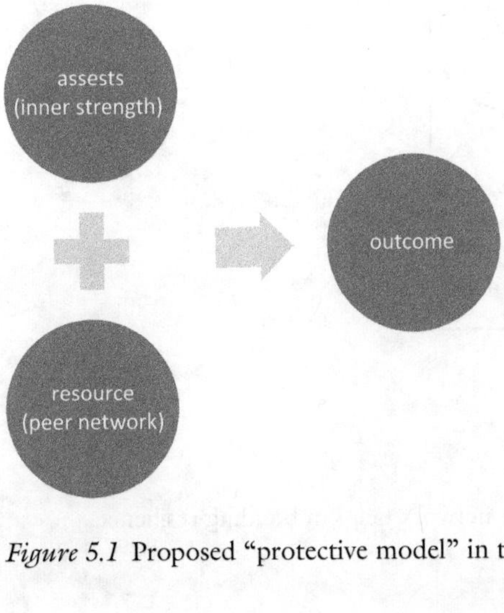

Figure 5.1 Proposed "protective model" in the context of this study.

the household structure by virtue of earning an income. However, it is not simply that autonomy arising from income makes them resilient. Rather, it is the peer network that plays a significant role in accentuating the psychological assets of the participants – such as self-esteem, self-confidence, and the ability to imagine and to aspire to a better future – by providing collective support through initiatives including skills development training, socio-psychological support, and access to credit and savings schemes. Hence, based on the discussions outlined in the study, I propose the following model to demonstrate how resilience has led to an empowering process for the participants.

Looking at how resilience and well-being interact from the social ecology perspective, Allison, Armitage, Béné, Charles, and Johnson (2012) argue that the well-being of an individual does not depend solely on their income, but it is instead an outcome and a process dependent on three other dimensions: material, relational, and subjective well-being (Sen, 1999; Gough et al., 2007). The three dimensions are particularly useful in understanding ways in which the different facets of a "life well lived" come together (Allison, Armitage, Béné, Charles, & Johnson, 2012, p. 4).

In the context of this study, the only material dimension that drives the participants is income, which acts as the first condition for choice. Their income comes through the exercise of choice in entering the sex and informal entertainment industry, which can be seen as a strategic choice. It is also strategic because, due to the lack of alternate skills and poor economic growth in Nepal, decent jobs are hard to come by. The 2015 earthquake that killed 8,000 people affected a further 5.6 million workers. Millions of people sought employment abroad, continuing

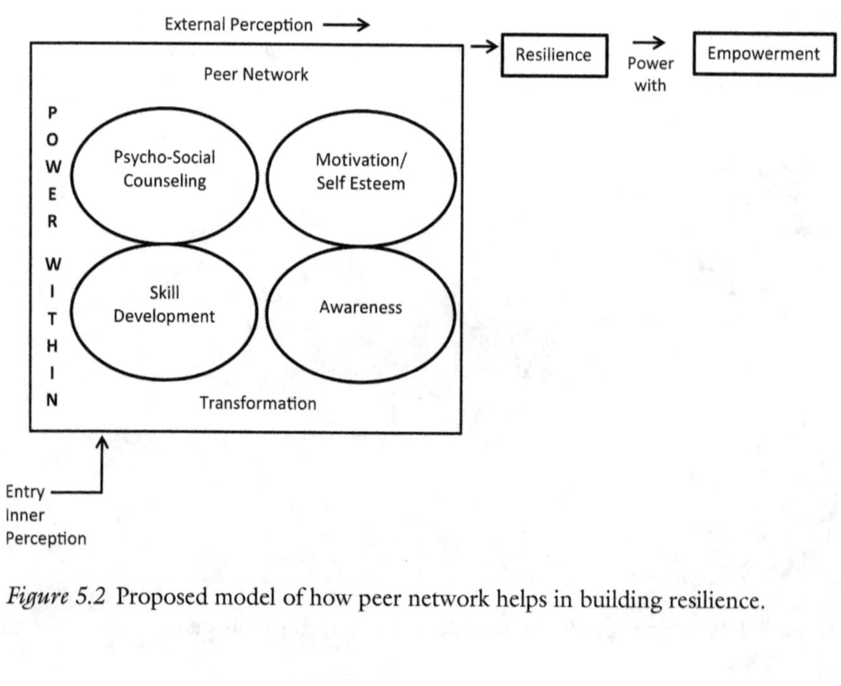

Figure 5.2 Proposed model of how peer network helps in building resilience.

Nepal's growing reliance on remittances for growth. As mentioned in Chapter 4, joining the informal entertainment industry was not necessarily the first choice of the participants, but other alternatives such as jobs in the construction sector or being a domestic maid were even more exploitative. However, as discussed above, after making this initial choice, some of participants have exercised a choice once again to learn new skills through peer networks with a view to leaving the sex and informal entertainment sector in the near future. It shows that they are capable of making hard decisions and looking at alternative livelihood options as they arise. As Participant 21 said, "spa training [provided by Raksha Nepal] has helped. It built my confidence, and I can get job even if I go abroad".

The women who participated in the study also made a choice to become a part of the peer networks, which are part of an informal opportunity structure. Organisations such as Raksha Nepal provide resources (contributing to the existence of choice) and allow the participants to make use of the resource (use of choice) for their well-being. As indicated in Chapter 4, Chen and Mahmud (1995) identify that there is more than one causal pathway – material, cognitive, perceptual, relational –through which resources are translated into agency, which is similar to what Allison, Armitage, Béné, Charles, and Johnson (2012) suggest. But these pathways can be experienced not only by the women themselves, but also by other agents or actors in their lives (Chen & Mahmud, 1995, p. 8). Relational changes here mean relationship building, which we see is forged through the participants' association with peer networks. The support that they derive from their peers helps them to increase their bargaining power, both with clients and with partners. They attain cognitive capacities by acquiring new skills through various training programmes. Permanent changes occur when they become more aware of their rights as women and assert that they are self-reliant as single women. In this study, it is evident that women experience material gain when they have access to and control over their income. We see cognitive changes in the levels of knowledge achieved through learning new skills and a greater awareness of the wider environment, which in turn adds to their self-esteem and brings about perceptual changes. Perceptual changes are both internal and external, and they happen as women begin to value themselves and their identity differently. The participants also demonstrate a subjective dimension of well-being when, even amidst fears, they harbour hope for a better future (Millennium Ecosystem Assessment, 2005).

In this context, we see the existence of two dimensions of power: relational changes, such as being associated with peer networks, is "power with" (Alkire & Ibrahim, 2007), which results in increased power from collective action, social mobilisation, and alliance building in the form of unions (discussed further in Chapter 7). The perceptual changes help bring forth "power from within" (Alkire & Ibrahim, 2007) that strengthens the self-esteem, confidence, and bargaining power of the participants, (especially with regard to clients), which in turn influences their perception and attitudes towards their adaptive capacities and, therefore, their resilience.

5.7 Conclusion

In the Transconceptual Model of Empowerment and Resilience, the resilience that the women who participated in this study demonstrate is positioned within the category of first-order changes, which are "hard-won changes". These changes have a decisive impact on the lives of the individuals concerned. They are hard won because the participants overcome a great deal of struggle, including violence at work and home, work-related stressors such as not getting paid, harassment from the police and other law enforcement agencies, and the overall stigma held by the community at large. They are first-order changes because, despite these challenges, the participants show an awareness of their situation and a desire to change or improve their lives (Brodsky & Cattaneo, 2013). The peer networks then give them the momentum to translate their desire into some sort of action and, in the process, the women acquire the strength to be more resilient. Whilst first-order changes are understood as being aimed towards adapting to, withstanding, or resisting ongoing problems and challenges through adopting a set of strategies, they might not necessarily change the status quo or the power differentials that are embedded in the ecosystem that supports social injustices. The participants have, however, created their own coping mechanisms and have learnt to deal with their daily challenges more effectively. The TMER argues that for true empowerment to take place there has to be a radical second-order change in relation to power dynamics and it must have a long-term transformative effect. In the context of the study, I have demonstrated that there is a considerable change in the power dynamics and that the participants are able to experience both "power within" and "power with". The benefits that they have derived from their associations have been significantly transformative, and we see that they make use of available resources (both internal and external) to adapt to vulnerable situations and withstand trauma and violence. They remain optimistic and make efforts to improve their lives by learning new skills and investing in the future.

This study establishes that for the participants, resilience, like empowerment, is an iterative and interactive process and its progress is not linear but spiral, which fits with observations made by other authors in relation to women working in different sectors (see e.g. Sarason, 1978, as cited in Brodsky & Cattaneo, 2013). In this chapter and in Chapter 4, the relational and processual perspectives on resilience have been unpacked by drawing on Rowland's conceptualisations of power. This chapter shows how "power within" and "power with" manifest in the lives of women in the resilience-building process. The proposed framework then shows that in peer networks women build their own community, which then acts as a protective lens: through this lens the women manage their external perceptions. The model indicates that, through their life experiences, the development of the participants' resilience is a product of inner strength (assets) *and* outer support (resources provided by peer networks). It is also a process, but it is one that has no single starting point. It involves multiple linked components and, as such, there has to be an understanding of the priorities and values of the persons or communities who are seeking empowerment. For example, peer networks have in-depth knowledge and understanding of the problems faced by the women in their community and are aware that resilience at times needs to be facilitated (as the peer network does in this context). In Chapter 6, I discuss how these peer networks came into being. It is the effort of a small number of women who decide to act differently in response to daily challenges that women face, acting as champions of change: they are "positive deviants" within the sector.

References

Alkire, S., & Ibrahim, S. (2007). Agency and empowerment: A proposal for internationally comparable indicators. *Oxford Development Studies, 35*(4), 379–403.

Allison, E. H., Armitage, D., Béné, C., Charles, A. T., & Johnson, D. (2012). The interplay of well-being and resilience in applying a social-ecological perspective. *Ecology and Society, 17*(4), 15.

Aspinwall, L. G., & Tedeschi, R. G. (2010). The value of positive psychology for health psychology: Progress and pitfalls in examining the relation of positive phenomena to health. *Annals of Behavioral Medicine, 39*(1), 4–15. doi:10.1007/s12160-009-9153-0

Best, K. M., Garmezy, N., & Masten, A. S. (1990). Resilience and development: Contributions from the study of children who overcome adversity. *Development and Psychopathology, 2*(4), 425–444.

Born, M., Jackson, S., & Jacob, M. N. (1997). Reflections on risk and resilience in adolescence. *Journal of Adolescence, 20*(6), 609–616.

Brodsky, A. E., & Cattaneo, L. B., (2013). A transconceptual model of empowerment and resilience: Divergence, convergence and interactions in kindred community concepts. *American Journal of Community Psychology, 52*(3–4), 333–346.

Burnes, T., Long, S. L., & Schept, R. A. (2012). Resilience-based lens of sex work: Implications for professional psychologists. *Professional Psychology Research and Practice, 43*(2), 137–144.

Canvin, K., Marttila, A., Burstrom, B., & Whitehead, M. (2009) Tales of the unexpected? Hidden resilience in poor households in Britain. *Social Science & Medicine, 69*(2), 238–245.

Carpenter, S. R., & Brock, W. A. (2004). Spatial complexity, resilience and policy diversity: Fishing on lake-rich landscapes. *Ecology and Society, 9*(1), 8.

Chen, M., & Mahmud, S. (1995). *Assessing Change in Women's Lives: A Conceptual Framework* (BRAC-ICDDR, B. Joint Research Project Working Paper No. 2).

Coy, M. (2009). Milkshakes, lady lumps and growing up to want boobies: How the sexualisation of popular culture limits girls' horizons. *Child Abuse Review, 18*(6), 372–383.

Fergus, S., & Zimmerman, M. A. (2005). Adolescent resilience: A framework for understanding healthy development in the face of risk. *Annual Review of Public Health, 26*, 399–419.

Fredrickson, B. L., & Tugade, M. M. (2004). Resilient individuals use positive emotions to bounce back from negative emotional experiences. *Journal of Personality and Social Psychology, 86*(2), 320–333.

Gable, S. L., & Haidt, J. (2005). What (and why) is positive psychology? *Review of General Psychology*, *9*(2), 103–110.

Gorry, J., Reilly, J., & Roen, K. (2010). Selling yourself? The psychological impact of street sex work and factors affecting support seeking. *Health & Social Care in the Community*, *18*(5), 492–499.

Gough, I., & McGregor, J. A. (Eds.) (2007). *Wellbeing in Developing Countries: From Theory to Research*. Cambridge University Press.

Graber, R., Pichon, F., & Carabine, E. (2015). *Psychological Resilience: State of Knowledge and Future Research Agendas* (Overseas Development Institute Working Paper 425). ODI.

Holroyd, E., Tang, C. S., Wong, W. C., & Yuen, W. W. (2014). Resilience in work-related stress among female sex workers in Hong Kong. *Qualitative Health Research*, *24*(9), 1232–1241.

Holroyd, E. A., Wong, W. C. W., Gray, A., & Ling, D. C. (2008). Environmental health and safety of Chinese sex workers: A cross-sectional study. *International Journal of Nursing Studies*, *45*(6), 932–941.

Kabeer, N. (1999). Resources, agency, achievements: Reflections on the measurement of women's empowerment. *Development and Change*, *30*, 435–464.

Lau, J. T., Tsui, H. Y., Ho, S. P., Wong, E., & Yang, X. (2010). Prevalence of psychological problems and relationships with condom use and HIV prevention behaviors among Chinese female sex workers in Hong Kong. *AIDS Care*, *22*(6), 659–668.

Lazarus, R. S., & Folkman, S. (1984). *Stress, Appraisal, and Coping*. New York: Springer.

Leder, S. (2016). *Linking Women's Empowerment and Resilience. Research Program on Water, Land and Ecosystems: Literature Review*. International Water Management Institute. cgspace.cgiar.org/handle/10568/72489

Luthar, S. S., & Zigler, E. (1991). Vulnerability and competence: A review of research on resilience in childhood. *American Journal of Orthopsychiatry*, *61*(1), 6–22.

Mann, T. (2001). Effects of future writing and optimism on health behaviors in HIV-infected women. *Annals of Behavioral Medicine*, *23*(1), 26–33.

Millennium Ecosystem Assessment (2005). *Ecosystem and Human Well-Being: Current State and Trends*. Island Press.

O'Neill, M. (2010). Cultural criminology and sex work: Resisting regulation through radical democracy and participatory action research (PAR). *Journal of Law and Society*, *37*, 210–232.

Sanders, T. (2004). A continuum of risk? The management of health, physical and emotional risks by female sex workers. *Sociology of Health & Illness*, *26*(5), 557–574.

Sarason, S. B. (1978). The nature of problem solving in social action. *American Psychologist*, *33*, 370–380.

Sen, A. K. (1999). *Development as Freedom*. Oxford University Press.

Sex Worker Education and Advocacy Task Force (2005). *Coping with Stigma, Discrimination, and Violence: Sex Workers Talk about Their Experiences*. SWEAT. www.sweat.org/za/docs/coping.pdf

Vanwesenbeeck, I. (2005). Burnout among female indoor sex workers. *Archives of Sexual Behavior*, *34*(6), 627–639.

Wood, A. M., & Tarrier, N. (2010). Positive clinical psychology: A new vision and strategy for integrated research and practice. *Clinical Psychology Review*, *30*(7), 819–829.

6 Positive deviance among Nepal's sex and informal entertainment workers

6.1 Introduction

In the first section of this chapter, I discuss the emergence of a positive deviance (PD) strategy as a concept and how it has come to be applied to various practical, theoretical, and disciplinary research domains. I argue that since the application of the PD strategy is seen to bring about an exceptionally high level of transformative results, it is now being afforded importance by donors within the international development industry. Following this, I examine the existing literature to demonstrate how PD strategies have been used in tackling social problems such as human trafficking in Indonesia and Nepal. The case studies mentioned in this section show that the application of a PD strategy varies depending on context and communities.

The chapter then goes on to document the lives of women who represent good examples of PD in the context of Nepal's sex and informal entertainment industry. In this section (6.4), I analyse the life trajectories of four women in order to identify the key attributes and skills that contribute to them becoming "positive deviants". I deconstruct the case studies of the four women discussed in order to broadly define the key common factors and the attributable qualities that contribute to these particular women taking on this role. In doing so, I propose a framework that demonstrates how PD qualities are enacted and applied in the context of women in the sex and informal entertainment industry. The latter part of the chapter discusses how the four organisations utilise a PD strategy by adopting a broader framework in relation to issues such as human immunodeficiency viruses/acquired immunodeficiency syndrome (HIV/AIDS), migration, and violence against women and girls (VAWG). I argue that adopting such frameworks helps them in two ways: firstly, it can deflect criticism from their work, which is viewed as promoting the interests of sex workers; secondly, the women who volunteer for these organisations tend to earn acceptance in society, though they might still be engaged in the sex and informal entertainment industry. In the concluding section, I note how the actions of positive deviants have facilitated three processes: social mobilisation, information gathering, and behavioural change, which I then go on to discuss in more detail in Chapter 7.

DOI: 10.4324/9781003156796-6

6.2 Positive deviance unpacked

The term "positive deviance" is used to identify people who succeed in difficult circumstances. It is a method of social inquiry grounded on the premise that in every community there are certain individuals or groups whose uncommon behaviour and strategies enable them to find better solutions to the same problems facing their peers. These individuals then lead by example and act as a "champion" for change (Herington & van de Fliert, 2018, p. 666)

In the last few decades, PD has emerged as a useful concept in understanding the nature of and potential solutions to complex social problems (Herington & van de Fliert, 2018). It emerged from the concept of deviance, which has long been used to analyse the attributes of individuals (Kohlborn, Kummer, Mertens, & Recker, 2016), but such studies have predominantly focused on negative forms of deviance. Negative deviance is described as behaviours or conditions that do not conform to acceptable social rules, therefore eliciting negative evaluations for a social group (Heckert & Heckert, 2002). In recent years, however, there has been a growing interest in PD (see e.g. Dodge, 1985; Heckert & Heckert, 2002; Shoenberger, Heckert, & Heckert, 2012). Ben-Yehuda (1990, as cited in Heckert & Heckert 2002, p. 455) called the concept, a significant strategy in opening "new and exciting theoretical and empirical windows for research", and since then, as noted by Heckert and Heckert (2002), PD has emerged as an established concept within the substantive literature on deviance. Bradley, Subramaniam, and Tomalin (2009) contend that the term PD can be broadly divided into two categories: a theoretical concept and a practical strategy. The theoretical application has its roots in the discipline of sociology and has been used to describe the voluntary behaviour of an individual or group that deviates from the norm (Sonenshein & Spreitzer, 2004, as cited in Herington & van de Fliert, 2018). When used in a theoretical sense, PD can be used as a lens through which to understand why and under what circumstances such behaviours occur.

PD is now used in research relating to a wide range of fields such as nutrition, criminology, education, and development and organisational scholarship (Kohlborn, Kummer, Mertens, & Recker, 2016). In these applications, PD has been defined as a practical strategy to identify and promote exceptionally high performance in a problematic domain of interest (Bradley et al., 2009, as cited in Herington & van de Fliert, 2018: 664).

When compared to other problem-based approaches to social enquiry, the focus of a PD strategy is to look at successful exceptions and to understand the factors that contribute to their success. Fliert and Herington (2018) argue that the steps involved in the PD strategy require defining the problem and determining desirable outcomes. It also means discovering individuals or groups who – either through their intrinsic behaviour such as leadership qualities, determination, persuasive power, or ability to stay motivated or through training or specific interventions – are able to achieve the desired goals and outcomes. A PD strategy in the context of development studies means identifying the behavioural factors that drive such individuals. This key question is now being given high priority by major funders including the Department for International Development (DFID), the United Nations Children's Fund (UNICEF), and Oxfam (Green, 2018; Albanna & Heeks, 2019).

6.3 Applying positive deviancy

A PD strategy has been applied to the study of a wide range of problems. Below, I provide examples of how it has been used to combat human trafficking because the organisations mapped in this study – though vocal about the rights of sex workers and of those engaged in the informal entertainment sector – through their activism also play a significant role in preventing girls from entering the informal entertainment sector, including through trafficking. For this reason, some parallels can be drawn when analysing their work through the PD framework.

Durá and Singhal (2009) used the PD approach to tackle the trafficking of girls in Indonesia. The strategy was based on the premise that in every community there are individuals whose uncommon practices or behaviours enable them to find better solutions to problems than their neighbours with access to the same resources. In this case, the PD strategy was implemented in the villages of East Java, where girls were systematically being trafficked. The purpose was to identify families who had, despite their poverty, found ways to keep their daughters at home. The importance of locating such families was to identify the methods and the practices of such families, which could then be encouraged and emulated by weaving them into the intervention programmes to combat the trafficking of girls. The PD process involves the foregrounding of such families, who had already been successful. Herington and van de Fliert (2018) argue that such methods force society to reflect on the prevailing views of what is considered customary or normal practice and enable consideration of alternative practices. In other words, as Durkheim's argument (1964[1895]) suggested, all social change begins with some form of deviance (Herington & van de Fliert, 2018, p. 665).

In the study above, the PD strategy was boosted through multiple communication processes, which included organising a workshop and asking the participants about the general problems of the community (defined as a dialogic introduction to PD). From the discussion, the main problem of the village was clear: many girls from poor families who leave the community and go to work outside end up in the sex industry. To tackle the problem, it was important to learn from those families that were successful in keeping their girls at home while other poor families were letting girls go to far-off places to work (Durá & Singhal, 2009, p. 7).

The authors underlined that through the PD mapping exercise:

> the community members began to take ownership of the 'silent' problem of missing girls, posing questions such as, 'why do girls leave the village, why not boys?' Realising that although an answer like 'they make money more easily' was a simple one, they probed further: 'but why? Where do they work?' And further: 'at a bar. What is a bar for you? A discotheque? Or perhaps a place where sex is bought and sold?' Through the detailed

house-by-house, street-by-street, village-level mapping, the community was able to identify the specific issues faced by vulnerable girls.

(Durá & Singhal, 2009, p. 9)

Accordingly, girls were identified as positive deviants based on stipulated criteria: that she had to be poor, under 18, and had made a conscious decision not to work in the sex industry despite an opportunity to do so. Two years after the PD project got underway, the village recorded dramatic progress in their efforts to combat child trafficking to such an extent that no new girls had entered sex work. Twenty averted attempts at girl trafficking were documented, and a mechanism had been put in place to ensure that travel documents were verified (Durá & Singhal, 2009).

Similarly, in Nepal, PD was experimented within the anti-trafficking context in 2002 by the Nuwakot District Development Committee with technical support from Save the Children US (Clawson, 2002, as cited in Brunovskis & Surtees, 2015). Although the project could not be completed due to disruptions by Maoist insurgent groups, it used a positive deviance inquiry (PDI) approach to identify PD strategies to inform an overarching programme response. The core principles of the PD approach were then used to inform research methodology and research questions. Apart from political problems, the researchers faced resistance from the local communities who were not willing to acknowledge the problems of human trafficking. However, the project focused on drawing from the core principles of positive deviancy, rather than fully implementing a PD project. It was learnt that "the social, cultural or political environment may not always be conducive to implementing a PD approach [...] both because of resistance to the issue, or as in this case, because of security concerns" (Brunovskis & Surtees, 2015, p. 14). An evaluation of the above study shows that the PD initiative works when the community owns the problem and looks for an organic solution from within. This dynamic creates a new space for the role of an expert.

6.4 Mapping the organisations studied

For the purpose of this study, scoping work was conducted to map the organisations that work with the women in the sex and informal entertainment industry in the local area. The four organisations are

1. **Raksha Nepal:** a humanitarian organisation that has been working for sexually exploited girls, women, and their children since its establishment in 2004 (the scope and extent of its work were introduced in Chapter 5).
2. **Jagriti Mahila Maha Sangh** (JMMS): Nepal's first federation of female sex workers currently engaged in reducing vulnerability to and the impact of HIV among sex workers.
3. **Society for Women Awareness in Nepal** (SWAN): a group of female sex workers whose aim is to create awareness around sexually transmitted diseases and HIV/AIDS. It also addresses the issues of sexual exploitation,

domestic violence, creating economic opportunities, capacity-building skills, and human rights awareness.

4. **Biswas Nepal**: committed to working against violence, injustice, and the exploitation of workers who are engaged in the adult entertainment industry. Through advocacy, it has been working on unifying and empowering workers by providing various forms of support.

These originations were considered as they are specifically led by women who themselves have worked in the sex and informal entertainment industry. In-depth interviews were conducted to understand the factors that enabled them to move out of the sector and set up non-governmental organisations (NGOs) that work for the welfare and protection of the rights of women engaged in the sex and informal entertainment industry in different capacities.

As a result of their unique position and experiences, the leaders of these organisations – Menuka Thapa of Raksha Nepal, Bijaya Dhakal of JMMS, Sobha Dangal of SWAN, and Bal Kumari Ale from Biswas Nepal – have a first-hand understanding of the complex problems and challenges that women in this sector face. This helps them to efficiently relate to, connect with, and mobilise women who work in sex and informal entertainment. The leadership of these women is increasingly recognised by all stakeholders, and they have become key actors for women working in the sector.

6.4.1 Case study 1: Bijaya Dhakal of Jagriti Mahila Maha Sangh

Bijaya Dhakal, aged 49, is the president of JMMS. She worked as a sex worker after her husband's sudden death. She was then 18 years old and was pregnant with her second child. For a while, Dhakal worked in a garment factory, but her income was never enough to feed her extended family. In 2002, the General Welfare Pratisthan (GWP), an implementing NGO, came to her village to promote safe sex, condom use, and risk reduction strategies among sex workers. They started looking for someone from the sex workers' community who could motivate others. Dhakal says:

> They talked about the diseases and general health problems that women like us can face and how we can take precautions. The counsellor asked me a lot of questions about my life, and I ended up disclosing a lot of information.

The association with the NGO helped her to understand the importance of a collective voice, and she realised that if they worked in a group, they would have better negotiating power and could protect one another: "In those days talking about HIV was a stigma and no one knew anything about it. So, the focus was on sex workers and they came up with a strategy of group formation to attract more sex workers".

The women were given an incentive of 50 rupees to attend meetings. They would spend 20 rupees on travelling and were encouraged to save 30 rupees, and through this a number of groups were formed in villages.

Dhakal started taking an active interest in training and advocacy programmes. She began mobilising women and telling them about things like HIV prevention and how to protect themselves. She recalled:

> For the first time I understood the meaning of the term 'peer educator', and I wanted to be one. Becoming a peer educator was helpful because it gave me the freedom of mobility. As a young widow, my every single move was under scrutiny by the society but now I could move around more freely, and I felt there was chance to make a difference to the lives of women like me. In many ways, I felt empowered.

She was recruited by the GWP for her leadership:

> I was selected because I was very vocal and could motivate others. I would easily say that I am a sex worker, which no one would dare to say in villages even today. I was made to believe that work is work and there is no harm in doing sex work. I learnt that if you hide your identity, you don't get your rights.
>
> Earlier I had no bargaining power with clients, doing sex work was tough as it was difficult to go out, but as we organised ourselves into a group, our bargaining power increased and there was a sense of security.

Dhakal started creating awareness among sex workers of the measures they should take while with clients, including using condoms, keeping their clients' mobile numbers, taking money in advance, reducing their dependence on clients, not drinking too much, and not wearing any expensive jewellery.

Dhakal moved to Kathmandu in 2006 during the peak of the Maoist insurgency and started mobilising sex workers in the city. She says that she was very clear about what she wanted to do. It was not possible to ask women to give up sex work, but it was possible to ensure that they do it safely. So, with some funding and help from another organisation called Women Acting Together for Change (WATCH), she formed an informal organisation with seven other members.

Dhakal says that besides her leadership qualities, her perseverance, experience, and determination kept her motivated. JMMS, which was formed in 2011, is now a federation of 27 NGOs working in 21 districts, all led by sex workers. One of their key strategies is to shed the stigma attached to sex workers and make them socially acceptable. Since sex work is banned in Nepal, they officially position themselves as an organisation promoting the rights and voices of marginalised women and orphan girls, but their main target group is sex workers who are the members of the federation.

Dhakal emphasises that women who work as sex workers are aware of the fact that they are not perceived as good women in the eyes of society but associating with an organisation helps counteract this because it enhances their image in society. They earn respect because they are more visible due to their participation in campaigns such as those against VAWG. Because of this, other women come to them for help when they encounter problems. This leads to a greater degree of social acceptance. She points out that this social acceptance in turn gives them negotiating power with their clients. A woman is in a position to find less abusive clients and earn more, which makes her more economically empowered. Dhakal states that:

> Due to economic realities of Nepal, it is not practical to tell a woman to stop sex work because she has to feed her family, but when she is educated, made aware of risks and is a part of a network seen to be doing social work it has a positive impact.

6.4.2 Case study 2: Balkumari Ale of Biswas Nepal

Balkumari Ale once worked in a cabin restaurant and is now the executive director of Biswas Nepal. She had come to Kathmandu to pursue higher studies after finishing higher secondary school. Since she came from a poor family, she joined the informal entertainment industry to meet her living expenses and save money to pay her tuition fees. She had joined a trade union, and through it she came in contact with a well-known organisation called Maiti Nepal, known for its work in preventing human trafficking. Along with a group of 23 other women, she attended a 10-day life skills training programme, known as "non-formal life education training", which was organised by Maiti Nepal.

The training programme was a defining moment in her life. Ale said that

> they spoke to us very politely and were always very patient with us. They always supported us, which really touched us. Since we came from poor families our lives were full of hardships. While working in Kathmandu, we kept ourselves confined to cabin restaurants where we worked and lived. We did not get any opportunity for exposure. We never really experienced love and respect. And so, the training session was good. We felt important and got lot of affection and love for the first time.
>
> They taught us about our identity; about things like "who am I?" It was about recognising our strength and our capabilities. At that point of time, we were low in confidence. When we looked at ourselves, we felt totally hopeless like degraded human beings, but the training gave us some hope. We began to think in a more positive way and believed that we too have skills like the ability to work as waitresses. The whole idea was to motivate us and to make us realise our potential. They taught us about positive thinking.

According to Ale, this had a great impact on her and on the other women who attended:

> we felt as if we were reborn. Earlier we were so ashamed of our work that we led almost a secretive life. The society looked down upon us. But after

> the training we felt motivated. Without that opportunity, we have no idea where we would be today. We were educated until class 12, so we had the desire to do something. We needed an opportunity but didn't have one. We also learnt things like problem solving, decision making, creative thinking, empathy, sympathy, and stress management.

Ale started imparting the basic education and life skills training that she had received to other women working in bars and cabin restaurants. She said that in those days 75% of women working in this sector were illiterate. She (along with her colleagues) taught them how to write their name and address and provided them with some elementary training. Since she herself was working in a restaurant, it was a challenge to go about meeting women and motivating them. The girls would often remain very frustrated about their work, so it was important to motivate them. Ale said: "We told them about the importance of education and the need to demand things like fair wages and fixed number of working hours. We tried to work on their self-confidence".

Seeing her motivation and hard work, Maiti Nepal encouraged Ale to start her own organisation in 2010 and offered her the seed money of INR 25,000. Looking back on that time, Ale went on to add:

> We (she and her colleagues) did not know what to do with the money initially as we did not have any support. We had no office. We used to organise meetings on roads and the seed money wasn't used. Then after a few months, Maiti Nepal called us and gave us INR 150,000 and with that money we were able to rent a room where we started legal counselling for girls who needed help.

Soon after, Biswas Nepal received a big international grant based on a proposal to rescue underage girls from the sector and to make provisions for their education.

She says that the grant was a game changer, and since then, there has been no looking back. Biswas Nepal has grown in strength, now employing 20 staff members and receiving funds from three donors to work on protection and advocacy and the prevention of child trafficking and entrapment in the adult entertainment industry. The organisation today is part of the National Coordination for Controlling Human Trafficking in Nepal. It runs two savings and credit groups that have 135 members, and it manages two drop-in centres and an adolescent centre. It also runs a trade union group that has 60 members.

Ale maintains that her personal stories have been a source of inspiration for many women. Since she herself worked in the sector, she is able to relate to women and girls who now work in the sex and informal entertainment industry. Her organisation provides them with individual counselling and motivation and helps them to cope with depression. It also offers financial assistance to women who want to start their own businesses. Ale said:

> It is about making them aware about their rights. Girls never come out openly to tell that they are working in the entertainment industry. So, we

> tell them not to be ashamed about their jobs. If there are some serious problems like someone not getting paid or being exploited at work, then we collectively raise our voice to take action, and this has helped a lot in building confidence in us.

As a woman-led organisation, run by people who had previously worked in the sector, Biswas Nepal has a good reputation among its three major donors. Ale concluded that

> We see ourselves as activists and we are happy. We speak about our life positively and think positively. We now work in five districts and people look up to us and respect us. In villages they tell us to help with jobs for their children in Kathmandu. We are seen as role models. There is a positive influence.

6.4.3 Case study 3: Menuka Thapa of Raksha Nepal

Menuka Thapa is the chairperson of Raksha Nepal. Since its inception in 2004, the NGO has worked to protect women and young girls working in the informal entertainment sector from trafficking and sexual violence. Menuka Thapa's father died in an accident just before she was born. She was the youngest of nine siblings: all girls. Her father's family wanted a boy, and soon after her birth, her mother and sisters were thrown out of their house. Thapa's in-laws saw her as a bad omen and blamed her for the untimely death of her father. Despite very limited resources, Thapa's mother was determined to give her an education. But when she was in high school, her mother died. As a result, in 1999, at the age of 16, she had to give up her studies and move to Kathmandu to earn a living.

Thapa knocked on the doors of charities for help, but there was little they could do as her problems did not fall under their mandates: she was not a victim of sexual abuse or trafficking. She took a part-time job as a singer in a restaurant. It was while working there that she witnessed first-hand the exploitation of girls and women working in dance bars and restaurants. She said: "They were forced to have sex with the customers by the owners of the restaurants. The girls went for days without getting paid but could not raise their voice against their employers for fear of losing their job".

Horrified by what she saw, Thapa rounded up a group of women and girls who worked there and encouraged them to speak up for their rights. She says this helped them feel more confident in firmly saying no to advances from the customers and owners, and they also began to demand their full wages. Hearing about her initiative, women and girls from different dance bars, restaurants, and massage parlours in Kathmandu began contacting her.

Realising that she had hit upon something important, Thapa started the NGO Raksha Nepal ("Protect Nepal") in 2004. By then, she was out of the restaurant industry and now had the goal of empowering women working in the sex and informal entertainment sector. Over the past 16 years, she says, her charity has helped 1,623 women and girls escape from sexual exploitation in brothels, massage parlours, so-called "duet restaurants", and "cabin restaurants".

Raksha Nepal rescues minors, girls under the age of 18, from brothels and massage parlours and brings them to their shelter where they are first given psychosocial counselling and offered healing through yoga and meditation. They are then provided with legal support and skills development courses in organic farming, driving, massage therapy, and housekeeping. Thapa ensures that the children go to a proper school.

In 2015, Raksha Nepal formed a union of women working in the informal entertainment industry. Thapa says that

> Through the union, we are trying to protect the rights of women engaged in sex work and those employed in massage parlours, duet restaurants, dance bars, and cabins.
>
> Society thinks women who are working in this sector are untouchables and doomed to live a miserable life that they can never change. So, I give my example and tell them that we stand by you and ask them what they want. Most women would say that they want to change their profession and do not want to be in this sector.
>
> I am committed to their cause. I see myself as the voice of voiceless women. They see me as a role model. We are very dedicated because everyone in Raksha Nepal is from the informal entertainment industry, so we understand their pain.

6.4.4 *Case study 4: Shova Dangol of the Society for Women Awareness in Nepal*

Shova Dangol is 36 years old and is president of SWAN. She grew up in Kathmandu and started working in the sex and informal entertainment industry. She began by working in bars and restaurants when she was 15 years old. The industry was booming in those days, and it was easier to make quick money, she says. Seeing her friends and neighbours working in the sector, she too was attracted. It was only after working for many years that she realised that she too was labelled a female sex worker and was seen as a deviant by society.

A group of women from an organisation called General Welfare Pratisthan, an implementing development agency, started visiting them in bars. They talked to the girls about their health and safety, HIV/AIDS, and the importance of using condoms.

Dangol attended a workshop and was immediately interested. She says:

> In the two days' workshop, I made friends, the organisers treated us with a lot of affection. I learnt about peer network and about the importance of using condoms. Fifteen years back, not many people knew about condoms and HIV. These trainings were life changing because we understood a lot

> of things. They were intense. While working in the restaurant, we did not have any knowledge and neither did we know about the existence of such organisations.
>
> My job was to reach out to women and girls who were at the high risk. They would work in places like dance bar, cabin restaurant et cetera. I also worked there and was one of them, so our first task was to reach out to women and girls who were in the sector. It was always easier for me to reach out to women rather than someone who is an outsider.

Dangol then worked as a peer worker for four years. She recalls:

> They used to just give us travel cost. So, I started distributing condoms and take women for treatment. I attended training programmes like advocacy for change, leadership training, capacity building and also went to Kolkata in India to meet other sex workers. These things made a huge difference. In India, I saw there is unity among sex workers and felt that we needed to have that sort of unity in Nepal. I felt that there was need for an organisation that could unite women working in this sector.

Dangol's activism and leadership qualities were spotted by a number of people. She was popular among the women and girls working in the sector. She believed that people who are not part of the informal entertainment industry could never really help the women and girls working in this sector. She says:

> Even where I was working as a peer worker I was always stigmatised and bullied. I talked about it with the director of the parent organisation that provided me all the training. I wanted to raise my voice. One day they asked us what else can be done to motivate us. No one raised their hands. I said that we are at risk. We have been lucky to understand few things. So, I told them I wanted to help my community. I wanted to start my own organisation. I had it in me and that was the beginning.

She was then invited by the United States Agency for International Development (USAID), who further trained her as per their guidelines and also granted her some funds to begin. Since 2006, the organisation has been receiving funds regularly from donors such as FHI360 (a global non-profit organisation working with vulnerable populations supporting HIV programmes in Nepal) for their HIV prevention and awareness work. Apart from HIV prevention work, Dangol's organisation, SWAN, also teaches women and girls working in the sector how to build their confidence and survival strategies.

When asked about the importance of organisations like hers, she says that women and girls trust her because she talks to them frankly:

> I tell them that I am one of you. I tell them about my story and motivate them to openly discuss their problems with me. I never tell them to quit

> because that is not a practical advice. I would tell them not to be ashamed of their work. There are no jobs in Nepal, as the economy is not developed. So, I counsel them and teach them things like how to maximise their earning by taking adequate precautions.

6.5 Pathways to positive deviance: applying a framework

The case studies of the four women above show how their pathways into PD began with HIV/AIDS interventions between 2000 and 2005. One of the steps involved in the PD strategy is to design behaviour change activities to encourage community adoption of the new behaviours and observe people in order to discover uncommon behaviours or enabling factors that could explain the intended outcome (Marsh, Schroeder, Dearden, Sternin, & Sternin, 2004). Sternin (2002) views PD as a new paradigm for addressing the pressing development problems of the world.

Although the PD approach has mainly been used in the field of nutrition, it can also be widely used in programme design where the focus is on social or behavioural change with regard to current practices. It needs to be facilitated by individuals who themselves exhibit the desired qualities required for change, and they differ vastly from other members of the communities. Sternin (2002, p. 59) argues that it is important to note that PD is most appropriately utilised where the problem to be addressed is a widespread norm and those exhibiting the desired qualities are in the minority. The PD paradigm described by Sternin supports the four women discussed above being designated as good examples of PD. They not only exhibit exceptional qualities that differ from other women who are engaged in the sex and informal entertainment industry in various capacities, but they have now also taken the lead as experts in tackling the wide-ranging problems encountered by members of the community. This approach can inform other interventions aimed at women in the informal entertainment and sex industry.

Based on the case studies of the women described above, Table 6.1 shows the unique qualities that I have broadly identified as the exceptional factors that contributed to their success. Accordingly, I created four labels: trigger moments, determination/perseverance, organisational capacity, and motivation. All four women demonstrated exceptional behaviour in terms of their ability to learn and then become agents of change by partnering with the communities of women working in the informal entertainment sector. Table 6.1 shows that each woman had unique qualities that made their behaviour exceptional when compared to other women in the community. Their process of self-discovery, which allowed them to identify and use these qualities to achieve their goals, began when presented with opportunities by the interventions (trigger moments) that they all encountered during their teenage years.

Kohlborn, Kummer, Mertens, and Recker (2016) provide another framework to study PD in relation to organisational behaviour, which can be applied here to further illustrate the PD of the four women discussed above. The authors state

Table 6.1 Unique qualities and exceptional factors of positive deviants

Name	*Trigger moment*	*Determination/perseverance*	*Organisational capacity*	*Motivation*
Bijaya Dhakal	Her association with the NGO was the defining moment as it helped her to discover her potential.	Following counselling sessions, she spoke openly about her identity as a sex worker and in the process connected with other sex workers in her village.	Set up JMMS, which is now a federation of 27 NGOs all run by sex workers. She now serves as a role model for other women and girls.	Says, "I have had a lot of opportunities and exposure. I have attended so many training sessions when I was young and all that helped me to stand out. But I worry about young girls and I feel that I must help them and that motivates me".
Balkumari Ale & team	Life skills training offered by Maiti Nepal. "We felt as if we were reborn. Earlier we were so ashamed of our work".	Inspired other women to be motivated and know about their rights. When given an opportunity, persevered hard to organise meetings on the streets.	Started NGO Biswas Nepal, which works for the welfare of women working in cabin restaurants and bars. Receives funds from five donors.	Ale maintains that her personal stories have been sources of inspiration for many women. They are committed to helping women from being exploited at work.
Menuka Thapa	Coming to the city and seeing the suffering of women and girls working in the industry. Realised she was able to raise her voice.	Was determined to help others and struggled hard to set up her own NGO.	Manages NGO Raksha Nepal and shelter homes for children of sex workers. Involved in advocacy, prevention, rescue, rehabilitation, and the general welfare of women working in the entertainment industry.	The ability to help the children of sex workers and see them growing up in a secure environment. "I feel motivated when I see the women and children smile. I have dedicated my life in helping the women working in this sector".
Shova Dangol	Workshop organised by NGO changed her perspective.	Was outspoken and realised the importance of collective action through training, research, and exposure programmes.	Set up and manages NGO SWAN, which works on HIV/AIDS and offers other counselling services to sex workers.	She says she was determined to help the members of her community. "I wanted to start my own (organisation). I had it in me and that was the beginning".

that PD can be observed in outcome (achieving things differently), behaviour (doing things differently), or both (doing things differently, thereby achieving different things). PD, then, needs to be explored to examine the possible determinants (i.e. the factors that trigger PD behaviour) and consequences (any positive effect of PD behaviour on peers, the group/community, or on society more broadly).

In the context of the four women referred to in this chapter, a PD can be described as a person who is exposed to violence and exploitation and is vulnerable to high-risk diseases (such as HIV/AIDS) by engaging in a high-risk profession (i.e. sex work), but who changes her trajectory with the help of interventions aimed at raising awareness of high-risk behaviour. The awareness campaigns serve as a platform for their deviance, and they then become the agents of change (new expert actors) and work towards the mitigation of risk factors within their community. Hence, I propose the following framework to analyse PD in respect of this study.

So, based on the case studies described above, the determination/perseverance, organisational capacity, and the motivations of the participants become the determinants of interest: that is to say, they are the factors that triggered positive behaviour, which has had consequences for other women and girls working in the sector. As indicated above, the women were determined to make changes in their lives and have demonstrated a great deal of perseverance, tenacity, and vision to sustain the early campaigns of which they became part. They assumed leadership roles and later started their own organisations with the help of established NGOs in Kathmandu. The initiatives undertaken by them now encompass a wide range of areas such as working on HIV/AIDS, rescue and rehabilitation, counselling, skills development, and advocacy for a change in policy to formally recognise women's rights in this sector. They also make efforts to stop young girls from migrating to Kathmandu by educating them about the risks and challenges. The unique point here is that all four organisations are run by and employ women and girls who have worked in this sector, and they too have become the agents of change, thereby enhancing the agency of the community members and making them more resilient and empowered. This represents a turning point in the campaign for women's rights in the sex and informal entertainment industry in Nepal, as well for other issues such as the trafficking and migration of young girls to the city.

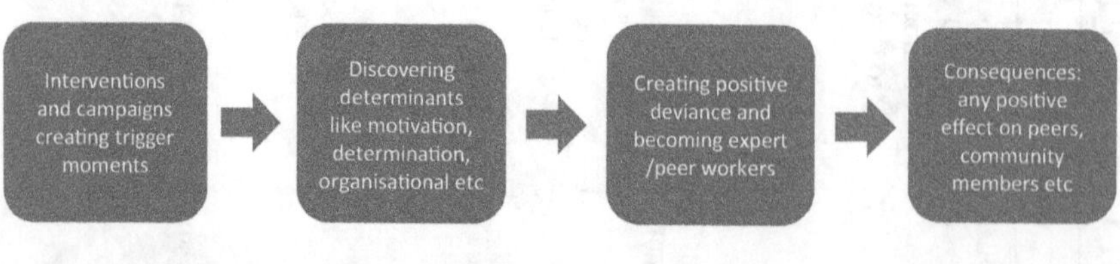

Figure 6.1 Proposed framework in respect of the four women discussed in this chapter derived from the framework for the study of positive deviance (Kohlborn, Kummer, Mertens, & Recker, 2016).

6.6 Applying the positive deviance strategy

It must be noted that the PD strategy referred to above differs from the strategies used to tackle the problems of human trafficking where "community" typically means a general target group made up of people living in a village that has been identified as a place where the problem exists. In the context of this study, the "community" refers to the women who are working in the informal entertainment sector, which includes sex workers (both street based and those working in small establishments such as brothels and cabin restaurants) and women working in dance bars and massage parlours. The above-mentioned organisations may not be adopting the PD strategy consciously, but elements of their work can be analysed through the PD framework.

The work of Raksha Nepal, whose primary focus, in the words of its chairperson Menuka Thapa, is to "help women escape abuse in the Nepal's informal entertainment industry", is a good example. It has been carrying out a range of activities towards that cause such as helping women learn through vocational courses, providing shelter to the children of women working in the sector, and providing legal aid and psychosocial counselling, but one of their recently launched initiatives is to prevent girls from getting into the sex industry in the first place. This resonates with the PD strategy used in reducing human trafficking cases at the source level (Brunovskis & Surtees, 2015). Menuka says:

> we are now running workshops in 12 districts in Nepal. We invite parents and tell them that they should be aware of what their daughters are doing in the city, and the risks they might be exposed to. We seek their support to help stop the migration of girls to the cities by creating work opportunities in the villages, especially in agriculture or animal husbandry.
>
> We have formed groups of outreach workers and employ rehabilitated girls to convince other girls in the villages are not lured by agents and middlemen who promise jobs and good life in the city. We use radio, brochures, and individual counselling to reach out. Our radio program, 'Voice of Raksha', is aired twice a week and has been a very effective medium to reach out to girls in remote areas. After every program, we get calls from girls across the country who are in dangerous situations, but we don't always have the resources to help them. This is what we feel bad about, especially after raising their hopes. We need more resources, funds, and support from the government to help women trapped in sex work.

From the above example, it can be seen that Raksha Nepal's strategy when deconstructed can be aligned with the PD strategy that was created to tackle the problems of human trafficking at the source level. The PD strategy in the context of Indonesia, as outlined above, involved mapping the patterns of disappearances and then working with the community to make sure that girls did not go missing. It meant identifying families whose daughters had remained in the village as "positive deviants" and then using their example to develop a coherent strategy to control the trafficking of girls. The reason I have emphasised human trafficking as an example is that it is widely believed that the trafficking of girls is tied to the process of girls being lured into the informal entertainment industry in Nepal's context, as is claimed by most stakeholders and donors. But, in reality, it might not be the case. The organisations discussed argue that because of their activism and vigilance very few are trafficked into the sector. As argued above, the application of the PD strategy is context specific, and it involves a range of measures. For the positive deviants discussed in this chapter, the scale of their organisations' work goes beyond the immediate scope of just the women working in the informal sector. Raksha Nepal's wider role is also to stop underage girls from becoming sex workers or being trapped in the entertainment industry. So, Menuka Thapa, the founder of Raksha has taken initiatives that involve working with the village community to problematise the issue of girls' unplanned migration to cities.

PD is a potentially useful framework for working with a community over time; however, tackling the complex issues of women engaged in the informal entertainment industry involves adjusting the PD approach to the context and its needs (Brunovskis & Surtees, 2015). It is important to note here that, despite a consensus that there is systematic exploitation of women in the sector, the objectives of the organisations vary, and they are somewhat ambiguous when asked to state their position with regard to sex work. While Raksha Nepal and Biswas Nepal categorically state that they are *against prostitution*, they mentioned that they do not force anyone to leave sex work. They also agree that women engaged in other forms of the informal entertainment industry are indirectly involved in paid sex. It must also be noted that the socio-economic vulnerability of women and girls can be so deeply entrenched that getting involved in this sector represents the only option available to them. This underlines the variety of mechanisms that are needed to address the wide range of interlinking problems encountered by the women working in this sector and that one singular approach to prevention alone will not be effective in all cases.

JMMS and SWAN have been working under the more general and less sensitive framework of HIV/AIDS, though in reality, their primary aim is to work with sex workers. Anita Subba, the technical officer of JMMS, says:

> we never use the term sex workers in our organisation's constitution. We use words like 'marginalised group', 'backward class', 'orphan girls', but in reality, most of the girls are sex workers, otherwise it becomes very difficult to register the organisation since sex work is banned in Nepal.

As indicated above, JMMS is a federation of 27 NGOs working in 21 districts, all led by sex workers. At the central level, it helps the federation in capacity building but at the grassroots level the members – all of them sex workers – are engaged in advocacy work related to violence against women, gender equality, and raising awareness about HIV/AIDS, which is a part of the USAID-funded linkages programme. Likewise, SWAN uses HIV/AIDS as an umbrella under which to reach out to the wider community of sex workers.

Brunovskis and Surtees (2015) argue that using a broader framework has several advantages: it facilitates more openness to the issue, particularly in a community where quitting the profession is not always an option due to economic reasons. Utilising broad narratives – working to raise awareness about HIV/AIDS for the marginalised group, for example – rather than focusing solely on sex work (which is banned in Nepal) is perceived as relevant to the wider community and the aims of the institutions. This is especially critical, as the informal entertainment industry in Nepal is often addressed in the context of the trafficking of women and girls for prostitution, with less focus on and knowledge about why the informal entertainment industry remains attractive and cannot be suddenly eliminated.

Further, outreach from the organisations discussed in this chapter has the ability to reach deep into the community and identify girls who are likely to migrate and potentially join the informal entertainment sector or become victims of human trafficking. It allows them to talk through the risks involved in migration, the dangers entailed in this sector, and the measures they need to adopt in order to protect themselves. Since they are more visible because of their wide range of advocacy work on HIV/AIDS prevention, they earn a level of trust and confidence among the women in the community. "Many of the sex workers are now community leaders, and when other women face violence, they consult them", says Bijaya Dhakal. She further underlines that being associated with an NGO helps a sex worker because it gives them a sense of identity and self-confidence. Addressing the issues of sex workers within a HIV/AIDS approach also offsets the potential for the stigmatisation of these women and those seeking help. Furthermore, as indicated by Brunovskis and Surtees (2015), using the PD approach in this way helps young women to foresee the potential pitfalls of migration and (in the context of this study) of joining the informal entertainment sector, which can help to avoid future exploitation and abuse.

6.7 Conclusion

The case studies presented in this chapter of individual women and the work of the organisations they lead are offered as illustrative examples of PD in the context of Nepal's informal entertainment sector: their actions and initiatives meet the principles of PD as suggested by Brunovskis and Surtees (2015). All four women are experts in their own way and, as such, are best placed to address the problems of women and girls working in the sector. This also provides them with a credible voice when working with other actors. For example, their projects are funded by international donor agencies and, when asked if the donors trust them, Ale of Biswas Nepal says:

> they trust us because we work hard, we are women, and have been a part of the informal entertainment sector. We feel good and feel motivated when people see us working for an organisation and doing good work. Yes, we speak about our life; we speak positively and think positively. We give priority

to women working in the sector. We have a high regard for their dignity and believe that all women should be treated with respect.

Respect for the community, its members, and its culture is at the foundation of PD, and the approach recognises the importance of focusing on interactive engagement and capacity building (Brunovskis & Surtees, 2015, p. 9), which is evident in the processes and approaches of the organisations discussed in this chapter. There is a great deal of community organisation, as indicated above. These organisations are run by women who have been a part of the community, and the mobilisers and outreach workers are currently or have been engaged in the sector. They demonstrate successful behaviour and strategies that bring about notable changes in terms of empowerment and agency. All individuals or groups who are part of the "problem" are also, therefore, potentially part of the solution. For this reason, the PD process necessarily involves engagement with all parties who are affected by the problem (Brunovskis & Surtees, 2015, p. 9). The actions of the women described in this chapter, as well as the achievements of their organisations, can be described as positive deviants as they have facilitated three key processes that define the approach as outlined by Brunovskis and Surtees (2015, p. 9): social mobilisation, information gathering, and behaviour change.

We see social mobilisation around the issues of the recognition of the labour rights of the women engaged in the informal entertainment sector, registration of business entities that offer them employment opportunities, standing up against violence and unfair treatment by employers or clients, and responding to police abuse. The community in general is motivated by the fact that there are those within the community (i.e. positive deviants) who are doing something and that a solution to the problem already exists among their peers. Information gathering is undertaken to identify women and girls who need help or want to be rescued. As discussed, this is being done in numerous ways, but Raksha Nepal's radio programme is helping them reach out to a wider population across the country. Finally, there is considerable evidence of behaviour change taking place in the community through the application of PD strategies. Women have access to credit and savings schemes, are better informed about the HIV/AIDS epidemic, and have even taken up other entrepreneurial work with the support of NGOs. In Chapter 7, I explain how the initiatives started by the positive deviants described above have resulted in creating strong peer networks and how women use these to bring about change in their lives and in their community. The most pronounced behavioural change that has emerged from these forums is the increased ability of women in the sex and informal entertainment industry in Nepal to speak collectively against violence and for their rights.

References

Albanna, B., & Heeks, R. (2019). Positive deviance, big data, and development: A systematic literature review. *The Electronic Journal of Information Systems in Developing Countries*, *85*(1), e12063.

Ben-Yehuda, N. (1990). Positive and negative deviance: More fuel for a controversy. *Deviant Behavior, 11*, 221–243.

Bradley, T., Subramaniam, M., & Tomalin, E. (2009). *Dowry: Bridging the Gap between Theory and Practice*. Zed Books.

Brunovskis, A., & Surtees, R. (2015). *Preventing Human Trafficking. Positive Deviancy Methodology in Practice*. Fafo and Nexus Institute. https://fafo.no/en/publications/fafo-reports/item/preventing-human-trafficking?category_id=204

Clawson, V. (2002). *Application of the Positive Deviance Approach to Anti-trafficking Programming in Nepal – a Trial in Nuwakot District*. Nepal: Save the Children.

Dodge, D. (1985). The over-negativized conceptualization of deviance: A programmatic exploration. *Deviant Behavior, 6*, 17–37.

Durá, L., & Singhal, A. (2009). Utilizing a positive deviance approach to reduce girls' trafficking in Indonesia: Asset-based communicative acts that make a difference. *Journal of Creative Communications, 4*(1), 1–17.

Durkheim, E. 1964 [1895]. *The Rules of Sociological Method. Vol. 8; translated by Sarah A. Solovay and John H. Mueller; and edited by George E.G. Catlin*. New York: The Free Press.

Green, D. (2018). *Should Positive Deviance be My Next Big Thing*. oxfamblogs.org/fp2p/should-positive-deviance-be-my-next-big-thing/

Heckert, A., & Heckert, D. M. (2002). A new typology of deviance: Integrating normative and reactivist definitions of deviance. *Deviant Behavior, 23*(5), 449–479.

Herington, M. J., & van de Fliert, E. (2018). Positive deviance in theory and practice: A conceptual review. *Deviant Behavior, 39*(5), 664–678.

Kohlborn, T., Kummer, T. F., Mertens, W., & Recker, J. (2016). A framework for the study of positive deviance in organizations. *Deviant Behavior, 37*(11), 1288–1307.

Marsh, D.R., Schroeder, D.G., Dearden, K.A., Sternin, J., & Sternin, M. (2004). The power of positive deviance. BMJ; 329:1177-79.

Shoenberger, N., Heckert, A., & Heckert, D. (2012). Techniques of neutralization theory and positive deviance. *Deviant Behavior, 33*, 774–779.

Sonenshein, S., & Spreitzer, G. M. (2004). Toward the construct definition of positive deviance. *American Behavioral Scientist, 47*(6), 828–847.

Sternin, J. (2002). Positive deviance: A new paradigm for addressing today's problems today. *The Journal of Corporate Citizenship, 5*, 57–62.

7 Peer networks and capacity building

7.1 Introduction

This chapter discusses the wider role of peer networks in creating an alternative narrative that resists the hegemonic discourse that labels sex workers as subaltern and as a stigmatised community, devoid of dignity and incapable of expressing agency (Basu & Dutta, 2008; Basu, 2011, 2017). Subaltern in this context refers to marginalised and poor communities such as sex workers whose voices are absent from discourse formation that informs policies that might directly impact their lives. Their voices remain absent because they are deemed incapable of making worthwhile contributions to the prevailing discourse (Beverly, 2004 as cited in Basu, 2011, p. 392). The dominant discourses are usually framed by people external to the environment of the subaltern community. Such discourses subsume the locally constructed cultural meaning that the "subaltern" community attaches to their daily needs and living conditions. To discuss how alternative resistance to such narratives takes place, I use the culture-centred approach (Basu, 2011, 2017; Basu & Dutta, 2008), which has previously been used to study how sex workers in Kolkata, India, challenge the hegemonic discourse and the structures that constrain their lives. In the culture-centred approach (which is explained in detail below) the narratives of the cultural participants (in this case the women working in the sex and informal entertainment industry in Nepal) are used to reconstitute discourses that contextualise the cultural meanings and structures of their lives. The studies by Basu and Dutta (2008) and Basu (2011, 2017) show that sex worker communities strategise their own tactical responses to the violence that characterises their work. They demonstrate serious concerns for their own health and their children's futures, contrary to the beliefs of researchers, campaign designers, and filmmakers that they possess no agency and that they have no understanding of the importance of good health and education (Kauffman & Briski, 2004; Basu & Dutta, 2008).

Peer network movements like those examined in this chapter create a chain of volunteers from within the community to spread health messages to other women who work in this sector. Doing so undermines the need for an external "expert" as proposed by the dominant discourses shaped by academics and health professionals working in the areas of human immunodeficiency viruses

DOI: 10.4324/9781003156796-7

(HIV) prevention. It needs to be appreciated that though these women might not be leaders, as such, their deviancy allows them to draw another positive identity – that of a social worker. Out of this deviance a number of organised activities and forums have emerged including unions, adult literacy schools, and credit and savings schemes. These are managed by the members and are designed to support the specific needs of the women working in the sex and informal entertainment industry. This is significant because peer networks that are managed and run by someone who has formerly been in the profession provide a more nuanced understanding of how these women interpret their own lives, as well as their health needs, their insecurities, the areas in which they need more support, and how they choose to advocate for themselves and their rights when both the social and political space is occupied by men who are hostile to their interests (Kempadoo, 2001 as cited in Lalini, 2014). In this chapter, I explore how the networks examined for this study directly contribute to a knowledge production process that is allowing women in the informal entertainment industry to resolutely express their voice and agency at both the personal and the social level.

7.2 The culture-centred approach

Basu and Dutta (2008) and Basu (2011, 2017) applied the culture-centred approach to health communication to study how sex worker collectives create communication structures to enhance their agency and develop resistance to prescriptive socially dominant discourses that underscore the lives of marginalised women. This approach is relevant in the context of examining the work of peer networks because they create an alternative organically emerging voice that tackles issues such as HIV, condom use, and other risk factors, including violence, that have a direct or indirect impact on marginalised women's health, security, and safety. Basu has positioned the culture-centred approach within the research context of subaltern studies (see Guha, 1988) in order to acknowledge that the voices of the marginalised are resistant to the dominant discourses that typically treat groups like sex workers as *objects* of campaigns in much of the international and development communication work (Basu & Dutta, 2008, p. 108). Subaltern theory notes that to be "subaltern" is not a static condition. It states that a person who occupies the marginalised position gradually comprehends and internalises the structures that are designed to keep them in perpetual dispossession and subordination and in doing so becomes more able to formulate ways to resist those structures through "collaboration and resistance" (Bhadra, 1997 as cited in Basu, 2017). Basu (2017) points out that resistance is enacted through a communication process which can

> be theorised along a spectrum that could include challenges to the dominant discursive constructions, the ownership of agency in determining community-relevant solutions, the mobilization of resources to create alternative communicative frameworks, structural resources and the overt

> confrontational practices that seek to challenge and fight violence that is imposed on subaltern spaces.
>
> (Pal & Dutta, 2008 as cited in Basu, 2017, p. 1508)

In the next section, I illustrate how these characteristics appeared in the context of this study's participants. But first I discuss how culture-centred approaches have been applied in the context of sex workers in studies in India and one study in Nepal.

Based on interviews with 38 women in a red-light district in Kolkata, India, Basu (2011) demonstrates how sex workers express what the author terms "autonomous subaltern rationality" to meet their health needs. Basu argues that, as opposed to the dominant view that portrays sex workers as people who are not concerned about their health, the sex workers demonstrate significant awareness of their health and extract the best out of the available resources to cater to their health needs and those of their children. However, the author also points out that for a sex worker in Kolkata, this might not mean visiting a doctor, but instead choosing local or alternative treatments. This is described as a "polymorphic approach", which means locally evolved community-based practices that are based on traditional knowledge or known remedies to common diseases. This approach is seen as critical in the context of resource deprivation as it offers multiple pathways through which to harness all available resources to help cultural participants achieve their desired health-related goals (Basu, 2011, p. 398). Prior to this study, Basu and Dutta (2008) analysed participant narratives in two sex worker communities in Kolkata. Their research points to the variety of ways in which members of a marginalised culture find opportunities to voice concerns and work towards empowerment and change. The study observed that forming a peer network was the first step towards addressing the wide range of issues with which sex workers are confronted. Their peer networks encouraged them to use condoms and to go for regular health check-ups, and it also instilled trust in the community by providing a common platform from which sex workers could launch and sustain their unified struggle against exploitation.

Basu (2017) conducted a more recent study that

> based on 12 weeks of field study in a sex worker community in India, foregrounds how sex workers communicatively frame and enact resistance and hence formulate insurgent texts, along a continuum–from overt violence to covert negotiation on issues such as condom and alcohol use.
>
> (Basu, 2017, p. 1507)

The author calls it insurgent and resistive because they go against the dominant notion that the subaltern is powerless, and in the context of sex workers, they are deemed as submissive and inclined to engage in unprotected and risky sexual practices for monetary benefits, thereby spreading human immunodeficiency viruses/acquired immunodeficiency syndrome (HIV/AIDS). The author engaged in open-ended dialogue on issues including:

> how meanings on health and HIV/AIDS are made and shared, negotiation practices related to illness, practices related to sex work and HIV/AIDS, communicative framing of relationships with colleagues, children, lovers/partners, clients, and the influence of NGOs such as New Light on addressing issues on health in the community.
>
> (Basu, 2017, p. 1510)

As a community, sex workers worry considerably about their health and the issue is a central part of their overall strategy of resistance to violence from clients. For example, the study cited above found that not using a condom is non-negotiable and, as a group, they came together to tackle difficult and violent clients who might force them to not use a condom. Similarly, as noted in this study, managing alcohol use becomes a strategy to resist attempts by clients to get sex workers inebriated and violate them by disregarding their concerns about HIV/AIDS and engaging in unsafe sex. These examples show that sex workers collectively are capable of expressing agency by enacting a localised discourse in their own space.

Basnyat (2014) documents the accounts of sex workers in Kathmandu, who describe their work as their *pasha*, meaning "profession". The study is based on 35 in-depth, semi-structured interviews that were conducted with street-based female sex workers. The women contend that they have found ways to overcome stigma by accepting what they do and that their profession as a sex worker is tied to their primary identities as caretakers of their children and providers for their family, which is the top priority for them. They negotiate their marginalised spaces by articulating that they have learnt to cope with stigma, abuse, and danger. Basnyat notes that

> This everyday agency involved women locating, negotiating and enacting their choices within structures of limitations, transforming these into the possibilities that enable the women to earn a living, provide for their family and save a little for the future.
>
> Their lived experiences illustrate the need to move away from traditional, top-down, linear behaviour-change health campaigns to reconstitute health interventions within a participatory bottom-up approach that includes the voices of participants and is situated within their own context and needs.
>
> (Basnyat, 2014, pp. 1040 & 1047)

7.3 Applying a culture-centred approach to the analysis of peer networks

The peer networks examined for this study help women in the sex and informal entertainment industry to create their own autonomous voice and agency for resistance, and this section addresses how they do so. The "structures", in this context, refer to problems faced at the micro, meso, and national levels, which can include a lack of job opportunities, harassment by law enforcement agencies, lack of access to education and healthcare, as well as the social problems faced by the participants such as violence, oppression, patriarchy, and a lack of access to the basic needs of life (Basu, Jana, Newman, & Rotheram-Borus, 2004; Jenkins, 2000; Karim, Karim, Soldan, & Zondi, 1995). As Basu and Dutta note:

> "Agency is enacted in its interaction with the structures at these different levels and embodies a variety of communicative actions and processes that challenge, navigate, and attempt to change these structures that constrain the lives of subaltern participants"
>
> (Basu & Dutta, 2008, p. 108).

Therefore, the collectives that women form give them the space to devise alternative pathways for their well-being based on what they perceive to be good for them rather than what outsiders think is good for them.

7.3.1 Health discourse

Narratives emerge more strongly through interactions and dialogues in the space provided by the peer networks through the formation of collectives. As all participants contend, the single biggest benefit of such an association is that they have a space in which they can freely discuss problems and even find solutions, and it gives them the strength to support each other. The participants say that health communication messages are more effectively received if they are discussed and communicated by peers, rather than being delivered through structured interventions designed by outsiders. Karim, Karim, Soldan, and Zondi (1995) argue that in the context of sex workers, due to their marginalised status, the women have limited access to basic resources and information, meaning they cannot negotiate alone for safer sex practices. However, their association with peer networks can make a difference.

My research found that since women and girls are part of multiple peer networks, there is often a flow and a sharing of information among them and across these spaces, allowing them to organise into a collective unit. For example, Participant 6 (age 23, upper caste Hindu, not married) discussed the use of condoms, which she learnt about from her association with another peer network (Jagriti Mahila Maha Sangh [JMMS], discussed in Chapter 6). She shares the vital information in informal gatherings when the members of Raksha Nepal meet:

> They tell us about condoms, they talk about all health risks and teach us where to go, where to seek support, they tell us not to go to the client's house et cetera. I share this information with my peers.

As indicated in the introduction, this study conducted two focus group interviews. These were designed to more broadly validate the responses of the individual participants and to understand what the participants think should be done to improve the lives of the women working in the sector. Accordingly, the questions were interrogative in nature in order to initiate a discussion, while the researcher simply remained an observer in the process. Thus, when questions were asked about access to health information and treatment, the women said that from time to time they go to free health camps run by another non-governmental organisation (NGO) "STEP Nepal", as well as those provided by the Society for Women Awareness in Nepal (SWAN, mentioned in Chapter 6 on positive deviance). Peers who work as volunteers then circulate the information. For health advocacy and awareness, Shova Dangol of SWAN provides insights into how the health programmes are relayed to the women. They work on awareness campaigns, which are run by former sex workers. Dangol said:

> We distribute brochures. Based on our own experience, we know how to identify girls who work as a sex worker. We ask them to visit the clinics and once they have visited, we also ask for feedback and they tell them to spread the message. Our job is to link them with treatment centres, so they know it exists and they can access it without hesitation. Lots of girls go with their clients. In such a situation it is important to make the girls aware about how to protect themselves and remain safe. Girls, nowadays, take adequate precaution and due to extensive awareness, less girls are becoming pregnant due to sex work.

But it is not just about the precautions that the women take against contracting HIV/AIDS. Participants in the focus group also mentioned that their greater awareness of health facilities has enabled them to access government hospitals during childbirth, for example. As a community, women in the informal entertainment industry are well informed of their own health needs and this marks a structural shift in the communication process. The peer networks have mobilised to deconstruct and reframe the health communication discourse in a manner that women can relate to and can adopt willingly, albeit through the external support of international agencies. So, the top-down approach, which has been problematised in the studies mentioned above, has become more localised, and subaltern groups such as sex workers are more able to access basic health programmes from and within their marginalised space.

7.3.2 Self-serving mechanisms

Raksha Nepal demonstrates a great understanding of the cultural factors and socioultural capabilities of the women with whom they deal. Menuka Thapa says that interventions to economically empower women in the sex and informal entertainment sector, such as skills development, are not prescriptive but are designed in consultation with the women who want them. Accordingly, its training programme includes non-conventional courses such as driving lessons and certified spa training. The certificates from these courses not only help women to become professionally qualified, but they also help them to avoid police harassment. As Participant 7 (age 33, lower caste, living separately, has three children) puts it:

> professional spa training has enabled me to get certificate and earn more. Now when police come, I show them the certificate that proves that I am a professional therapist and helps me to avoid getting arrested. Earlier, I couldn't speak with anyone. But after associating with peers, I feel much confident. I feel good as we provide moral support to each other.

For many women, their ability to keep their children in the Raksha shelter home has given them peace of mind because they are kept out of harm's way. This, they say, allows them to concentrate on other things, like learning a new skill for alternative employment.

The participants in the research attach great importance to education. Their children's education is of paramount importance because they hope that, if their children do well, their misery and suffering will not be in vain. The participants clearly understand that good education is a pathway to a good job and a good life. Participant 19 (age 32, upper caste, not living with husband, has two children) explained, "I don't have any desires. If my children grow up well and are happy, that would be my biggest benefit". To that end, Raksha Nepal has been running a shelter home for the children of women working in this sector, and its chairperson ensures that all the children go to school. However, some mothers have attempted to admit their children to the shelter, but due to limited resources the organisation can only take a limited number. In addition, Raksha Nepal has set up a weekend school for adult women (mostly those working in the sex and informal entertainment sector) to enable them to learn basic literacy skills, and women of all age groups attend in very high numbers. Participant 1 (age 41, upper caste Hindu, not living with husband, has three children) says:

> If I was educated well and had not married early, then I wouldn't have suffered the same fate. I never had the chance to study but now I am learning whatever I can and it's helpful. I at least know how to sign my name.

The adult literacy programme that women access by attending the school gives them privilege over other women from mainstream society who might not have the same opportunity or have the agency to exercise such choices. As such, the dominant discourse in the media that associates the women in the sex and informal entertainment sector with depravity and ineptitude is fundamentally challenged by women expressing their agency to exercise their choice and add cultural meaning to opportunities that they were previously denied.

The credit and savings schemes set up by Raksha Nepal provide another example of how subaltern communities can bypass mainstream financial institutions that deny them access because of their marginalised status and sometimes due to a lack of proof of a permanent address. Women who are part of the savings and credit schemes said that they could never have opened a formal bank account because of insufficient identity papers. The banks also require them to maintain a minimum savings balance, which the women might not be able to do. The credit and savings schemes give loans that are easily accessible at low interest rates. Since it is mostly composed of women working in the informal entertainment sector, the background of each woman and their addresses are known, thereby minimising the chances of default.

The chairperson of the credit and savings scheme, Menuka Thapa, says:

> In 2004, I met a number of women who were facing violence. They were earning but their income was not enough to support their families. So, I came up with the idea because we thought if we could pool our savings, it could be a lot of money. I cannot help everyone, but everyone can help someone. The women frequently worried about their children's future. I told them that if they save fifty rupees a day, they can gradually save enough to do something in a few years and that can be used to pay for children's education. We took ten rupees from every woman to start with, and in four years, it became 850,000 rupees, and that served as a collateral to open the credit and savings.

Raksha Nepal's credit and savings scheme is a network of 4,000 women, most of whom are engaged in the sex and informal entertainment sector. The women came together to form microfinance groups, each one made up of between 20 and 25 women. Each group has a treasurer and a chairperson, who are elected based on their skills and leadership abilities. In the early stages, the groups are oriented with the system and how it functions. The women are then taught the advantages of the credit and savings schemes and how they can access loans. They then receive a passbook and are taught how to maintain it. The groups meet once a month, collect the savings, and loans are given to women who need them the most. The decision on who needs a loan is based on a consensus.

Some of the women said that the savings and credit schemes also serve as a platform where women can discuss their personal problems, and where they can seek advice from each other on how to deal with them. There is a sense of solidarity and friendship. They stress that they are able to relate to each other's problems as they tend to face similar issues and can empathise with each other's struggles. One member of the savings scheme (this person was not part of the sample group, but offered to tell the researcher about her experience) who worked in the informal entertainment sector and now runs her own corner grocery shop, said:

> I have been a member for ten years. On an average I saved two-hundred rupees a day. I took out a loan of 50,000 rupees two years back and invested it in a tea shop and now I have expanded it to a grocery shop. The tea shop has enabled me to stand on my own feet. Due to my age, I could no longer work in the informal entertainment sector. My son and other members of the family refused to take care of me. If this system didn't exist, my life would have been more difficult.

Another woman (also not part of the sample group) who was 46 years old offered to share her experience:

> I have been a part of the women's co-operative for six years and saved five-hundred rupees a month. I took a loan of one lakh [100,000] rupees and set up my own spa business. It is my main source of income, which helps me to send my children to school. If I work for someone else, the pay would be less, and I could have never saved enough. Now I spend, save, and am able to send children to school. Because of Raksha Nepal, I was able to get some training on business management skills by attending the Raksha Women's School.

The above examples demonstrate the ability of the women in the sex and informal entertainment sector in Kathmandu to devise mechanisms that cater to their specific needs and also show their ability to create parallel subaltern discourses that are not represented in the mainstream narratives.

7.3.3 Solidarity and agency

For most of the participants, "it is the process of communication that demonstrates an opportunity to enact agency" (Basu & Dutta, 2008). The women who participated not only began to question social structures, but they also had strong opinions about strengthening existing programmes. This phenomenon, as described in Chapter 5, is referred to as "power from within" (Alkire & Ibrahim, 2007)). Their discussions and the views they express shed light on complex issues at the micro level that often create barriers to operating freely in a market environment. Communication allows these issues to be discussed and helps in shaping the agenda. For example, Participant 1 (age 41, upper caste, married but lives separately, has three children) who runs a restaurant but formerly worked in the sex and informal entertainment industry says that the government needs to do more to make markets safer for women and to sensitise the police on gender issues:

> I employ seven women, due to which I face constant harassment from the police. They ask me what the women are doing in the restaurant. If you work in the restaurant that doesn't mean you are a woman of bad character. I have been taken away by the police a number of times for no reason. Police should be there to protect us not harass us.

Raising one's voice against police atrocities is now an important campaign area, not just for Raksha Nepal but also for other NGOs discussed in this study.

The women interviewed have hope and expectations for a better future. Their ability to express their opinions demonstrates a sense of awareness, much of which is gained through interactions with peers. Some women expressed the view that the government should do more to create economic opportunities for less privileged people like themselves. Participant 7 (age 33, low caste, sometimes lives with husband, has three children), for example, said, "The government should provide monetary support to those who want to learn new professional skills", while Participant 3 (age 20, Buddhist, widow, has one child) said:

> my message to the government is to help the victims of the earthquake [around 9000 people were killed in an earthquake that struck Nepal in April 2015]. There are so many women. Some are disabled, some are old, some have no homes. If the government helps, they don't have to come to the city.

Platforms like those provided by Raksha Nepal allow women to come together and deliberate on these issues. The bonds that they develop enable them to build trust and organise as a collective in order to articulate the critical issues faced by the community as described above. They then collectively stand up to respond to issues such as police harassment or dealing with exploitative customers (Basu & Dutta, 2008). Participant 9 (age 28, upper caste, lives separately, has one child) said that those who commit crimes against women should face severe repercussions:

> people should treat women engaged in the entertainment and sex sector with respect. All work should be accorded dignity. I think government should hang rapists, that will serve as a deterrent. Men who commit violence against women should be shamed in the media, that might also help to reduce crime against women.

In this context, Basu and Dutta (2008) in their study argue that the power to communicate becomes the motivating tool that enables them to come together to engage in a unified struggle against exploitation. Thus, concepts of community participation are related to agency, as it gives them the voice to question the social structures that undermine their lives and that of other women. They learn to "optimise the available resources, and at the same time extract a share of those resources, of which they have traditionally been deprived" (Basu & Dutta, 2008). The participants have become aware of their rights and understand that being women does not mean that they have to be subservient to the homogeneous masculine power. All participants said that they are willing to stand up if any other women, in their profession or otherwise, are seen to be facing violence. This phenomenon is referred to as "power with".

Table 7.1 shows that while sharing their experiences and offering solidarity, the women come to think of themselves as people who share something in common. Such experiences give the women the strength to develop strategies to cope with violence at work. The process triggers a "shift in consciousness" that Cornwall (2016) describes as one of the first steps towards empowerment. The agency that the women gain through the supportive network helps them to create a platform for social change in a marginalised space. They question the normative beliefs and institutional barriers that sustain inequality and keep them in a subordinated position. There is a new-found confidence and a determination to emerge out of

Table 7.1 Willingness to stand up against violence

Participant 14: age 40, has three children, lower caste, married.	"I am willing to help women who face violence and even fight or die for younger girls who are in the same profession and are helpless".
Participant 3: age 20, has one child, Buddhist, widow.	"Yes, sometimes when the owner forces my colleagues to work even when they are ill, I go and protest to protect my colleagues".
Participant 16: age 23, has one child, Buddhist, living separately.	"Yes, will help other women. I am in this profession not by choice. I have been forced by my circumstances and I feel other women are in a similar situation too".
Participant 13: age 32, has four children, lower caste, not living with husband.	"Yes, I have learnt about self-defence and I want to teach other girls so that they can protect themselves".
Participant 4: Age 28, has one child, lower caste, married.	"Yes, I will protest if I see any woman being harassed […] violence at home is higher than at workplace […] Many women work here (massage parlours) because of violence at home".

the predetermined social construct of women perceived as weak and dependent: the participants outright reject such limitations on the basis of gender.

Table 7.1 provides the responses given by some of the participants when asked if they would stand up if they saw other women facing violence.

The measures that peer networks such as Raksha Nepal have taken to bolster this level of confidence and self-belief are highly significant. Researchers have argued that a woman is said to be on the path to true empowerment when she takes control of the process of change rather than act merely as a recipient of it. To that effect, the peer networks described in this study are significant actors in facilitating "bottom-up" rather than "top-down" approaches to development (Baden & Oxaal, 1997; Narayan, 2000; Rowlands, 1997). We see from the above examples that the respondents not only demonstrate both "power within" and "power with" (Alkire & Ibrahim, 2007), but also that they gain an understanding of the structures that constrain them. Thus, the benefits derived from their association with peer networks have had a transformative effect on their lives.

7.4 Dealing with violence: the role of the union

Politically, Raksha Nepal as a peer network has been actively campaigning for the rights of women working in the sex and informal entertainment industry. They have been lobbying with the government to formally recognise the sector and they work closely with committees that have been formed by the government to come up with directives to regulate the industry. This is significant because they have otherwise limited or no access to the policy platforms and civil society organisations that determine their fate through the regulation and implementation of policies. This is once again the manifestation of "power with" in regard to political and legal capabilities and the union. Below, I present a brief review of the emergence of the union of sex workers around the world.

The global movement for the recognition of the rights of sex workers began in parts of Europe and North America in the late 1970s. This was mainly in response to the increasing levels of violence, harassment, and oppression of women who were engaged in the sex trade. In 1975, a sex worker protest event was held in Lyon, France. This was soon followed by the emergence of the first prostitutes' rights collective, Call Off Your Old Tired Ethics (COYOTE), in San Francisco, California. The two events drew international attention to the conditions faced by sex workers (Jenness, 1993, p. 42; Mathieu, 2003, p. 54). Around the same time, sex workers' groups started emerging in Canada. These were small, loosely affiliated groups that sex workers at the local level formed to promote their rights by denouncing criminalisation, stigmatisation, harassment, and violence directed at people who work in the sex industry (Brock, 1998). The first national organisation "Better End All Vicious Erotic Repression" (the name chosen for its acronym: BEAVER) emerged in Toronto, Ontario, in 1977 with the mandate to "Legitimize the female sex, decriminalize prostitution" (Brock, 1998, p. 41). The first international conference for sex workers was held in Amsterdam in 1985, where the attendants produced the World Charter for Prostitutes' Rights (Pheterson, 1989). These events ushered in a new period of activism for sex workers and taken together are seen as a historic milestone for the international movement of sex workers' rights (as cited by Beer & Trembley, 2014, p. 289).

Despite the growing momentum to recognise the rights of sex workers globally, there has been opposition to such movements, mainly due to sociocultural, religious, and political factors. For example, sex workers do not have autonomous organisations in many Eastern European countries, and the struggle for sex workers' rights is organised mainly either through gay and lesbian organisations, health projects, or anti-trafficking groups (Garofalo, 2010, p. 224). Even in countries where the sex industry is regulated, the basic human rights of sex workers are routinely violated. This has been further aggravated by the issues of increased illegal migration into Europe and human trafficking. That said, there is a growing trend towards seeing all migrant women who work in the sex trade as victims of organised crime. There is also a growing recognition that, in the developing world, sex workers are part of the informal economy where women in general constitute a significant part of the overall labour force. The women working in the informal economy receive irregular and unpredictable returns on their labour and work under highly exploitative conditions. While the income may, to a degree, empower women and help in enhancing their self-worth and in negotiating important aspects of their life, it does little to enhance their legal status as citizens who can enjoy equal rights as women, as workers, and as human beings. It has also not promoted their organised capacity to struggle for the recognition and realisation of their rights (Kabeer, Milward, & Sudarshan, 2013, p. 2).

Through various studies, Gall (2006, 2007, 2009, 2014) has noted that the unionisation of sex workers has been a slow and fragile process because, for the most part, sex workers are not employed. The author points out that sex workers often have no contracts of employment and do not work together in large numbers. Instead, they often work alone and do not have a fixed place of work. In other words, the characteristics of sex workers' places of work are not like those of other workplaces (such as factories) where unionisation has been a relatively straightforward process. Further to that, in many parts of the world, sex workers themselves resist the idea of unions as it carries with it the risk of being identified *as* a sex worker, rather than as a businesswoman who is engaged in the profession to earn a living and gain access to a better life *through* sex work. Some even aspire to become operators of brothels, saunas, and the like. Consequently, their "right to do business" as entrepreneurs and their view of themselves as individuals does not necessarily sit well with the collectivist principles of unionisation.

Among sex workers, commentators, and social scientists, the sex work discourse has now been sufficiently established and accepted, and one of the significant issues emanating from it concerns the representation of sex workers' interests at work (Gall, 2014). Gall (2014), argues that the context of studying any form of sex workers collective self-organisation differs from other forms of labour in the sense that sex work (in this case as part of the sex and informal entertainment industry) is not regulated by the state in the same way as other work; but at the same time, it tends to be heavily regulated through criminal codes and hostile public policies that are rooted in value systems that view it as a form of (negative) deviancy and as a social problem.

For the purpose of this study, I looked at the Workers' Protection Union, which was formed in 2015 as an independent arm of Raksha Nepal. The rationale behind creating a union was to help women working in the informal entertainment sector to realise their emancipatory potential so that they are not sexually exploited and there is a greater recognition of their work, which is not to be confused with sex work. I met with some of the members of the union on two occasions in December 2015 and April 2018. The membership of the union had grown considerably during this time, increasing from around 3,500 members in 2015 to 7,800 active members as of April 2018. There is a nominal fee of NR 105 for general members and NR 1,000 for a lifetime membership. It also raises the question of whether creating a union leads to the formalisation of NGOs as advocacy groups. It is notable that all members of Raksha Nepal are invariably also members of the union. So, by creating a union and a credit and savings body, NGOs like Raksha Nepal can potentially offer the informal entertainment sector much of the benefits of being a "formalised" industry in Nepal.

The union has 14 board members who are elected through a voting system. It is registered with the Ministry of Labour and is also working in collaboration with other organisations with similar objectives in Eastern Nepal. The constitution of the union (translated from Nepali) outlines that its main objective is to campaign for the recognition of the informal entertainment sector like any other profession so that those who are working in the sector are treated with dignity. In line with this, it has the following objectives:

- To represent all other organisations working in the sector.
- To ensure the economic empowerment of all its members.

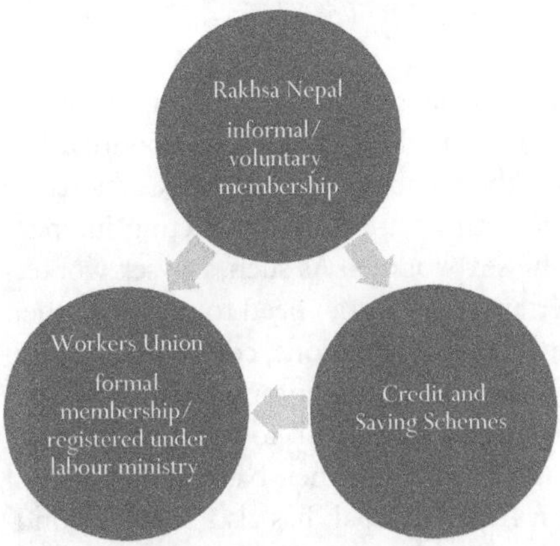

Figure 7.1 Structure of Raksha Nepal.

- To make members aware of their rights through workshops.
- To raise a voice against and to end coercive sexual exploitation.
- To provide skills training for alternative jobs.
- To deliver initiatives for creating employment opportunities.
- To network with national and international organisations.
- To advocate for formulating laws for the entertainment sector (fixed working hours and minimum wage).
- To partnership with other organisations in implementing programmes.
- To raise a voice on violence against women.

Since its inception, the union has been campaigning on a number of issues. One of its key campaign objectives is that women working in this sector should be treated with dignity; they should have a minimum monthly wage of NR 8,000, and their working time should be limited to eight hours a day.

When asked about their most successful campaigns, its president, Sabina Limbu, cites an example in which the union secured the release of women owners of massage parlours who were detained by the police and their businesses shut down, while no such measures were taken against the businesses owned by their male counterparts. The women came together and protested outside the police station against such arbitrary arrests: "A number of our members worked in such parlours, so we felt that they cannot lose their jobs because of such arbitrary gendered action by the police".

Campaigning against police abuses has been one of the primary concerns for the union. One member says:

> Earlier we were afraid of the police as they would conduct raids, detain us and even harassed us. We were the scapegoats but now as the union has grown in strength, we are becoming more vocal and the relationship with the police has somewhat improved. Now they tend to cooperate with us if

> they come to know that we are a part of the union. This has been one of our biggest achievement.

Another successful campaign was to secure the wages of 40 women from the owner of a *dhori* (cabin bar/restaurant) who had not paid their wages for six months. The union collectively protested and compelled the owner to pay up. These actions are small but significant. As Gall (2014) notes, there are often conflicting interests between the operators of sex work and the sex workers. As such, the sex workers (in this case, women in the informal entertainment sector) need to represent their needs independently through other means. In such situations, collective organisation can be helpful. Since the owners of businesses in the informal entertainment industry are often powerful and influential, it can be difficult to stand up to them, but by coming together the women are able to enhance their bargaining power.

The union, like its parent organisation Raksha Nepal, has also been responding to calls from women in distress, including those suffering from domestic violence or intimate partner violence (IPV). While this might not necessarily be the job of the union, as such, the strategy is adopted as a means to reach out to the maximum number of women to increase union membership. The union is not just campaigning for labour rights and economic rights, but also the civil, political, and human rights of the women engaged in the sector. In the Nepalese context, this is exemplary as even some of the big international collectives such as COYOTE in the United States, the English Collective of Prostitutes (ECP), and the Red Thread in the Netherlands initially concentrated on civil, political, and human rights rather than economic and labour rights (Gall, 2014).

Menuka Thapa explained that

> The reason we help women in distress is to show solidarity with them. This helps us to increase our membership. It is about rapport building. The women who are in this sector are not educated. It is a way of convincing them, so they can be attracted towards the union. We have problems with funding, and we rely on membership fees to run our day-to-day affairs. But we also have a shared value and that is to raise voice against any form of violence against women and girls.

The unionisation of informal entertainment workers occupies a unique position in the sense that its activities go beyond just campaigning for the rights and interests of the workers, as is the case of general unions. Firstly, there is an emphasis on the phrase "informal entertainment sector" and caution is exercised so as not to be seen as a collective that represents sex workers. This is because sex work is not legal in Nepal and is considered to be morally deviant, thus resulting in stigmatisation. There is a risk that it could reinforce the criminalisation of, and hostile public policies towards, members (Gall, 2014). Secondly, the union is made up of women who work in established businesses with signboards indicating "massage parlour", though they admit that systematic sex work happens through the conduit of massage parlours. In this context, Menuka Thapa explains:

> We have two objectives. At one level we are working with the government to make the environment safer for the women working in this sector. At another level, we help women who no longer want to be a part of the industry or work as a sex worker. The Supreme Court of Nepal has asked the government to promulgate law for the women working in this industry. The government has not taken any action, but we are campaigning, so it is important that we have more members. We want to engage with the workers, governments, and the employers to make them aware of their rights. Those who want to come out we will help them. But we do not want to force anyone.

Thapa says that as an organisation, the union is against forced prostitution, but also believes that if someone is engaged in prostitution, they should be open about it. She says that in Nepal, street-based prostitutes are those who are no longer granted access to entertainment establishments as they become old or are not considered good looking enough. So, they eventually end up working on the streets.

The union, by positioning itself as a collective that campaigns for the labour rights of women engaged in the informal entertainment sector, rather than as a union of sex workers, strategically deflects any criticism or the antagonism of society at large. In fact, the president of the union says that it is a collective of women who are vulnerable, and therefore it also operates as a self-help group. For example, one member, who is a single mother of three children, has been a member of the union for over 4 years. She says that before becoming a member, she was very weak and lacked the courage to speak out:

> I always thought, as a woman we have to be subservient to men but when my husband passed away, I had to look after my children, so I joined the entertainment industry and worked in massage parlour. [...] As a single woman, I had to face a lot of harassment. The society too looked down at me [...] I had to educate my children and look after them. There was no place where I would be treated with respect. I needed support and the union was the place for me. Here I learnt a lot from the company of other women, who too work in a similar profession. The union has made me strong and taught me to be confident and bold. I have taken courses on legal awareness and had exposure trips to India. If men are single, they have no problem, they have all the rights, but if a woman is single, she is almost treated as an outcast. If you are a woman then it is a problem. I wanted to change this. The union taught me to be strong and I feel really nice and confident.

Gall (2014) argues that collective organisation like Rakha Nepal's Workers' Protection Union is seen by sex workers an critical forum for collective expression of voice and solidarity, because individually they have almost no negotiating powers with clients, operators or regulators who technically control the lives of women working in this sector. However, Gall (2014) underlines collectivism should not be seen in contradiction to or incompatible with individualism, as a collective action is meant to champion the rights and dignity of individuals. Subsequently, the utility of collective interest (representation of workers' union in this case) is all the more salient because sex work, as indicated above, remains regulated by the state through criminalisation. This is not true for most other forms of work, and many segments of society still view this industry as a form of social and moral deviancy (Gall, 2014).

7.5 Conclusion

Macro secondary quantitative research conducted by Htun and Weldon (2012) has found that autonomous women's organisations that are working to end violence are critically important. They list three reasons why women's autonomous organisations can have such an impact. Firstly, "women organising as women generate social knowledge about women's position as a group in society" (Htun & Weldon, 2012, p. 553). The specific contextual understanding of violence that emerges from these groupings is part of the critical mass of knowledge needed to redirect action towards the most relevant entry points in order to bring about transformation. These entry points cannot be assumed to be the same for all groupings, even within the same cultural context. Secondly, ending violence against women and girls (VAWG) requires a shift in the unequal gender structures underpinning societies across the globe. This restructuring will not happen within pre-existing political institutions or political parties where the "gender issue" may struggle to make it onto the agenda in any sustained way. All too often, as Htun and Weldon (2012) point out, VAWG is marginalised in public debate. Thus, autonomous organisations that are focused on and committed to ending VAWG are the only realistic hope. Thirdly, women's organisations represent safe spaces within which women are able to vent their frustration regarding their marginalisation and seek support to strategise collectively and individually. Organisations that rest within state structures do not represent "safety" because they fall within the institutional eyes and ears of the government, which women (especially those whose work is criminalised) rightly do not always feel serves to protect and support them (Bradley & Sahariah, 2019).

From the interviews with the participants, as discussed throughout this research, it is evident that the work of peer network organisations is a vital resource for women, and it has an incredibly important empowering impact. The informal entertainment sector itself, does not represent a safe space for women, but by organising together some of the obstacles faced within the sector can be overcome. However, while resilience to violence at work is navigated through peer networks and supportive local organisations, ending the violence that sex and informal entertainment workers suffer at the hands of their clients is more challenging. Achieving this requires engagement with organisations that are free to act against violence and are unconstrained by differing and conflicting political agendas.

A number of women who took part in the study asserted that they are not ashamed of what they do, and that this sense of empowerment and resilience comes from collectivism. The peer networks help them develop the ability to challenge powerful people and deep-seated social norms, which evolve from changes in self-perception as the starting point (Murthy & Seshu, 2013, p. 244). According to Participant 17, most buyers of their services "are men in power like police or the army, and they are not ashamed of using their service, why should I be".

Kabeer, Milward, and Sudarshan's (2013) moving collection of the narratives of women organising women workers in the informal economy shows the extent of the violence faced by women in stigmatised jobs – rag pickers, domestic workers, sex workers. The common themes that emerged from the narratives of organising informal women workers resonate with the findings of this research, which are

- the power of collectivisation to end the isolation of sex workers and confront their exploitation and stigmatisation,
- the significance of collective critical analysis in changing women workers' consciousness of their right to have rights,
- the importance of having capacity to exercise a voice to claim those rights,
- the crucial role played by the organisations and individuals who accompanied and supported the process of organising.

In addition to their income, what has really helped to reassert their identity as independent women is their coming together as organised, informal groups and associations. The women in this study are associated with NGOs, which provide them with the platform to unite and draw solidarity and strength from each other. The autonomous organisations, which are partly supported by donors, enable them to learn new skills and give them access to savings and credit schemes. They also offer shelter to their children and support their education. The association of peer networks is significant because it allows women to tackle the issue of their dignity more than their income (Kabeer, Milward, & Sudarshan, 2013). As women come together around the more practical concerns of their daily lives, their collective identity starts to grow and strengthen, and they tend to take up wider social and political issues. We see in this study that women are now voicing their concerns about police atrocities and a number of women have expressed their views regarding safety in the workplace, including the need to formalise the informal entertainment industry.

These peer networks also go some way towards erasing the multiple and intersecting inequalities including caste, age, marital status, and religion. It was observed throughout the study (as discussed in Chapter 3) that women of all castes found their way into the informal entertainment sector; all participants shared experiences of suffering and poor economic conditions: these experiences were a common denominator among the women in this research. The peer networks promote further integration among them by uniting them in speaking up for a common cause and also counselling them to deal with their own personal trauma and distress. The women are given scope for growth and learning, irrespective of their backgrounds. The leadership of women, especially in the credit and savings schemes and in the union, is not challenged by women from other castes. They begin to respect each other, and identities of caste or religion are diluted in the process. In the wider cosmopolitan environment of Thamel where these women operate, market forces play a role in redefining identities as socially divisive issues of caste and religion lose their meaning (Liechty, 2005). Peer networks, in general, respond to the needs of all women who experience violence, irrespective of their social background. Also, in the context of the positive deviants described in Chapter 6, it is notable that all four women come from different castes. Bijaya Dhakal is a high caste Hindu and Menuka Thapa is a Buddhist, while Shova Dangol and Balkumari Ale belong to the lower castes. All of these women now play a prominent role in public life, advocating for the cause of the women they represent. They speak up for the rights of all women, which has given them a shared identity and a set of common goals.

References

Alkire, S. & Ibrahim, S. (2007). Agency and empowerment: A proposal for internationally comparable indicators. *Oxford Development Studies, 35*(4), 379–403.

Basnyat, I. (2014). Lived experiences of street-based female sex workers in Kathmandu: implications for the health intervention strategies. *Culture, Health & Sexuality 16*(9), 1040–1051.

Basu, A. (2011). HIV/AIDS and subaltern autonomous rationality: A call to recenter health communication in marginalized sex worker spaces. *Communication Monographs, 78*(3), 391–408.

Basu, A. (2017). Reba and her insurgent prose: Sex work, HIV/AIDS, and subaltern narratives. *Qualitative Health Research, 27*(10), 1507–1517.

Basu, A., & Dutta, M. J. (2008). Participatory change in a campaign led by sex workers: Connecting resistance to action-oriented agency. *Qualitative Health Research, 18*(1), 106–119.

Basu, I., Jana, S., Newman, P. A., & Rotheram-Borus, M. J. (2004). The Sonagachi project: A sustainable community intervention program. *AIDS Education & Prevention, 16*(5), 405–414.

Beer, S., & Tremblay, F. (2014). Sex workers' rights organizations and government funding in Canada. In C. R. Showden & S. Majic (Ed.), *Negotiating Sex Work: Unintended Consequences of Policy and Activism* (pp. 287–303). University of Minnesota Press.

Beverly, J. (2004). *Subalternity and Representation: Arguments in Cultural Theory.* Durham, NC: Duke University Press.

Bhadra, G. (1997). The mentality of the subaltern. In R. Guha (Ed.), *A subaltern studies Reader, 1986–1995* (pp. 63–99). Minneapolis, MN: University of Minnesota Press.

Bradley, T., & Sahariah, S. (2019). Tales of suffering and strength: Women's experiences of working in Nepal's informal entertainment industry. *International Journal of Gender Studies in Developing Societies, 3*(1), 20–36.

Brock, D. R. (1998). *Making Work, Making Trouble: Prostitution as a Social Problem.* University of Toronto Press.

Cornwall, A. (2016). Women's empowerment: What works? *Journal of International Development, 28*(3), 342–359.

Gall, G. (2006). *Sex Worker Union Organizing: An International Study*. Palgrave Macmillan.

Gall, G. (2007). *Sex Worker Collective Organisation: Between Advocacy Group and Labour Union?* Centre for Research in Employment Studies.

Gall, G. (2009). Union organising with "old" and "new" industrial relations actors: The cases of sex workers in Australia and the United States. In G. Gall (Ed.), *The Future of Union Organising: Building for Tomorrow* (pp. 173–84). Palgrave Macmillan.

Gall, G. (2014). Collective interest organisation among sex workers. In C. R. Showden & S. Majic (Eds.), *Negotiating Sex Work: Unintended Consequences of Policy and Activism*. University of Minnesota Press.

Garofalo, G. (2010). Sex workers' rights activism in Europe: Orientations from Brussels. In M. Ditmore, A. Levy, & A. Willman (Eds.), *Sex Work Matters* (pp. 221–238). Zed Books.

Guha, R. (1988). The prose of counter-insurgency. In G. Spivak & R. Guha (Eds.), *Subaltern Studies* (pp. 37–44). Oxford University Press.

Htun, M., & Weldon, L. (2012). The civic origins of progressive policy change: Combatting violence against women in global perspective, 1975–2005. *American Political Science Review*, *106*(3), 548–569.

Jenkins, C. (2000). *Female Sex Worker HIV Prevention Projects: Lessons Learnt from Papua New Guinea, India and Bangladesh* (UNAIDS Case Study). unaids.org/sites/default/files/media_asset/jc438-femsexwork_en_3.pdf

Jenness, V. (1993). *Making It Work: The Prostitutes' Rights Movement in Perspective*. De Gruyter.

Kabeer, N., Milward, K., & Sudarshan, R. (2013). Organising women workers in the informal economy. *Gender & Development*, *21*(2), 249–263.

Karim, S. S. A., Karim, Q. A., Soldan, K., & Zondi, M. (1995). Reducing the risk of HIV infection among South African sex workers. *American Journal of Public Health*, *85*(11), 1521–1527.

Kauffman, R. (Writer/Director), & Briski, Z. (Writer/Director). (2004). *Born into Brothels* [Motion picture]. HINKFilm.

Lalini, Y. (2014). Gender relations and HIV/AIDS: Female sex worker activists creating community. In C. R. Showden & S. Majic (Eds.), *Negotiating Sex Work: Unintended Consequences of Policy and Activism* (pp. 287–286). University of Minnesota Press.

Liechty, M. (2005). Carnal economies: The commodification of food and sex in Kathmandu. *Cultural Anthropology*, *20*(1), 1–38.

Mathieu, L. (2003). The emergence and uncertain outcomes of prostitutes' social movements. *European Journal of Women's Studies*, *10*(1), 29–50.

Murthy, L., & Seshu, M. S. (2013). *The Business of Sex*. Zuban.

Narayan, D. (2000). *Voices of the Poor: Can Anyone Hear Us?* Oxford University Press.

Oxaal, Z., & Baden, S. (1997). *Gender and Empowerment: Definitions, Approaches and Implications for Policy*. Swedish International Development Co-operation Agency.

Pal, M., & Dutta, M. J. (2008). Theorizing resistance in a global context: Processes, strategies and tactics in communication scholarship. In C. Beck (Ed.), Communication Yearbook, (vol. 32, pp. 41–87). New York, NY: Routledge.

Pheterson, G. (Ed.). (1989). *A Vindication of the Rights of Whores*. Seal Press.

Rowlands, J. (1997). *Questioning Empowerment: Working with Women in Honduras*. Oxfam.

8 COVID-19 and the human rights movement of sex workers in Nepal

8.1 Introduction

As a group, sex workers have been among the worst affected by the COVID-19 pandemic. As the pandemic evolved and restrictions on movement and activities were put in place, the income avenues for sex workers and those engaged in the informal entertainment sector abruptly disappeared. Governments around the world closed down massage parlours, bars, spa centres, and other similar establishments suspected to be high-risk areas for the spread of the virus. Whilst the pandemic in itself has exposed the vulnerability of migrant and informal workers and those from marginalised sectors of society worldwide, sex workers in particular remain even further towards the margins; alienated because their work lacks legal recognition. Their plight during the pandemic has been further aggravated by the existing systematic social discrimination and stigma that the group faces, even under normal circumstances. This meant that sex workers found it especially difficult to access social welfare measures aimed at the poor and economically weaker sections of society (UNAIDS, 2020; Lam, 2020; Platt et al., 2020). Jozaghi and Bird (2020) note that even in developed economies like Canada, sex workers were omitted from the emergency economic assistance announced during the pandemic.

In addition to economic hardship, sex workers' organisations have alleged that there have been systematic violations of their human rights including arbitrary arrests, raids, and use of criminal law to enforce COVID-19 restrictions (NSWP, 2020; Platt et al., 2020). In response to the enormous challenges that sex workers faced globally, the Network of Sex Workers Projects (NSWP) and the Joint United Nations Programme on HIV/AIDS (UNAIDS) issued a joint statement urging immediate action to protect the rights of all sex workers during the pandemic (NSWP & UNAIDS, 2020) and appealed to governments to ensure protection under the law to provide equal access to health care and income schemes (UNAIDS, 2020; Lam, 2020).

Lam (2020) notes that, in the face of such adversary, sex workers' groups around the world were able to mobilise what resources they had available to them, which went a long way towards building resilience within the community. Sex worker communities developed rapid response strategies, including setting

DOI: 10.4324/9781003156796-8

up emergency and mutual aid funds and developing resources, programmes, and campaigns to address the various vulnerabilities that emerged as a result of COVID-19 (Lam, 2020, p. 779).

In Nepal, local sex workers' organisations worked with human rights groups, lawyers, and the police to demand relief in the form of material and health support for community members, as well as protection from violence.

8.2 The human rights movement and sex workers in Nepal during COVID-19

The COVID-19 pandemic has highlighted how, in a time of crisis, the criminalisation of sex work and the failure to recognise and uphold the human and labour rights of women working in the sex industry can pose severe challenges to the community. In a press statement during the pandemic, UNAIDS (2020) stated:

> the criminalization of various aspects of sex work in the majority of countries serves to magnify the already precarious situation of sex workers in the informal economy. As sex workers and their clients self-isolate, sex workers are left unprotected, increasingly vulnerable and unable to provide for themselves and their families.

However, in Nepal (and across India, Sri Lanka, and Bangladesh) there has been a call for the human rights of sex workers to be recognised, which has been accompanied by a growing activist movement. In Nepal, the movement has been gaining momentum since 2018 and is aimed at building the capacity of sex workers' organisations in order to fight for their basic human rights at the grassroots level. Although the movement is still at an early stage, during the COVID-19 pandemic the local sex workers' organisations were able to demand health care and other relief assistance from the authorities. They were also able to devise strategies to support their peers. In this section, I discuss how the movement for the recognition of the human rights of sex workers across South Asia gained momentum and consider its impact on sex workers during the pandemic.

Sampada Grameen Mahila Sanstha (SANGRAM), an India-based non-governmental organisation (NGO) working for sex workers' rights since 1992, has been leading the way in promoting the human rights of sex workers by tackling the issues of stigma and discrimination that the community at large faces across South Asia. SANGRAM co-created Sex Workers Allies South Asia (SWASA) in 2014 with the objective to promote the human rights of sex workers by building alliances with women's rights groups, human rights organisations, activists, LGBT leaders, and sex workers' leaders. In Nepal, it is registered as Social Work Allies for Sustainable Approaches (SWASA) to prevent any backlash for directly supporting the cause of sex workers.

During the follow-up interviews conducted for this chapter, Meena Seshu, a prominent sex workers' rights activist and director of SANGRAM, explained the genesis of SWASA's movement for promoting the human rights of sex workers:

> our key demand is that sex workers should be treated as part of the workforce. The state must not discriminate them based on their occupation and must remove harmful laws and policies that criminalise them. Our campaign is about bringing an end of all forms of violence that women working in this sector systematically face by both state and non-state actors. We demand full decriminalisation of sex work.

Seshu added that the movement for the recognition of the human rights of sex workers in South Asia has suffered repeated setbacks because the narrative is routinely hijacked by abolitionists, some radical feminists, and anti-trafficking activists. Groups that conflate sex work with trafficking, despite various court judgements and directives by international organisations, argue that all sex workers are victims of trafficking. SWASA firmly believes that such conflation between sex work and trafficking prevents either group from accessing justice or their rights.

Seshu gave a recent example whereby the National Human Rights Commission in India issued an advisory in October 2020 recognising sex workers in India as informal workers. The Human Rights Advisory on Rights of Women in Context of COVID-19 listed recommendations for sex workers under the women at work section. The recommendations in the advisory were met with approval from the sex worker community, with the National Network of Sex Workers (NNSW) describing the inclusion in the advisory as "the most critical victory for sex workers" (NSPW, 2020). However, a month later, the commission was pushed to change its recommendation following a campaign opposing the move by anti-trafficking activists. Ultimately, the commission argued that sex workers should be given help on "humanitarian grounds" during the pandemic as informal workers and did not remove sex workers from the women and work section.

SWASA's movement aims to build the capacity of sex workers and allies so that the fight for the human rights of sex workers is fought together across movements. As Meena Seshu explained:

> We aim to build capacity so that sex workers and their allies are able to organise in such a way that advocacy is possible at all levels. Sex workers should have the ability to converse with national governments on laws and policies that impact them and present their argument from a rights perspective.

The organisation was formed in 2014 when a group of sex workers' organisations from India, Nepal, Bangladesh, and Sri Lanka converged on New Delhi to create a strategic framework for action to be ratified by their communities in their respective countries. The four countries identified the need for empowering the sex workers in each country by making them aware of the laws and their rights. There was consensus that sex workers should not be at the mercy of groups who neither know about sex work nor have any interest in the rights of sex workers. The idea was to empower sex workers (including those who are female, transgender, or male) so that they can speak up against violence and demand their human rights. To achieve this, national teams identified country-specific partners who could strategically push the sex worker rights debate with women's rights groups and human rights organisations, academics, activists, and government committees. Subsequently, SWASA built alliances with the Sex Workers Network in Bangladesh, the National Network of Sex Workers in India, and the Stand Up movement in Sri Lanka. Alliances were built with two sex worker groups in Nepal: Jagriti Mahila Mahasangh (JMMS), which has 27 sex workers' organisations affiliated to its network, and the Society of Women Awareness Nepal (SWAN) (see Chapter 7).

In the second round of interviews, Shanti Tiwari, chairperson of SWASA Nepal, said:

> In Nepal there has been a lot of focus on HIV prevention, but there has been no efforts to talk about the human rights of sex workers [...] the issue of human rights of sex workers is a global issue and since it was not going to come easily to the community, the idea of the movement is to make the community members aware of their rights so that they can assert and claim their basic rights for themselves.

In 2018, with funding from the Foundation for a Just Society (FJS) and technical support from SANGRAM, SWASA (South Asia), and Veshya Anyay Mukti Parishad (VAMP) India, SWASA Nepal started capacity-building work for JMMS and SWAN. Shanti Tiwari explained the work as follows:

> our programme is focussed on building the capacity of sex workers organisations. We mapped 27 community based organisations [CBOs] across twenty-three districts in Nepal. Each of these CBOs are directly run by sex workers. We provided them grants anything between USD 1000-5000. Our programme is designed is such a way that female sex workers are able change the perception about their work and are able to understand the basic human rights not just in theoretical sense but by engaging in a dialogue with peers.

Accordingly, SWASA Nepal encouraged sex workers' leaders to organise focus group discussions with members of the sex worker community. Tiwari explains that the idea of the focus groups is to make the sex workers aware of their rights by holding discussions around the following questions:

- What do you think about sex work?
- Have you ever heard of human rights?
- Can you say what comes under human rights?
- Have you ever heard of women's rights?
- Can you say what comes under women's rights?
- What kind of rights should a sex worker get?
- What kinds of violence have you been facing as a sex worker?

During the discussions, the participants are provided with a range of information about their social and legal rights. Community-based organisations (CBOs) also organise interactive sessions with human rights lawyers, representatives of women's groups, and the police. During these meetings there is a candid discussion about the various challenges that sex workers face at work and the legal and social remedies from which they can avail. The meeting with the police serves a crucial confidence-building measure as there is usually mistrust and suspicion on both sides. They are made to understand that by engaging in sex work, they are in no way selling their body but merely providing a service. The participants are also made aware of concepts such as the "criminalisation" and "decriminalisation" of sex work.

In 2018, SWASA provided technical support to sex workers' groups in Nepal affiliated to JMMS to make their first ever presentation to the Convention on the Elimination of All Forms of Discrimination Against Women (CEDAW) in Geneva. In their presentation, the sex workers from Nepal highlighted the key issues that they routinely face, for example violence at work and lack of access to justice and health services. They also made recommendations, calling for the reform of punitive laws that are used to detain and harass sex workers, the introduction of policies and law enforcement practices to protect sex workers' rights, and for their right to be free from violence to be upheld. This was seen as a significant step as it was the first time that sex workers in Nepal had been able to take the issue of human rights to an international forum of this kind.

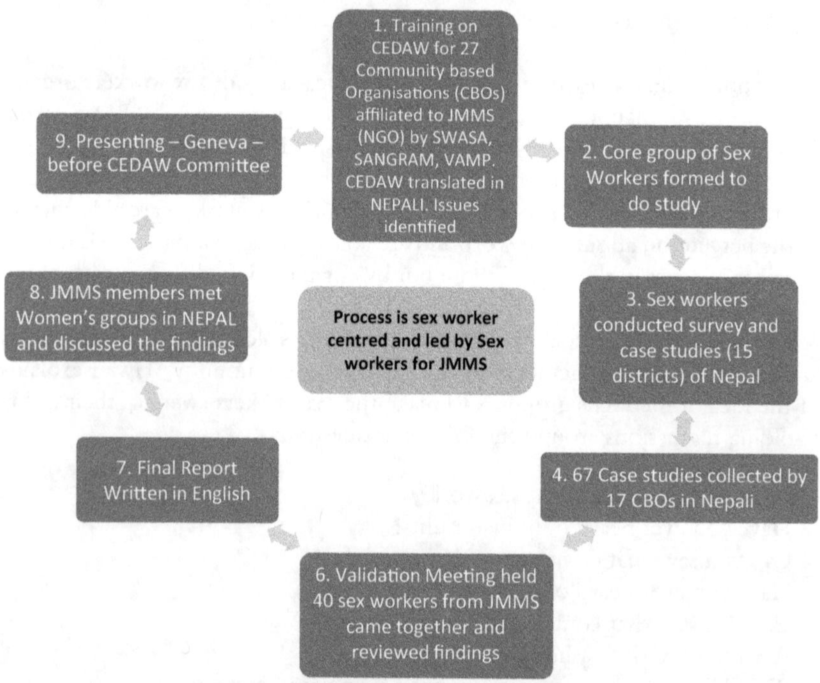

The diagram shows the process of how SWASA provided technical support to JMMS to prepare the presentation for the CEDAW in Geneva.

Shanti Tiwari says it was a small victory in itself:

> A number of community-based organisations have existed for long, but they lacked the capacity to really organise and speak up on issues like human rights as they were not really informed about it earlier so our first task was to build the capacities of leaders. It also helped them – for the first time – to voice their concerns directly at an international forum.

SWASA introduced me to the leaders of seven sex workers' CBOs from different districts in Nepal; however, due to COVID-19, these introductions and the interactions that followed were conducted online. Nonetheless, the accounts provided allowed me to better understand how awareness of their human rights was helping sex workers to create strategies to support their peers during the pandemic. Below are excerpts from the interviews.

8.2.1 Sex workers' leader, Mahila Sachetana Samaj, Mahottari

> SWASA helped us to structure our organisation and gave us clear direction on issues that we should be campaigning for. It trained us on leadership, and we then took the message to over 200 sex workers in our district.
>
> Earlier we worked on our own and often clueless how to raise our issues with the district authorities. We did not have the courage or the capacity to speak up about our rights. We constantly lived under the shadow of violence from clients and the local police. We tolerated silently. Due to various programmes conducted by SWASA we gained confidence and now aware of our rights.
>
> We understand as sex workers we are not selling our bodies but merely providing a service. Earlier we could not access any government schemes because as sex workers we thought we are not entitled to it, but that perception has changed. We were able to claim certain benefits as citizens during the pandemic, though it was not easy.
>
> In our focus group discussions, we discussed extensively about COVID-19 pandemic and how as sex workers we must get all possible help. We took lead in educating our community members about that the precautions that we need to take like wearing a mask, using sanitisers, and maintaining social distancing. We mapped other women's organisations in the area and discussed how we should approach them for help. We were able to get rations for our community members during the lockdown. We also have a counsellor as one of our board members. We were able to provide counselling session in groups virtually to help women cope with stress due to loss of livelihood. There were a number of other problems: community members were not able to pay rent or buy food. We did our utmost to help with support from and funding received from SWASA, South Asia. It did make our community members resilient.

8.2.2 Sex workers' leader, Mahila Sahayogi Samuha, Sunsari

We had frequent interaction with human rights groups. During the discussions we told them about the kind of violence we face at work. We also explained the stigma and discrimination we face from the society at large.

Earlier we never heard of human rights. SWASA and others helped us in realising that we have the basic legal and social rights like everyone else. We never had a plan of action on issues that we should focus and raise our voice. During the focus groups we learn from each other's experience and this gives us confidence. We further interacted with women activists and the police officials. For the first time, we were able to raise our concerns with the police about the arbitrary arrests and harassment we constantly face. The lawyers' groups explained to use the various legal recourse that we can take when we are taken into custody illegally.

Now, when we face violence, we reach to various organisations simultaneously. There is greater coordination. We used the funds that we received from SWASA to organise meetings with the law enforcing agencies. The extensive and candid dialogue helped in fostering a good relationship with the police.

The police harassment has drastically reduced. One positive thing that has happened is that when a sex worker is arrested and taken to the police station, the police themselves ring and inform us. They tell us "Please come and take your sister". This is a positive outcome. We too are careful to restrict our work with a specific area and during the COVID-19 lockdown we followed the government guidelines wherever possible. The relief material we received from SWASA and other NGOs helped us survive.

8.2.3 Sex workers' leader, Gorato Nepal, Pokhara

We are able to understand concepts like decriminalisation. We were always treated like criminals, but we were not aware of legal terminologies and our rights. Now we are fully able to comprehend that it is important to claim our rights and we have been able to ramp up our activism. We have reached out to over 200 sex workers in Pokhara alone and we are taking our campaign to neighbouring Kaski district. It feels empowering to think that we are not really criminals.

Another positive development is that there has been a much stronger co-ordination with the various levels of the local government. During the COVID-19 outbreak, we have been able to procure relief martial and ration from the government authorities and distributed it amongst some of the sex workers. We also spoke with the health authorities and ensured that our members access to health facilities including COVID-19 tests during the lockdown. We would not have the courage to demand these rights a year back, but now we know we can and it is our right.

8.2.4 Sex workers' leader, Ekarikkrit Mahila Samuha, Tanahu

Our campaigns and activism has made us more visible in public space and this has helped. We are able to demonstrate that as women we too have agency and not at the mercy of anyone. Our meetings with the police has helped: we are treated with respect and this is mutual. Earlier we used to shiver whenever we confronted the police. Earlier when were arrested they would also let go the client and we could not say anything but now we do not let this happen. We ring our lawyers and fight our case. The clients know that they cannot abuse us at will. We are collective of 150 sex workers and we always speak in a unity. During the COVID-19 lockdown, we were able to demand some food from the government authorities. Many of our members do not have citizenship papers, but that didn't mean that they could be deprived of food during the pandemic.

8.2.5 Sex workers' leader, Jeevan Jyoti Mahila Sangh, Lalitpur

We as sex workers are now able to appreciate our work and body. We understand we do not have to live under constant fear and abuse – we can fight back too. We choose to be sex workers because of circumstances, but we are not criminals. We have made a choice in our life based on our agency. I feel proud that as a sex workers' leader I stand up for the protection of the rights of my community. Our main goal is to achieve decriminalisation of sex work. It is going to be long battle, but building allies with various rights group I am confident that one day we will get there… one day. COVID-19 was a challenge, many women were harassed by the landlords, they were thrown out and even sexually abused. We tried to help our sisters wherever we could. And in most instances police cooperated.

8.2.6 Sex workers' leader, Niggadh Mahila Samuha, Bara

Our organisation is 12 years old, but we have never had any discussion about our human rights because we never heard of it. Also because of the discrimination and abuse we face at the hands of the society, we always remain demoralised. SWASA's approach was different as it not only built our capacities but made us realise that the only way we can strengthen our voice is by building alliances with other human and women rights groups. We learnt that just because we are sex workers it does not mean that we can be discriminated. Like all citizens we must be protected from violence.

During the Covid-19 pandemic, a number of sex workers were not able to work. We were able to secure the service a psychologist and provide counselling sessions virtually. We engaged actively with the local government bodies and made them aware of our problems. When any of our community member contracted the COVID-19 virus we acted immediately and ensured they had access to medical facilities.

We conducted meeting with the local municipality and was able to get some ration for the community members during the lockdown. We realised that when we spoke collectively, are more successful in convincing the authorities to help us. The problem is that we never spoke earlier. We are determined to take campaign to the next level when things normalise post COVID-19. Our campaign is about "my body, my right" – we have a right to make a choice about how we want to earn our livelihood. Our agency must not be underestimated and our human rights must be respected. This is our key demand.

8.2.7 *Sex workers' leader, Sangarsha Mahila Samuha, Bhaktapur*

Earlier the focus of our work was on HIV testing. Ever since we came in contact with SWASA Nepal, we received a lot of their support; our sisters [co-sex workers] have realised that we too have bodily and human rights. We have the agency to choose our profession and it is our right.

Since we understand our rights, we are in a much stronger position to articulate our position strongly and even respond to violence with reason. When we face discrimination or violence, we respond peacefully, "we ask why you are behaving with us in this way?"

We tell them we are just doing our job and not disturbing anyone. We assert that since we are poor, not educated or skilled we do sex work to support our families. Please do not assume that we are being forced into sex work.

We have been able to gain this level of confidence because of the regular interactions with human rights and women activists. Such meetings in groups embolden our capacity to respond to injustice and violence.

When police detain and disrespect us, we tell them to treat us more soberly. We remind them that there is no provision in law that gives them [the police] the liberty to touch or abuse us. We have learnt his from our interaction with human rights lawyers. We tell the police that we have not robbed or murdered anyone so why should we be treated as criminals. They should go after those people who use our bodily service and then refuse to pay and eventually resort to violence. This happens every day, but rather than punishing them we are humiliated in front them. They let the clients go and detain us until we pay. Due to our activism this is changing. The police know that we are not going to sit silently and tolerate injustice.

The men who use our services must realise that we too have working hours and we are not readily available all the time. We provide a service, which cost money and it is not free.

Our fight for the recognition of our basic human right and decriminalisation. In our group meetings we deliberate how we should raise our voice and who it should be targeted to. Raising our voices in vacuum will not help. It is strange that government makes policies for us without consulting us. We are literally kept out from all forums because of status of sex workers. So, it is essential to build allies; we are much stronger when we unite and speak collectively.

During COVID-19 pandemic it was almost impossible for sex workers to get any kind of ration and assistance from the government authorities. The provisions were only for those who had proper citizenship papers but many of our sisters [co-sex workers] do not have any kind of identity papers. This was not an excuse from denying them basic humanitarian support. We spoke up and were to get some ration from the authorities. Now more sex workers have confidence in us. Our human rights can be achieved when we stand up and claim every other right meant for the poor, women, or ordinary citizens.

8.3 The impact of COVID-19 on sex workers and women in the informal entertainment sector in Kathmandu

The fallout from the COVID-19 pandemic on the lives of women and girls working as sex workers or in the wider informal entertainment sector has already been severe. An independent survey of 690 sex workers across Nepal – conducted collectively by 17 sex workers' CBOs, Jagriti Mahila Mahasangh, and the Society of Women Awareness Nepal with technical support from SWASA Nepal – showed that livelihood, survival, and the ability to provide care for their children were the main concerns for most women. This was mainly because the income of all the respondents had stopped abruptly as soon as the lockdown was announced in March 2020 across Nepal. In an interview, Shanti Tiwari, chairperson of SWASA Nepal, said that the survey was unique because it was done by the sex workers themselves – it was a part of their capacity-building exercise: "The community leaders are in position to meet and interact with their peers. We provided technical support and trained community leaders how to collect data. It based on semi-structured interviews and focus groups conducted during September–December 2020".

The study revealed first-hand information about the wide range of challenges that female sex workers faced during the pandemic in the city of Kathmandu. In the study, 50% of the respondents were aged between 18 and 30, with over 70% of the women sharing that they were engaged in "high-risk sex work", even during the lockdown. Of the respondents, 93% said that it had been difficult to find customers since the start of the pandemic.

Over 60% of the respondents said that they were victims of exploitation and violence, mainly perpetuated by customers who refused to pay. The other perpetrators of violence were the police, hotel owners, landlords, intimate partners, and family members. During the lockdown, three quarters of the respondents faced severe violence, which in some cases included rape. When asked about the nature of the violence, 67% of the respondents said they experienced "mental trauma" as they feared eviction by their landlords from their homes due to their inability pay rent. Of the respondents, 20% said they experienced physical violence from their clients, family members, or the police. Lack of a safe place to work and access to condoms and other health services were other common challenges faced by the majority of sex workers.

Menuka Thapa of Raksha Nepal (see Chapter 7), who has been campaigning for the labour rights of women working in spas, massage parlours, and cabin restaurants, confirmed that since women in this sector are not permanent employees, they do not earn a salary or any kind of benefits from their employer. Unable to pay any rent, most women returned to their native villages where they faced acute food shortages. During the course of the pandemic, Raksha Nepal was in regular contact with 300 women in the Thamel area of Kathmandu. All these women (including some of those mentioned in the previous chapters) are part of the Raksha women's group and work in the informal entertainment sector. Thapa says her organisation provided food and other essentials and psychological support to women and girls but there was not enough to help everyone. A number of women did not have proper citizenship papers so they were unable to access the relief provided by the government and had to rely on hand-outs from charities. Thapa explained:

> We found the that majority of women had no choice but to get into sex work even during the lockdown down. They kept in touch with their clients through social media platforms. They said clients would ask them to perform live erotic acts on mobile phones. They were paid through mobile banking services. A lot of young girls [women] migrated online to earn money this way.

Shova Dangol, president of SWAN (see Chapter 6), conducted a field survey with 107 women working as sex workers or employed in the informal entertainment sector in the Lalitpur area during the pandemic. During her interactions, she found that almost 80% of the women and girls had gone back to their village during the lockdown (March–June 2020), but had returned when the lockdown was eased and businesses gradually reopened. At this time, there was a surge of new women in the sector following the lockdown but there was absolutely no demand for their services as there were no tourists. Thapa and Dongal also facilitated remote online interviews with five women (three of whom had been interviewed during my research). I asked them about the impact of COVID-19 on their lives and work:

Participant 1:

> When the lockdown was announced we had no choice but to go back home. I was welcomed by my family members. We have a small agricultural land, and I was helping my family with my farming work but my family kept asking me about my job and I felt uneasy. I returned to the city immediately after the lockdown was lifted but situation was even worse in the city. Customers stopped coming to the dance bars, so out of desperation I had to engage in street based sex work. I need money to survive in the city.

Participant 2:

> I have been working as a sex worker and in massage parlour for fourteen years. I have a daughter to feed. Before the lockdown I was earning on an average 20,000 rupees but that suddenly stopped. I have a rent to pay, so I took the risk of working even during the lockdown. I was even arrested.

When asked if she received any form of support, she said "I once received relief material that was distributed by SWAN and that was only support I received. When I need help I approach NGOs like SWAN for my health and other needs".

Participant 3:

This participant is a street-based sex worker. She talked about the violence and harassment she faced from clients and the police even after the lockdown was lifted. Many new women had chosen to work as sex workers because they needed money and this had disrupted the market as clients had more choice and they refused to pay the usual amount. She said that the police did their job during the lockdown and were legally right in stopping women from working on the streets, but even after the lockdown was lifted they continued to intimidate sex workers: "They come in civil dress and arrest us. They keep us in detention and let us go after extorting some money". She added that she struggled for food during the pandemic: "As sex workers we did not receive any direct support from the government, whatever relief we have received has been through NGOs".

Participant 4:

A single mother of two children, she said that she had nowhere to go and had to stay in her rented apartment. She had been involved in sex work during the lockdown but said it was very difficult to get clients: "For me it was the question of survival and feeding my children. I managed to keep afloat with some monetary support that from my known clients. They paid me even though they did not use my service".

She also talked about clients who simply refused to pay her and physically abused her instead: "I have always worked in massage parlour and never worked on the street. Since the establishments were closed, I had no other option".

Participant 5:

This participant had worked in a spa centre in downtown Kathmandu. She said she had to get involved in sex work after the start of the COVID pandemic because her husband was abusive:

> He worked as a security guard and lost his job. He would force me to go out an earn. I got in touch with my known clients, and they were generous and was able to provide my services in a secured place. It was too risky to be out in the street. We are still suffering. We urge the government to help us.

Dongal highlighted that the situation for female and transgender sex workers and those working in the informal entertainment sector was equally bad:

> Women in general are worst suffers not the people we are talking about are most marginalised and oppressed [...] Parents of many young women who work in this sector usually do not know where their daughters actually work, and many women who returned home during the pandemic, found themselves in an awkward situation when asked about their job situation.

There was also a steady rise in domestic violence as men became unemployed – this put additional pressure on women to go out to work. She said that a number of women had to borrow money from their friends or from clients, and the ones who are now in debt are going to suffer for a long time.

Dongal went on to stress that despite the violence and challenges, sex work remained relatively profitable compared to other low paid jobs during the pandemic. She said that a number of the women she had interacted with had tried working in brick kilns, but it did not pay enough.

> For a lot of women sex work is more profitable, especially if they are already into the profession; women have ownership of their bodies. Other informal jobs are exploitative for women. Due to sudden economic crisis triggered by the pandemic, the [informal] market is overcrowded and difficult for women without experience to compete. A few women tried selling masks and vegetables but could not make ends meet.

Dongal says her organisation had distributed relief supplies that it received from SWASA Nepal, UN Women, FHI360, and other private donors. It also raised money from its own staff members to help sex workers in distress: "We feel bad that we were only able to help a few women. At least at the time of pandemic sex workers should not have been discriminated. After all they are humans too".

When asked about the main health issues that sex workers and those engaged in the informal entertainment sector faced during the pandemic, Menuka Thapa of Raksha Nepal highlighted that (in addition to the risk of contracting COVID-19) issues of menstrual hygiene were a concern as free sanitary napkins were not available, and unintended pregnancy was also a risk due to the unavailability of contraception.

> Most younger women who could barely earn could no longer afford to buy sanitary pads. Menstrual hygiene and management were not adequately addressed even in quarantine camps [...] we found that sex workers had no access to contraceptive measures during the lockdown and risked unintended pregnancy. Many health facilities had stopped providing care services due to the on-going fear of COVID-19 transmission. The women continue to face challenges in accessing safe abortion services and other reproductive health services. Many workers faced discrimination. They were not able to access

the basic health care services during that period since the hospitals were open only for emergency cases.

Thapa added that the pandemic has derailed the progress made in advancing the rights of women and girls working in the informal entertainment sector through their union and networks. Due to the restrictions imposed on the movement, women have lost access to their social space and peer support, both of which are essential to ensuring their rights: "Most of the women are reeling under anxiety and mental trauma about the long-term consequences on their future prospects, financial security, and the ability to support their families and the dependents, including the education of their children".

8.4 Conclusion

COVID-19 has had a devastating impact on sex workers globally, but despite the challenges posed due to loss of income and harassment owing to the criminal status of their work, sex workers have been able to create their own coping strategies to overcome the challenges (Lam, 2020). This chapter demonstrates how efforts to make sex workers aware of their basic human rights in Nepal have meant that they can use their voice and agency more effectively to defend themselves against violence and arbitrary police arrests, and even demand relief assistance from the authorities during the COVID-19 pandemic. This increased confidence has been achieved through an innovative process of forming alliances with other local groups that champion women's rights and human rights more broadly. It is innovative in the context of Nepal because by using the human rights paradigm they have been able to focus their activism directly on issues that matter to them, such as violence and arbitrary detention by police. Further, though their activism is in the nascent stage, by employing human rights discourse, they have been able to demand access to welfare schemes by classifying themselves as a "needful" category during the COVID-19 pandemic (Kotiswaran, 2021). Through their movement, sex workers in Nepal (and the rest of South Asia with support from SWASA) are sending out a message of inclusiveness and social justice. They argue that they are not only sex workers, but also women, poor, and marginalised, so they too should be entitled to the economic support and welfare schemes announced during the pandemic: they should not be discriminated against simply because of their work.

Similar sentiment was echoed by UNAIDS during the early stages of the COVID-19 pandemic. The organisation called on countries to take "immediate, critical action, grounded in human rights principles, to protect the health and rights of sex workers" during the pandemic and beyond (UNAIDS, 2020). Further, the sex workers themselves (with training and technical support from SWASA Nepal) have undertaken research to document the fallout of the pandemic on the lives of its community members. This is a significant achievement because, as Shanti Tiwari put it, "for the first time sex workers groups in Nepal have control over their narrative as they have first-hand understanding of the challenges that they have confronted during the pandemic". It also reinforces the arguments discussed in the previous chapters that marginalised women like sex workers are not devoid of agency and they are capable of devising their own strategies for survival. Meena Seshu argues that for the human rights of sex workers to be recognised it is important for the community members to develop local articulation on issues that they (i.e. the community of sex workers) face. An understanding of such issues within the context of the human rights paradigm will strengthen their voice and capacity to converse with local and national governments on future laws and policies that will have a direct impact on their lives.

Despite the ongoing consequences of COVID-19, some hope has emerged. Activism among sex workers to defend their human rights has been growing, and they have seized the moment to be heard, which has had an influence on policy. For example, similar activism by their counterparts in neighbouring India has resulted in a positive outcome. In the Indian state of Maharashtra, the government provided financial aid during the COVID-19 pandemic to ensure the "Right to Livelihood" of 5,000 rupees (approximately £50) per month to sex workers with identity cards issued by the National AIDS Control Organisation. The state government further pledged an additional 2,500 (£25) for school-going children of sex workers. A total of 30,901 women and 6,451 children will benefit from the scheme as per media reports. Meena Seshu recognised the importance of international movements for women in Nepal: "today it is India, tomorrow it can be in Nepal. The idea is to be persistent and to support our counterparts across South Asia".

From the above narratives provided by sex workers' leaders and a number of other participants mentioned through the book, it is evident that sex workers do not necessarily want to give up their work, but instead demand that they should be treated with dignity and should be able to work free from violence (Kotiswaran, 2014). It is also observed that strengthening the sex workers' movement and their human rights can go a long way towards combating the trafficking of women and girls in the sex and informal entertainment sector. As discussed in Chapter 6 on positive deviance, when empowered and educated about their rights, sex workers can also play an active role in stopping girls from joining the sector.

Sex worker activists also argue that sex workers themselves do not support the idea of any woman or girl being coerced into the sector. For this reason, the victimisation and stigmatisation narratives that depict all sex work as a crime against women are counterproductive. They contend that the focus should be on recognising that sex work is *work* first, and then, in specific cases, it should be denounced when criminal exploitation takes place. These arguments find further support from human rights groups that call for the complete decriminalisation of sex work. Organisations such as Human Rights Watch and Amnesty International argue that criminalising sex work subverts the basic human right to personal autonomy and privacy (see www.hrw.org).

Meena Seshu argues that when girls migrate from poorer regions to bigger cities to work in premises where sex work may take place, such as dance bars and spa centres (defined as the informal entertainment sector in this volume), they have some idea of what the job entails but they are unaware of the associated level of exploitation and violence. There is a need to create awareness about the dangers of such jobs and put in place support systems that are available to women and girls who are in distress. Rather than simply creating more policies to control sex work, the state needs to invest more in devising mechanisms to widely disseminate such information. As Meena Seshu put it:

> This is where the state needs to step in and that is where the state fails us. The state has the capacity to reach out to vulnerable populations. There is a greater need to strengthen the knowledge and information base and creating systems to reach out to women who find themselves in dangerous situations. This should be the first step in realising the human rights of not just sex workers but all women who work in poor conditions and are exploited.

References

Global Network of Sex Work Projects (NSWP). (2019). *Policy Brief: The Impact of Anti-Trafficking Legislation and Initiatives on Sex Workers.* NSWP. www.nswp.org/resource/policybrief-the-impact-anti-trafficking-legislation-and-initiatives-sex-workers

Jozaghi, E., & Bird L. (2020). COVID-19 and sex workers: Human rights, the struggle for safety and minimum income. *Canadian Journal of Public Health, 111*(2), 406–407.

Kotiswaran, P. (2014). Beyond the allures of criminalisation: Rethinking the regulation of sex work in India. *Criminology and Criminal Justice, 14*(5), 565–579.

Kotiswaran, P. (2021). The sexual politics of anti-trafficking discourse. *Feminist Legal Studies, 29*, 43–65.

Lam, E. (2020). Pandemic sex workers' resilience: COVID-19 crisis met with rapid responses by sex worker communities. *International Social Work, 63*(6), 777–781.

NSWP. (2020). *COVID-19: Sex Workers Community Responses.* Global Network of Sex Work Projects. www.nswp.org/page/covid-19

NSWP & UNAIDS. (2020). *Joint Statement: Sex Workers Must Not Be Left behind in the Response to COVID-19.* Global Network of Sex Work Projects & United Nations Programme on HIV/AIDS (UNAIDS). www.unaids.org/en/resources/presscentre/pressreleaseandstatementarchive/2020/april/20200408_sex-workers-covid-19

Platt, L., Elmes, J., Stevenson, L., Holt, V., Rolles, S., & Stuart, R. (2020). Sex workers must not be forgotten in the COVID-19 response. *Lancet, 396*(10243), 9–11.

9 Conclusion

9.1 Strengthening the voices of women: the liberal and pro-work approach

In this volume, I have attempted to develop a nuanced understanding of what empowerment and resilience could mean for the women working in the sex and informal entertainment industry in Kathmandu, Nepal. It is well understood that the life of sex workers is not only fraught with violence, but it is also complex. Sex workers and those working in the informal entertainment industry negotiate their own space, oscillating between their private and professional life. This book offers evidence of the experiences of the women working in this highly volatile sector. Their narratives discuss a wide range of themes including migration, income generation, empowerment, resilience to violence, stigma and social norms, motherhood, citizenship, transitional justice, and human rights. Each of these themes is a lens through which a person's life can be understood, and together they offer nuanced insights into how women engaged in this sector build their lives around their families and peers and find meaning, despite the high levels of violence and abuse that characterise their work. Further, the ways in which these various factors intersect can shape or define their sense of identity and ability to make choices.

Although the study is situated in Nepal, the underlying themes that the volume explores have global relevance. It is well known that sex work and associated activities (defined in this volume as the informal entertainment sector) play a vital role in supporting the tourism and hospitality industry, and the number of venues in which informal entertainment takes place is quickly growing, especially across major cities in Nepal and in neighbouring India. The regional and global context of the sex and informal entertainment industry and the key theoretical debates underlining the business of sex work were discussed in the introduction; the notions of empowerment, resilience, and positive deviance were then referred to widely in relation to different contexts and themes. From this it became clear that, while there is a consensus that violence is inherent in sex work and that it commodifies a woman's body by bringing them to the marketplace to be exploited by men, there is a greater need to look at the sex industry from a broader social, economic, and political perspective. In terms

DOI: 10.4324/9781003156796-9

of the law, the various national approaches to commercial sex work worldwide differ, ranging from criminalising, decriminalising, or legalising to many countries leaving this area entirely unregulated by not designating sex work as legal or illegal.

The experiences of the four women discussed in Chapter 6 on positive deviance are important because they illustrate how positive deviance strategies can bring about exceptional, high level, and transformative results. Their individual narratives and achievements can help donors analyse the mission and objectives of the organisations they run and the specific needs of the community, which can then help to better inform future programming in relation to issues of women's economic empowerment (WEE), human trafficking, and violence.

The chapters in this volume also provide space for considering the full spectrum of participant experiences and how they deal with different facets of their lives. To better understand this, the research analysed the lives of the participants in two parts: life before and after migration to Kathmandu (as discussed in Chapters 2 and 3), where this study was conducted. The primary purpose of the former was to understand the social, cultural, and political factors that lead women to work in Nepal's sex and informal entertainment sector. The participants were asked about when they first migrated to Kathmandu and under what circumstances. They were then asked to explain how their lives changed immediately after their migration and what were their initial struggles. This allowed the key factors that eventually drove the study participants to enter the highly vulnerable sex and informal entertainment industry to be identified and contextualised, and it provided a nuanced understanding of their motivations and personal circumstances prior to doing so.

While it is widely believed that poverty and a lack of economic opportunity are the main reasons for many women entering the sex and informal entertainment industry, this study has found credible evidence that, in addition to those factors, armed political conflicts (like the Maoist conflict described in Chapter 2) can have far-reaching consequences for women (especially those who are already poor or vulnerable) who get caught up in such conflicts and even find themselves on the frontline. The crucial point taken from these chapters is that it is not economic factors alone, but different constellations of factors and pathways, rooted in social, cultural, and patriarchal norms, that can converge to create situations in which women find themselves exposed to different forms of violence, which in turn can push women to join the sex and informal entertainment industry. A large number of participants divulged that they had faced high levels of violence within their families, which had compelled them to leave home and look for jobs purely for the sake of survival. From the data presented in this study, a complex picture emerges, illustrating the many dimensions that need to be in place in order to push for greater gender equality. The normalisation of violence remains deeply rooted, not least in the "everyday" experiences of intimate partner violence (IPV) reported by the participants. It is clear that past traumatic experiences of abuse drove many of the women who participated in the study out of rural areas and into Kathmandu's growing sex and informal entertainment sector.

Despite poverty being only one of many factors that matter, it is also very clear that independent income generation played a vital role – even if it is from the socially stigmatised sex and informal entertainment sector – in helping these women to break away from the shackles of patriarchy and harmful cultural practices that tolerate humiliation and violence against women within the household. The second part of this volume (Chapters 4–7) looked at the lives of the participants after they joined the sex and informal entertainment sector. Subsequently, the focus of the questions was on the relevance of earning an income and if it had an empowering effect on their lives. The questions addressed in this part included: What constitutes violence at work and how do the participants respond to it? What are the ways in which they exhibit resilience to past trauma and daily violence? What allows them to be positive about their future? And what measures do they think should be taken in order to improve their working conditions so that they can earn an income with dignity?

Central to my theoretical inquiry was an exploration of what agency, resilience, and empowerment actually mean in the lives of women who work in a sector that is seen as a harmful and vulnerable environment for women. This study thus presented detailed insights into the complex and often contradictory experiences of both violence and earning an income for women working in Nepal's sex and informal entertainment sector. In particular, it explored if income allows women to build greater resilience towards various forms of violence and whether they feel more empowered to exercise agency on issues ranging from how to spend their money to challenging the abuses that they and their peers suffer.

The analysis of the interviews revealed the pivotal role that peer networks play in helping build the resilience of the participants by providing them with resource capacities such as social networks, vocational training courses, and psychosocial counselling. In particular, this study found that local women's organisations that campaign to end violence against women are critical in bridging the gap between income and increased resilience to violence. The picture is, of course, non-linear; women record many forms of violence (according to global definitions) while not always regarding them as such (Bradley & Sahariah, 2019, p. 21). The study further revealed the importance of peer networks and specialist support organisations that, alongside income, contribute to women feeling more empowered to lead autonomous lives.

Furthermore, while examining the literature on sex work it became evident that a large proportion of the literature approached the issue of sex work from the empowerment and oppressive paradigms rather than looking at the *business* of sex work. Such ideological positions are often informed by empirical data, which in these circumstances is not necessarily conclusive, making the debate even more fragmented (Bradley & Szablewska, 2014, p. 247). Attempts to bridge these opposing views will always encounter major difficulties and the issue is further complicated by the fact that – as this study shows – no single common factor can be identified to explain why women enter the industry. Equally, there is also no singular response to addressing it effectively. The numerous empirical studies examining the routes that lead women into the sex industry show the diversity of motivations as well as the diversity of means by which women enter the profession. It is, therefore, rather the combination of various socio-economic and cultural factors that affect decision-making, and these differ between countries, regions, and even individuals (Bradley & Szablewska, 2014, p. 246).

Further, such studies have not analysed the broader debates of violence within families or migration, which often acts as the trigger or cause for a woman's decision to work in the sex and informal entertainment sector. In particular, such studies do not consider income as an independent variable and driver of women's decisions to work in this industry. Studies on WEE reveal that income is seen not only as a way to survive physically but also as a means through which to enhance one's voice and agency in domestic and personal spheres (Klugman et al., 2014). A critical question that has largely remained unanswered in the context of sex and informal entertainment work in the developing world is the extent to which earning an income through this sector can be described as empowering.

From the voices of the women in this volume, it became abundantly clear that the majority of women currently engaged in sex work do not want to exit the profession, at least not until their children grow up. Kotiswaran (2021) cautions that such a statement should not be read as simply rejecting the radical feminist focus on rehabilitation, which is ultimately aimed at abolishing sex work, but should be seen from what she refers to as a "redistributive standpoint", meaning that if a woman wants to exit the profession on her own terms she can do so with dignity. Decriminalising sex work can go some way towards realising that goal. Women assert that they are not criminals; they have children to feed and demand a working environment free of violence so that they can work with dignity and provide for themselves and their families. Kotiswaran (2021) adds to this and highlights the importance of reaching a better understanding of how sex workers can protect themselves by earning more, and by improving their working conditions and bargaining power within sex work.

Chapter 8 documents how an emerging sex workers' human rights movement is gaining momentum, through which sex workers are now demanding the decriminalisation of their status. During the COVID-19 pandemic, sex worker groups framed their own survival strategy, at times rallying authorities to demand relief assistance for themselves and their peers. The decriminalisation of sex work remains a vexed issued: as discussed earlier, it faces severe opposition from radical feminist groups and human trafficking activists who see sex workers as victims of male sexual subjugation and exploitation. The global sex workers' movement is often silent about the rights of women engaged in the informal entertainment sector and see it as a distinct category. At the same time, women working in these venues do not like to be associated with the sex workers' movement because they do not want to be labelled as sex workers. In developing economies, governments and law enforcement agencies tend to overlook the sector too, as these businesses operate in close proximity to the police and often have the patronage of powerful politicians and businesspersons. Kotiswaran (2021) states that sex workers' movements have done a commendable job over the last two decades in resisting the discourse of radical feminist groups and human trafficking activists that call for the abolition of sex work, and they have garnered considerable global support for the decriminalisation of sex work. However, she is also critical of such movements for their inability to recognise the "informality and heterogeneity of sex markets world over" and their failure "to produce a sophisticated theory of regulation to reduce levels of exploitation within sex work".

Kapur (2002) argues that the victimisation framework overlooks the structural factors that shape and constrain both the agency and the exploitation of sex workers. This point is strongly reinforced by the activists and other participants in this study, but at the same time there is also an acceptance that widespread violence, abuse, and exploitation remain inherent in the profession. In the context of India, Sadage and Foster (2018, p. 39) argue that legal responses to sex work would benefit from a more nuanced understanding of sex workers' lived experiences, and this holds true for Nepal since sex workers in both countries operate in a similar sociocultural environment. The authors advocate for partial decriminalisation and a pro-work model and argue that a combination of these can strike a balance between a woman's human rights approach to regulating sex work, punishing and preventing exploitation, and supporting and recognising empowerment and autonomy (2018, p. 39). The pro-work model offers a potential avenue through which sex workers can avail of the benefits of employment laws and occupational health and safety legislation, and also gain access to the protections afforded by criminal law and human rights (Sagade & Forster, 2018, p. 32). Further, the model requires the operators of such businesses to be registered and ensure that standard employee benefits, including decent wages and hours, are well defined. Decriminalisation, the author argues (as is broadly asserted by sex workers and human rights activists), can potentially make the business of sex more transparent and can significantly reduce the violence perpetrated by clients and also by state actors, particularly the police. This point has been raised again and again by sex workers' leaders and other participants throughout the course of this study. The other potential benefits of decriminalisation are better access to health information, enhancing the negotiation power of sex workers, and better implementation of HIV programmes.

The pro-work model can potentially serve the interests of those working in the informal entertainment side of the business in particular. Although those advocating for the rights of women and girls working in dance bars and other similar establishments distinguish themselves from sex work (i.e. that which is conducted from a brothel or street-based prostitution), there is clear evidence – as this study suggests – that women engaged in the informal entertainment sector or the hospitality/tourism sector, which sustains and promotes bodily labour of women, are equally exposed to wide-scale abuse and sexual violence. Further, as mentioned above, these closed-door establishments promoting "erotic" entertainment (which are often surreptitiously run by powerful interest groups such as politicians and business lobbies) require greater scrutiny as it is suspected these centres are hotbeds of coercion of women into sex work. Organisations such as Raksha Nepal have strenuously demanded better working conditions including minimum wage and fixed hours of work for women working in massage parlours, dance bars, and live entertainment restaurants. Many of these licensed establishments are registered under the Ministry of Labour, but sexual exploitation and abuse continue unabated. Despite the hopes of some activists, sex work, in itself, is not going to be abolished in Nepal whether it is legal or not and, as such, efforts must be made to improve working conditions and make such establishments safer for women.

The pro-work model also undermines the notion that sex workers lack agency, are powerless, and hence need to be rescued and/or rehabilitated (Over & Hawkins, 2011). The case studies in this volume also challenge this notion (see Chapter 7): it is true that many women may have joined the sector unaware of what it entailed, but for many others joining or remaining in the sector represents a strategic life choice. At no point have they suggested that they want to be rescued or rehabilitated, but at the same time they welcome measures that could provide more social protection and bring dignity to their work. The peer networks, they say, have given them a renewed sense of identity and increased confidence to tackle the challenges they face on a daily basis. For the pro-work model to be meaningful, however, there will also need to be a dramatic improvement in terms of the physical working conditions of those engaged in this sector (Sadage & Foster, 2018), not just in Nepal but all over the world. And to achieve this, it is imperative that in developing economies like Nepal, tourism and hospitality stakeholders play a more active role and are legally accountable for safeguarding the women whose labour enables the industry to thrive and make a profit. It is well understood that there is a nexus between the sex and informal entertainment industry and the hospitality/tourism industry. Studies have documented that hospitality and tourism are usually hotspots of sex trafficking globally (Carolin, Lindsay, & Victor, 2015). As such, there is an urgent need for a concerted international effort to make the tourism and hospitality industries more transparent. Programmes need to be introduced to educate industry stakeholders so that proper mechanisms can be adopted to stop the exploitation of women associated with the hospitality and tourism sector. Carolin et al. (2015) point out that more research is needed to better understand the scope of sex trafficking and the role of the hospitality industry in it.

Throughout this volume, I have alluded to discourses on human trafficking to argue that the link between human trafficking and sex work is often overstated (see the Introduction). It is also worth noting that in the last few years a range of empirical studies have evidenced the negative effects of anti-trafficking policy (Kotiswaran, 2021; Sangram, 2018). I also pointed out how the organisations discussed in the volume, such as Raksha Nepal and JMMS, devise their own strategies to educate parents and young girls to be alert to the potential threat of trafficking that takes place under the pretext of offering young women jobs. In this study, I do not claim that trafficking into sex work does not happen at all, but rather I oppose using trafficking laws to criminalise sex workers and to strip them of their basic human rights. Kotiswaran (2021) criticises the Western media for being complicit in blowing human trafficking out of proportion by portraying horrific images of women being rescued from brothels in developing countries.

She alleges that such coverage of the issue creates a "sex panic" that strengthens the position of human rights activists and reinforces the problematic colonial era construct of the Third World victim "as thoroughly disempowered, brutalised and victimized" (Kapur, 2005).

As a journalist who has reported on human trafficking stories for the Western media in the past, I agree (despite have contributed to it myself) that there is a problematic approach to the manner in which the stories are documented and reported. These stories are often told with the help of a small number of prominent NGOs that have the resources and staff to facilitate the distribution of such stories and even take the journalists along on rescue missions. The NGOs have a clear agenda of getting the maximum publicity out of the story. In most cases, this means waiting months for an opportunity when all the elements of a dramatic rescue mission can be pieced together to make the story visually powerful. Sometimes, the journalist goes to the extent of documenting the agony of the survivor, even filming their reunification with their family. In one incident, while filming for a BBC documentary on human trafficking, the entire village had surrounded the survivor's family out of curiosity when they saw a foreign crew, thus ruthlessly exposing the rescued woman and her family. The ability of such stories to shock an audience rests on what Bernstein (2018) terms "militarised humanitarianism", which refers to neo-colonial humanitarian intervention in the Global South using undercover raid, rescue, and rehabilitation missions (cited by Kotiswaran, 2021). What is even more problematic is that the survivor is typically forgotten once the purpose of the story has been served.

9.2 Limitations

This study has argued that income generation is a positive force in the lives of the women who participated in the research as it has enabled them to take control of their lives, build resilience to their past trauma, and connect with other women who share similar backgrounds in order to challenge the ongoing violence that they face. It has also allowed them to bring about a dramatic shift in the day-to-day structure of their lives, moving from conventional family units into new all-women peer networks. In part, this is because they have been able to leave behind violent husbands and destructive family and community contexts and take control of their decision-making. However, because the study took a woman-centred approach, it does not document the views of the men who might have been the perpetrators of violence or the perspectives of the families the women left behind; nor was it possible to interview clients or customers of the women who participated in this study. Documenting these voices is imperative if we are to seek further insights into how to combat the rigid gender norms and harmful perspectives that encourage men to engage in high-risk behaviour and that grant them the power to abuse and dictate the terms of sex. Such studies could inform how to better engage with men and boys to combat violence, rape, and human trafficking in the sex and informal entertainment industry.

This study also explored how women build resilience and respond to trauma. It illustrated the ways in which the participants have gained awareness of the injustices that are embedded in social power structures, as well as identifying how gendered practices within a particular cultural context are reproduced. During the course of the research, I noticed that the issue of psychological trauma among women working in this sector represented a gap in the existing literature. This research noted that the women who participated have often undergone deep trauma as children or adolescents, but as the questions of this research were not originally designed to explore such trauma, its impact on the mental or physical well-being of the participants has only been touched upon.

Although it was not the objective of the study, it is worth noting that Karuna Konwar, a psychologist who has been providing psychosocial therapy to some of the women in the NGO Raksha Nepal, pointed out that women who have gone through suffering tend to be hopeful about their future when they become part of peer networks because they experience a sense of bonding and care. The support they find in each other helps them to become more resilient. She added that the deep scars left behind by past trauma take time to heal, and sometimes can even be exacerbated by additional violent experiences. Konwar also cautions that raising one's voice or fighting for one's rights are not necessarily signs of having healed from past trauma: sometimes, it can also be a sign of ongoing trauma, which tends to resurface when they are on their own. Additionally, further methodological work is needed to develop indicators to evaluate resilience. In this study, I have demonstrated that the participants have been able to exhibit resilience when they have received external support from peer networks, but questions still remain regarding how, and indeed if, such resiliency can be sustained in future, especially in the absence of leaders who are identified as positive deviants, such as Menuka Thapa (Chapter 6).

This research did consider the role of unionisation among sex workers, albeit only with regard to one union (run by Raksha Nepal), but during the research it came to light that other NGOs are gradually setting up independent unions. Further research is needed to learn about their affiliations and their capacity for political advocacy. There is also a need for evaluation and impact studies of the various interventions mentioned in this volume. Future research also needs to focus on empirical evidence as there remains a lack of disaggregated data, particularly with regard to gender-based violence (GBV), human trafficking, exploitation in sex work/prostitution, and employment. The murkiness of the empirical data can prevent the effective assessment of planned or existing policies and programmes that seek to ensure the protection of women's human rights, including those of sex workers.

9.3 Recommendations

In Chapter 4, I argued that transformative change cannot truly take place if social structures limit the opportunities of individuals. Numerous studies have shown that for women, empowerment in terms of income and other qualifications might not be reflected in other aspects of a woman's life (Becker, Mahmud, & Shah, 2012; Goetz & Sen Gupta, 1996; Hashemi, Riley, & Schuler, 1996; Jejeebhoy, 2000; Kishor, 2000). A woman might feel empowered at the individual or household level, for example, but this might not translate to the marketplace or the community level. Although these first-order changes are meaningful gains that can contribute to resilience and may help develop agency, they also require a radical second-order change in relation to power dynamics in order to bring about economic and social justice. This can only be achieved by addressing structural barriers (as discussed in Chapter 5) such as the transformation of social attitudes, and legislation. The Committee on the Elimination of Discrimination Against Women (CEDAW) reviewed the sixth periodic report on Nepal (November 2018) and has expressed concern that the Human Trafficking and Transportation (Control) Act punishes women in sex work rather than punishing exploitation within prostitution. There is an absence of regulations and monitoring of the entertainment and hospitality service sector in general, and there is also a lack of reporting of harassment and violence against women in prostitution perpetrated by law enforcement officers. The recommendations of the report encouraged the Government of Nepal:

1. to formulate a comprehensive policy, legislative and regulatory framework that ensures monitoring and legal protection from exploitation of women who engage in prostitution and ensure that they are not prosecuted for engaging in such activities.
2. investigate, prosecute and punish law enforcement officers for the harassment and extortion of women in prostitution, and ensure that victims are provided with gender-sensitive protection and support.
3. strengthen exit programmes for women who wish to leave prostitution.

(Thapa, 2018)

Based on the research presented in this volume, I propose the following additional recommendations:

- The Government of Nepal needs to guarantee that women and girls who have been victims of the armed conflict have access to interim relief and full and effective reparations, including restitution, compensation, rehabilitation, and guarantees of non-recurrence.
- This study found that social and cultural values surrounding women's sexuality, dowry, and patriarchy remain the key drivers for early marriage (Human Rights Watch, 2016). This is compounded by the ineffective implementation of existing legal provisions that ban child marriage and by barriers to accessing justice. In line with the CEDAW recommendations (Thapa, 2018), the Government of Nepal needs to ensure that marriage registration is mandatory and that child marriages are null and void.
- None of the participants in the study or their partners had completed high school. Research in 18 of the 20 countries with the highest rates of child

marriage has shown that a girl's level of education is the strongest predictor of her age at marriage (ICRW, 2016 as cited in Human Rights Watch, 2016). The Government of Nepal, therefore, needs to take further action to promote and reinforce equality and inclusion in education by enhancing support systems, scholarships, and incentives for girls from poor households and remote areas, lower castes, indigenous background, and religious and linguistic minorities, as well as for girls with disabilities.

- Significant resources must be made available to NGOs in order to offer psychosocial counselling and to treat the post-traumatic stress disorder (PTSD) of women and girls who have been victims of abuse, rape, and human trafficking. This area has been severely overlooked by international donors and does not appear to have even been considered by the government. The NGOs mapped in this study have asserted that due to limited funding they cannot afford to pay for the services of psychiatrists on a regular basis. Currently, the NGOs lack the means to take a medical or scientific approach to helping women build their resilience.
- Resources need to be made available to increase the capacity of shelter homes for the children of women working in the sex and informal entertainment industry. The initiatives of Raksha Nepal (which are supported by international donors) are a model worth emulating. Through these projects, Menuka Thapa, the chairperson of the NGO, has been able to ensure that the children go to a regular school. Very few shelter homes offer such levels of protection and care. More funding needs to be made available to build many more care homes like these, and interventions must be designed to ensure access to quality education for children of women engaged in this sector.
- There is scope for developing the hospitality industry in Nepal in a professional manner. Nepal is popular with international mountaineers and trekkers and there is a demand for massage, spa, and other forms of Ayurvedic treatment. The government could make efforts to develop the industry, which has the potential to create jobs and add value to the economy. Currently, the businesses offering entertainment and hospitality services, including massage and spa services, are not uniformly registered. There is no statutory body, and because of this some are registered under the Ministry of Labour, others under the Ministry of Tourism, and still others under the Department of Cottage and Small Industries. Such a confusing system leads to the manipulation of the system and laws being inconsistently enforced.
- The government must regulate the minimum wage and working hours for those working in this sector. It must create an environment in which women and girls engaged in this sector can work with dignity. The industry should be recognised as a formal service sector so that it falls under the remit of labour laws. The workers would then be able to access social protection schemes. This has been the primary demand of most women and girls working in this sector.

- Although women such as Menuka Thapa, Shova Dangol, Bijaya Dhakal, and Balkumari Ale (identified as positive deviants in Chapter 6) are doing outstanding and inspiring work, they lack the necessary skills and ideas to expand the capacities of their organisations to meet future challenges. For example, the leaders of such organisations broadly talk about labour rights but have little knowledge of what they really mean or how to strategise political communication, advocacy, and lobbying. There is a risk that their work and leadership qualities may be exploited by local political parties. It is therefore necessary to train them and their employees in management and communication skills. It is also important to train union leaders and build their capacities so that they can raise funds and clearly define their objectives.
- Appropriate strategies for the meaningful engagement of sex workers should be identified at the earliest opportunity. Such strategies will help programme planners to establish the needs of sex workers in terms of their objectives for participating, and to manage their expectations once they are involved in the programme. Meaningful engagement can contribute to effective capacity building with sex workers and can contribute to the overall success of these programmes.
- On a national level, communication and collaboration with financial institutions should be explored in order to promote the development of initiatives to improve the financial literacy of participants. While this approach contributes to the economic empowerment of sex workers, it also helps to increase sex workers' access to financial services. Furthermore, financial institutions should ensure that they do not discriminate against sex workers who want to access financial services.
- Some major international aid polices require that NGOs denounce prostitution if they wish to be eligible for funding. For example, this means that in Nepal the organisations that are engaged in sex workers empowerment and campaigns for better conditions are seen as inappropriate partners for United States Agency for International Development (USAID) anti-trafficking grants or contracts (Kempadoo, 2016). As discussed in Chapter 6, it was found that this type of policy could have an adverse effect on promoting WEE and on efforts to tackle the issues of violence perpetrated against women and girls who work in vulnerable professions. This is also self-defeating in the global fight against human immunodeficiency viruses/acquired immunodeficiency syndrome (HIV/AIDS) as sex workers are systematically denied access to and participation in intervention programmes. It also does not help efforts to combat human trafficking as the owners of adult entertainment businesses run a sophisticated chain in order to ensure that there is a constant supply of women to feed the growing demands of the industry, and this in turn leads to trafficking. Future policies must not marginalise sex workers by separating them from those working in the informal entertainment industry, and more resources need to be directed towards WEE programmes.

References

Becker, S., Mahmud, S., & Shah, M. N. (2012). Measurement of women's empowerment in rural Bangladesh. *World Development*, *40*(3), 610–619.

Bernstein, E. (2018). *Brokered Subjects: Sex Trafficking and the Politics of Freedom.* University of Chicago Press.

Bradley, T., & Sahariah, S. (2019). Tales of suffering and strength: Women's experiences of working in Nepal's informal entertainment industry. *International Journal of Gender Studies in Developing Societies*, *3*(1), 20–36.

Bradley, C., & Szablewska, N. (2014). Social justice within transitional justice: The case of human trafficking and sex-work in Cambodia and Myanmar. In N. Szablewska & S. D. Bachmann (Eds.), *Current Issues in Transitional Justice: Towards a More Holistic Approach* (pp. 261–287). Springer.

Carolin, L., Lindsay, A., & Victor, W. (2015). Sex trafficking in the tourism industry. *Journal of Tourism and Hospitality*, *4*(4), 166–171.

Goetz, A., & Sen Gupta, R. (1996). Who takes the credit? Gender, power and control over loan use in rural credit programs in Bangladesh. *World Development*, *24*(1), 45–63.

Hashemi, S. M., Riley, A. P., & Schuler, S. R. (1996). Rural credit programs and women's empowerment in Bangladesh. *World Development*, *24*, 635–653.

Human Rights Watch. (2016). *"Our Time to Sing and Play": Child Marriage in Nepal.* www.hrw.org/sites/default/files/report_pdf /nepal0816_web.pdf

Jejeebhoy, S. J. (2000). Women's autonomy in rural India: Its dimensions, determinants, and the influence of context. In G. Sen & H. Presser (Eds.), *Women's Empowerment and Demographic Processes: Moving Beyond Cairo.* Oxford University Press.

Kapur, R. (2002). The tragedy of victimisation rhetoric: Resurrecting the "native" subject in international/post-colonial feminist legal politics. *Harvard Human Rights Journal*, *15*(1), 1–38.

Kapur, R. (2005). *Erotic Justice Law and the New Politics of Postcolonialism.* London: The GlassHouse Press.

Kempadoo, K. (2016). *Trafficking and Prostitution Reconsidered.* New York: Routledge.

Kishor, S. (2000). Empowerment of women in Egypt and links to the survival and health of their infants. In G. Sen & H. Presser (Eds.), *Women's Empowerment and Demographic Processes: Moving Beyond Cairo.* Oxford University Press.

Klugman, J., Hanmer, L., Twigg, S., Hasan, T., McCleary-Sills, J., & Santamaria, J. (2014). *Voice and Agency: Empowering Women and Girls for Shared Prosperity.* The World Bank. www.worldbank.org/en/topic/gender/publication/voice-and-agency-empowering-women-and-girls-for-shared-prosperity

Kotiswaran, P. (2021). The sexual politics of anti-trafficking discourse. *Feminist Legal Studies*, *29*, 43–65.

Overs, C., & Hawkins, K. (2011). Can rights stop the wrongs? Exploring the connections between framings of sex workers' rights and sexual and reproductive health. *International Health and Human Rights*, *3*(6) Supplement 3, 1–10.

Sagade, J., & Forster, C. (2018). Recognising the human rights of female sex workers in India: Moving from prohibition to decriminalisation and a pro-work model. *Indian Journal of Gender Studies*, *25*(1), 26–46.

Sangram. (2018). *Raided: How Anti-trafficking Strategies Increase Sex Workers' Vulnerability to Exploitative Practices.* Sangli. https://sangram.org/upload/news/newsPdf/raided-e-book-4.pdf

Thapa, T. M. (2018). *Statement Delivered at the Sixth Periodic Review of Nepal at 71st Session of CEDAW Committee by the Leader of Nepali Delegation Hon'ble Minister for Women, Children and Senior Citizens Mrs. Tham Maya Thapa*. https://tbinternet.ohchr.org/Treaties/CEDAW/Shared%20Documents/NPL/INT_CEDAW_STA_NPL_32836_E.pdf

Index

For Product Safety Concerns and Information please contact our EU representative GPSR@taylorandfrancis.com
Taylor & Francis Verlag GmbH, Kaufingerstraße 24, 80331 München, Germany

www.ingramcontent.com/pod-product-compliance
Lightning Source LLC
LaVergne TN
LVHW021039011026
849160LV00008BA/624
* 9 7 8 0 3 6 7 7 4 2 5 4 6 *